Matt,

Romans 12:2 "And do not be conformed to this world, but be transformed by the renewing of your mind, that you may prove what is that good and acceptable and perfect will of God"

We need to renew our minds everyday. I have used this book in the past to be in His Word daily

T— Brea

TIME TO GET SERIOUS

TIME TO GET SERIOUS

*Daily Devotions
to Keep You Close to God*

◇

TONY EVANS

CROSSWAY BOOKS • WHEATON, ILLINOIS
A DIVISION OF GOOD NEWS PUBLISHERS

Time to Get Serious

Copyright © 1995 by Tony Evans

Published by Crossway Books
         a division of Good News Publishers
         1300 Crescent Street
         Wheaton, Illinois 60187.

Art Direction / Design: Brian Ondracek

Cover design: Cindy Kiple

First printing, 1995

Printed in the United States of America

Scripture verses marked KJV are taken from the King James Version.

Unless otherwise marked, Scripture quotations are from the *New American Standard Bible*, © 1960, 1962, 1963, 1968, 1971, 1972, 1973, 1975, and 1977 by The Lockman Foundation, and are used by permission.

Library of Congress Cataloging-in-Publication Data
Evans, Anthony T.
     Time to get serious: daily devotions to keep you close to God
    Tony Evans.
       p.   cm.
    ISBN 0-89107-866-5
    1. Devotional calendars.   2. Bible—Meditations. 3. Meditations.
    I. Title.
    BV4811.E87 1995
  242'.2—dc20   95-37964

04

16   15   14   13   12   11   10

*Posthumously dedicated
to my good friend and mentor
Tom Skinner
whose brand of serious Christianity
has been a great inspiration
to my own life and ministry.*

CONTENTS

PREFACE

Knowing and serving God is serious business. So serious in fact that the opportunity to do so cost God the life of His Son. When people become Christians and pledge themselves to the arduous demands of discipleship, they soon discover that the Christian life is a battleground and not a playground. It is a lifetime of challenges, conflicts, and spiritual confrontations. It involves victories and defeats (hopefully more of the former than the latter). It means becoming a special target for the enemy who makes it his business to zero in on those who would prioritize the kingdom of God.

To far too many the Christian life is like a trip to Disneyland—all fun, games, thrill rides, and cartoon characters. However, it is only when they leave the theme park that they enter the real world of sickness, death, poverty, divorce, debt, and crime. Because many Christians have successfully separated faith and life, they are often unprepared to deal with the real nitty-gritty matters of life our faith was designed to enable us to handle.

To prepare ourselves to address these matters victoriously can be a difficult and sometimes discouraging task. It involves the development of the daily discipline of the heart and mind that will equip us to face the ever-present challenges that continuously confront us. Preparing for life's challenges demands the regular refocusing of our priorities, dreams, desires, goals, and plans so that they are being brought in line with God's agenda. It involves counteracting the subtle and not-so-subtle attempts by the enemy to get us to think and operate independently of God.

This work was written to assist you in your pursuit of God and His will for your life. It is a call for serious Christians to set aside time, on a daily basis, to direct their hearts and minds to many of the important faith challenges and issues that await us each day.

You will find a reading for each weekday of the year and a special time for reflection each weekend. The book is divided into thirteen sections of four weeks each. You may start using the book on any day of the year, since (with the exception of Christmas) the material is not closely tied to specific months.

Time with God was meant to be more than just "a verse a day to keep the devil away." It is the deadly serious process of reorienting our thinking so that our lives are brought into alignment with the kingdom of God. It is seeking His power and grace to face the attempts of our adversary to overthrow us and those we love. It is the counterattack necessary to stand firm and steadfastly refuse to relinquish territory to the evil one.

It is my hope that God will use this volume to help equip you to meet the perplexities of life with the motivation and spiritual tenacity that only God can give. It is our prayer that each page of this work will provide you with the divine focus necessary for biblical, Spirit-led reflection and decision-making so that you experience the thrill of spiritual victory and not the agony of spiritual defeat.

In tough times God needs tough servants, and for all of us that means it's time to "get serious."

WITH GRATITUDE

I want to say a special word of thanks to my friend Philip Rawley for his excellent editorial help in the preparation of this manuscript, to Lane Dennis and Leonard Goss of Crossway Books for their ideas and their encouragement, and to Crossway editor Lila Bishop for her work on the manuscript.

ONE

KNOWING GOD

If God is the all-consuming, all-powerful, all-knowing, loving, and infinite Creator, Sustainer, and Redeemer of this universe, then nothing else we can do matters quite as much as getting to know Him— and to know Him well!

"Let him who boasts boast of this, that he understands and knows
Me, that I am the LORD." Jeremiah 9:24

LIFE'S GREATEST PURSUIT
Read It: Philippians 3:3-7

Here we are with a new year ahead of us—a whole year to learn and grow. So where do we start? How about at square one: the knowledge of God. That's where it all begins. Getting to know God is the greatest pursuit in life.

God said so Himself through the Prophet Jeremiah. In fact, in Jeremiah 9:23 God says, "'Let not a wise man boast of his wisdom, and let not the mighty man boast of his might, let not a rich man boast of his riches.'"

God says, "There is something in life worth bragging about, but it's not your bank account, your position in the marketplace, or your educational degrees." God says there is only one thing in life worth bragging about: "Do you know Me?"

It's amazing how we brag about everything else. Some of us can brag about our educational achievements. We've gone through school, and we graduated *magna cum laude,* or "Lord, come soon!" whichever was appropriate. People treat us respectfully; they give us titles to recognize our achievement, and if we are not careful, we might boast about that.

Or you may have started at the bottom of your company, and now you're in the executive suite. Now there's extra money in the account. The home is nice. The cars are new. The clothes are authentic. All of the data necessary to indicate success might tempt you to brag.

But God says, "If you really want something to shout about, can you brag that you know Me? Because if you can't talk about that, then it doesn't matter how much money is in your account, what degrees are on your wall, or what position you have in the company."

Pride is like growing a beard. It needs to be clipped daily. Every day you and I need to get up and look at our degrees, our careers, our money, and then say, "If it were not for the grace of God . . ."

See, the knowledge of God affects everything about you. God says, "If you are going to brag, brag that you know Me."

——— **Think About It** ———
Do you know God well enough that *He* could
brag on *you* if He wanted to?

"Sanctify them in the truth." John 17:17

TELLING THE TRUTH
Read It: Isaiah 6:1-7

Part of coming to know God intimately is hearing the truth about ourselves. We need someone who will tell us the truth.

We don't do that with each other. We don't tell people the truth because we don't want to offend them or make them mad at us. Besides, all of us like being lied to occasionally. No woman wants to ask, "How do you like my new dress?" and hear, "Worst thing I ever saw in my life."

No one wants to hear that! And even though we may think a piece of clothing or a hairstyle is the worst we have ever seen, we aren't about to say so because people don't want the truth. Therefore, our relationships are often shallow and never get to where they are supposed to be.

You don't have that problem with God. God calls it as He sees it. He's not going to tell you, "I'm okay, you're okay." He's going to tell you, "You are dead in your trespasses and in your sins." He's not going to make it comfortable or convenient for you. When God begins to unveil who He is, it also unveils who we are.

That's the problem Peter had when he ran into Jesus Christ at the lake and found out who he was. Peter fell on his face and said, "I am a sinful man" (Luke 5:8).

The Prophet Isaiah saw the Lord and cried out, "Woe is me!" (Isaiah 6:5). Why? Because if you want the real deal with God, you are going to get the truth, the whole truth, and nothing but the truth, and some of it's not going to be pleasant.

But God doesn't tell you the truth about yourself and then leave you where you are. Like a good doctor, He tells you you're sick so you will get the proper treatment. The proper treatment for sin is salvation through the blood of Jesus Christ, who provided forgiveness for our sins by His death on the cross.

You can never know God until you are properly related to Him through Christ. If you have never come to Jesus Christ in repentance and faith, today would be a great day to do that.

--------- **Think About It** ---------
Have you ever thanked God
for telling you the truth about yourself?

"God is spirit; and those who worship Him
must worship in spirit and truth." John 4:24

THE GOD WHO IS SPIRIT
Read It: John 4:19-26

During Jesus' encounter with the Samaritan woman in John 4, He made a very important statement about God's essential nature. They were talking about worship when Jesus said, "An hour is coming, and now is, when the true worshipers shall worship the Father in spirit and truth; for such people the Father seeks to be His worshipers" (v. 23).

Please notice that the phrase in John 4:24 has no article. God is not "the" Spirit; God is spirit. That is, spirit is His essence. That's who He is. This phrase is put at the front of the sentence in Greek for emphasis, so what Jesus is saying is, "I want to emphasize why you must worship God in spirit and truth."

You can't get very far in a quest to know God without talking about worshiping Him. And you can't worship God the way He wants to be worshiped until you understand that "God is spirit."

What does it mean to say something is spirit? First of all, it means that God is nonmaterial. He does not have a body. Spirits don't have bodies (Luke 24:39). You say, "But Jesus has a body."

Yes, but that's because He became man, not because that's who He is in His eternal essence. In God's essence, He is immaterial. Now the Bible knows we have trouble with that because we are material beings in a material world.

So the Bible speaks about God in human terms: "the hand of the Lord" or "the eyes of the Lord." These human descriptions are used to help us relate to a spirit being we could not relate to otherwise.

But when it comes to worship, God says, "You must worship Me in My essence"—that is, in spirit. That's why we don't make images of God and bow down to them. He forbids it, because nothing on earth could represent our awesome God properly.

That's also why worshiping God is a matter of what you do in your inner being, your spirit. What you do in your spirit is God's first concern, because everything else will flow out of that.

─────── **Think About It** ───────

The great God who is spirit is actually looking for people to worship Him in spirit and in truth! Want to join up?

"The heavens are telling of the glory of God." Psalm 19:1

GOD CAN HANDLE IT
Read It: Ephesians 1:1-6

Do you ever do anything just because it makes you feel good? You don't have to do it. There's no need to do it, but you just enjoy doing it.

Well, that's how God feels about all of creation! He created the universe out of His own good pleasure. He didn't have to do it, because one of the attributes of our God is that He is self-sufficient. He doesn't need anything or anyone to complete Him.

Psalm 19 invites us to see, by looking at what God has created, how glorious and sufficient He is. If you really want to know how sufficient, how good, how complete something is, look at what it produces. If what it produces is glorious, then the person responsible for that production must be more glorious than the thing produced and must be sufficient to produce it. Today's verse says we can look at nature and see God's fingerprints all over it.

That's why God does not spend time trying to prove His existence to atheists. Only a fool would reject the existence of God after looking at a creation as complex and orderly as this world. All of the things that make life what it is prove that we have an all-sufficient God and that there is none like Him.

The Bible declares that God is responsible for creation, which of necessity means that God precedes creation. The reason God precedes creation is that He "has life within Himself" (John 5:26). God has self-generating power, His own internal battery, by which He created everything.

And having created all things, God is more than sufficient to handle His creation. Referring to Jesus, Colossians 1:17 says that "in Him all things hold together." Jesus is the "cosmic glue" that keeps this universe from flying apart.

God's self-sufficiency is good news for us. Why? Because Ephesians 1:5-6 says that He saved us and adopted us as His children because it pleased Him to do so, not because we were worthy. That's what grace is all about, and that's why we can call God our Father.

————— **Think About It** —————
The self-sufficient power that God exercised in creation
and in our salvation is the same power by which He will keep us
secure until He comes for us.

"You shall be holy, for I am holy." 1 Peter 1:16

ENCOUNTERING A HOLY GOD
Read It: Psalm 11:4-7

If you were high above the earth and looked down on one man standing on a mountaintop and another standing in a valley, they would look to you as if they were standing side by side. You would be so high that the small matter of a mountain would be irrelevant.

God is so high that when He sees us in relation to sin, we are all standing on level ground. Our God is holy, totally separate from sin. He can't even stand to look at it (Habakkuk 1:13).

But most people's attitude toward sin is epitomized by the attitude of the famous naturalist, Henry David Thoreau. When urged to make his peace with God, Thoreau answered, "I did not know that we had ever quarreled."

There's been a quarrel, all right! God's got the quarrel with us, because we have all offended His holiness. All people need to be saved, because everyone has the same problem. The Bible says, "There is none righteous, not even one" (Romans 3:10).

Someone might object, "But that's not fair."

Sure it is. Suppose you were sick, and as the doctor was getting ready to operate on you, he said, "All of my scalpels are dirty. I've got one that I just picked up out of the mud. It's real dirty. I've got another one that's a little better, but it still has dirt on it. Now I've got this one scalpel that's just got a little spot of dirt on it. So I think we will chance this operation with this slightly dirty scalpel."

Not on me! All it takes is a few germs to contaminate your whole body. I want my doctor's scalpel to be absolutely clean when he cuts me open. In the same way, God is so holy that He is as offended by an evil thought as He is by murder. While there are differences in the consequences of sin, there is no difference in essence.

That's how holy God is, how totally unlike us. We have to do the adjusting. He's not going to change. When you understand the holiness of God, something's got to happen. Have you made the adjustment?

─────── **Think About It** ───────

If God were not perfectly holy, He would simply be a slightly better version of us, not a Person worthy of our worship.

REFLECTION

O ur first week together has been a loaded one. Whenever you decide to start getting to know God better, you quickly realize that He is infinite in His character and perfection. That's why getting to know God is really a lifelong pursuit.

But what better way to occupy yourself than with the study of our awesome God? He invites us to know Him, and the benefits are never-ending. No wonder Solomon wrote, "The fear of the LORD is the beginning of wisdom, and the knowledge of the Holy One is understanding" (Proverbs 9:10).

As you reflect this weekend on God's greatness, His truthfulness, His essence as spirit, His self-sufficiency, and His holiness, make some fundamental decisions:

1. *Let God be God*. Sounds pretty basic, doesn't it? But we have a tendency to box God in, trim Him down to fit our preconceived ideas. But even if we could shrink God to our size, we wouldn't like the result.

2. *Practice His presence*. Make worship a daily attitude of your heart, not a once-a-week performance you do for God.

3. *Seek to live a holy life*. The idea of trying to be holy sounds scary to a lot of people and it is. You don't try to be holy. If you know Christ, you are already declared righteous and holy in His sight. Being holy is a matter of living up to your standing: obeying and following Christ, taking the same attitude toward sin that He has. You can do it because you have the Holy Spirit inside of you to empower you to live in a holy manner.

*"Who has directed the Spirit of the LORD, or as His counselor
has informed Him?" Isaiah 40:13*

A TRUE KNOW-IT-ALL
Read It: Psalm 139:1-6

If your grade school was anything like mine, you had a "know-it-all" in your class. On any subject, Mister or Miss Know-it-all could expound at length. Nothing made you madder than to see some kid who acted like he knew everything, because you knew he didn't know half of it.

There's only one who knows it all in the universe, and it isn't that kid. It is the great God whose perfections we have been studying. One of the attributes of our God is His *omniscience*, a word made up of two words: *omni*, which means all, and *science*, which has to do with knowledge.

So when we talk about the omniscience of God, we are referring to His "all-knowingness," what God knows. This is one of a trilogy of God's "omni" attributes we will consider the next few days. A simple definition is that God's omniscience refers to His perfect knowledge of all things both actual and potential.

Let's make sure we get it down straight. The omniscience of God means that there is absolutely nothing He doesn't know—that there is no information system or set of data that exists anywhere outside of God's knowledge—nothing. He depends on no one outside of Himself for any knowledge about anything.

I like the story of the wealthy grandfather who was getting up in age. He was going deaf, but he went to the doctor and was fitted with a unique hearing aid. It not only overcame the old man's deafness, but it allowed him to hear perfectly. When he went back to the doctor for a checkup, the doctor commented, "Well, your family must be extremely happy to know that you can now hear."

The grandfather said, "No, I haven't told them about my hearing aid. I just sit around and listen to the conversations. I've already changed my will twice."

When folk don't think you know, it will greatly affect what they say and do! Are you living in light of the fact that God hears and sees everything you say and do? I hope so, because He does.

——— **Think About It** ———
God knows you intimately, every cell
in your body, and He loves you!

> *"Behold, heaven and the highest heaven cannot contain Thee." 1 Kings 8:27*

HE'S EVERYWHERE
Read It: Isaiah 43:1-7

God is everywhere. He's immense. Nothing can contain Him because He is *omnipresent*, present everywhere all at the same time. Theologians call it His immensity.

Many of us understand immensity when we go into the closet and put on our clothes, only to burst out of them. You know someone's gaining weight when a lot of new suits and dresses start showing up. That's one of the telltale signs that some dead monkey is on the line somewhere!

That's what happens when you stuff God into the universe. Solomon says, "You burst out of it. It cannot contain You." God's presence is so vast that not only is He everywhere in the known universe, but He bursts through its boundaries and fills the things we don't even know about.

God's presence is also distinct in that all of Him exists everywhere. He is not broken up into parts. Each little piece of the universe has the entire presence of God. The reason we know this is that God's being cannot be divided.

Yet even though God is equally present everywhere in all of His fullness, He is *not* equally related to everyone and everything. In other words, there is an equality of essence, but not of relationship. The Bible says, for example, that people need to call on God "while He is near" (Isaiah 55:6). That's not a statement about God's essence, but about the way He relates to people.

Again, the prophet says God's people "remove[d] their hearts far from Me" (Isaiah 29:13). This is a moral and spiritual statement, not a reflection on God's omnipresence. God the Father was there when Jesus died, yet Jesus said, "My God! My God! Why hast Thou forsaken Me?"

Isaiah 43:1-7 teaches that God takes care of His own. He is present with His children in a way that He is not present with those who don't know Him. If you know Jesus Christ, God treats you like one of the family. You enjoy His special relational presence. You can call Him "Abba," which means Daddy. Talk about benefits!

——————— **Think About It** ———————

It's one thing to say that God is everywhere. It's quite another to realize that because you are His child, He's with you everywhere you go.

"Thou hast made the heavens and the earth by Thy great power and by Thine outstretched arm! Nothing is too difficult for Thee."
Jeremiah 32:17

GOD'S GOT THE POWER
Read It: Job 38:1-7

One night I came out to my kitchen and found a roach on my counter. This was unlike any roach I had ever seen. It was a "jump bad in your face, get down" roach. When I walked up to this brother, he didn't run away. He just stood there as if to say, "Look, this is my house."

I couldn't believe it. It was just amazing to look at this thing. I would move my hand in front of it, and it did not budge. Obviously, it did not know who I am, because I squashed that boy flat!

You know, that's what autonomous man does to God. He gets "roachy" on God. He pops back like he is someone, like he has a little power. He's got a little degree behind his name. He's got some machines that can take him into outer space, and he thinks he's got power. But it's suicide to "jump bad" against God. He has *unlimited* power.

Monday we learned there is nothing God does not know; that's His omniscience. Yesterday we learned there is no place where He does not exist; that's His omnipresence. But that's not all. There is nothing God cannot do; that's His *omnipotence*.

People often say that God has to show them His power before they'll believe. He *has* shown us His power. God asked Job a very interesting question: "Where were you when I laid the foundation of the earth!" (Job 38:4). God was saying, "I didn't have to get any advice or help to pull any of this off."

Think about it. It takes no more effort for God to create a universe than it does for Him to create an ant. All He has to do is say, "Ant be," and you've got an ant. He says, "Universe be," and you've got a universe.

See, once you know God can make the universe, nothing else is hard. If He can pull that off, He can do anything you can ask and far beyond.

——————— **Think About It** ———————

Is there something in your life that's too big for you to deal with? Bring it to God, because nothing is too hard for Him!

"We were eyewitnesses of His majesty. . . . when we were with Him on the holy mountain." 2 Peter 1:16, 18

OUR GOD IS "HEAVY"
Read It: Matthew 17:1-8

Remember when we used to say, "That's heavy," when we heard something awesome? Well, that's an appropriate response to the glory of God. His glory is the visible manifestation of His attributes, character, and perfections. The word *glory* in the Old Testament is a very interesting word that means "to be weighted, to be heavy." Today we might respond, "Awesome!"

When we talk about glory, then, we are talking about someone with an awesome reputation because He has awesome splendor. God is glorious. You can see it in everything He has made. But His glory is most fully seen in the person of Jesus Christ. John 1:18 puts it this way: "No man has seen God at any time; the only begotten God [Jesus], who is in the bosom of the Father, He has explained [revealed] Him."

In His earthly life, Jesus Christ was God's glory in human flesh. That's why He did what only God could do: heal the sick, raise the dead, read people's minds, know the future. Jesus was God in human flesh. His glory was veiled, though, because no one can look on God and live.

But in Matthew 17 Jesus took Peter, James, and John up to a mountain. There Christ zipped down His humanity, so to speak. He took off the veil of flesh for just a minute, and bursting out of His humanity was a bright light. The voice from heaven was so awesome the apostles had to hide their faces because the glory of God was revealed on that mountain in the person of Jesus Christ, who was God become man.

There are only two groups of beings who won't voluntarily glorify God: fallen men and fallen angels. Both will someday be discarded from His presence because throughout all eternity, God will only fellowship with those who voluntarily bring Him glory.

You see, your claim that you esteem God will be validated by how you respond to the God you say you esteem. The proof that you glorify God, that you recognize His intrinsic value, will be the value that you ascribe to His glory.

———— **Think About It** ————

We have the privilege of bringing glory to the most glorious Being in the universe! What are you going to do today that will glorify God?

"Oh, the depth of the riches both of the wisdom
and knowledge of God!" Romans 11:33

THE WISDOM OF GOD
Read It: 1 Corinthians 1:18-31

Our God is all-wise. God's wisdom is His unique ability to so interrelate His attributes that He accomplishes His predetermined purpose by the best means possible. That's a big definition, so let's break it down.

God's wisdom is tied to His purpose. Paul makes this clear in Ephesians 1:8b-10, where he says that God's purpose is "the summing up of all things in Christ." Jesus Christ is the wisdom of God, just as we saw yesterday that He is the glory of God. Paul says that Christ "became to us wisdom from God" (1 Corinthians 1:30).

God's wisdom is seen in the plan He devised for our salvation. None of us would have come up with the plan God did. In our "wisdom" we would have made it much more confusing, complex, and inequitable. We would have devised a "lay-away" plan or an "earn-your-way-to-heaven" scheme.

But God in His wisdom came up with a salvation that is free to all and available to all by sending His Son to die for our sins. Yet the Cross looks foolish to a dying world that is depending on its own wisdom.

That's why in 1 Corinthians 1, Paul throws some jabs at folk who think they are smart: "The foolishness of God is wiser than men" (v. 25). "God has chosen the foolish things of the world to shame the wise" (v. 27). Why? So that "no man should boast before God" (v. 29).

You can see how God's attributes interact and interrelate here, because the reason He chooses what seems to be the foolish and the weak to accomplish His purpose is that He won't share His glory with anyone.

So God doesn't look just for the wise and the powerful. But does He call *any* wise or powerful to Himself? Of course He does. A noblewoman once told the British preacher John Wesley that she was saved by an *m*. Wesley wanted to know what she meant. "God says not many noble can be saved. He did not say not *any*," she replied. Smart lady!

─────── **Think About It** ───────

Wouldn't it be great to tap into God's wisdom to help you live
your life *today*? You can. Just ask Him for it (James 1:5).

REFLECTION

If you're starting to feel as if you're surrounded by the presence and power and knowledge and glory and wisdom of God, you're making some real progress in getting to know Him.

We've talked about a lot of great truths this week, the kind of stuff it will take you and me the rest of our lives to comprehend. But that's the exciting part about getting to know God. You never run out of new material, you never get bored, you never learn it all—because He is infinite in all of His attributes and perfections.

You may want to take the weekend just to reflect on what we've learned this week. That's fine, but let me give you something else to think about. Read Romans 8:31-39, and you'll see that our great and glorious God has given us some great and glorious blessings in Christ. Consider these benefits of knowing and serving Him:

1. No opposition (v. 31).

2. No deprivation (v. 32).

3. No condemnation (vv. 33-34).

4. No separation (vv. 35-39).

There's no one else in town offering a salvation like that! Be sure to spend some time praising and thanking God this weekend for what He's done for you.

"The judgments of the LORD . . . are more desirable than gold, yes, than much fine gold." Psalm 19:9-10

BETTER THAN GOLD
Read It: Psalm 19:7-14

We live in a world that has lost the value of God's Word. The Bible now plays second fiddle to many other things that have no lasting value attached to them.

But the problem is ours, not God's. It's almost impossible to overstate the importance of His revelation. It's the inerrant (errorless) means by which He reveals Himself to us. God says to us, "You want to know Me? Devour My Book." Job understood that. God's Word was more vital to him than his daily food (Job 23:12).

In other words, what God had to say was more important to Job than his fried chicken, greens, and corn bread. That's serious! It was the fuel by which Job lived—by which he was sustained during severe trial. We're in a time of severe trial today. Our need for the Bible is critical, because we're watching a generation "perish for the lack of knowledge."

The Bible addresses our dilemma. It answers our desperate need for something stable, solid, and dependable to guide us. Psalm 19 gives at least four examples of what the Word of God can do for us: (1) It is so comprehensive that it can transform your whole person (v. 7a). (2) It teaches you how to live skillfully; it imparts wisdom (v. 7b). (3) The Word shows you the true path to follow as you wind through life's maze. In fact, you will never see life as it really is until you see it through the lens of the Bible (v. 8). (4) There are no impurities in the Word, no errors that will lead you into a ditch if you follow it (v. 9). God's Word is the enduring standard against which everything is to be judged.

Sounds great, doesn't it? So what should you do about the good things in God's Word? Today's verse tells you. Go after them like a miner with gold fever!

Want to know how much you value the Word? Answer this question: What's more important to you, your Bible or your money? David was called a man after God's own heart because he valued God's Word more than his paycheck.

——— **Think About It** ———
David knew his paycheck couldn't give him life—and neither can your paycheck or mine give us life. But God's Word can.

"Thou art good and doest good." Psalm 119:68

GOD IS SO GOOD
Read It: Psalm 25:8; 34:8

Many of us grew up singing the little chorus, "God Is So Good." That song contains some profound theology, because the goodness of God is one of the infinite attributes of His character. If we're going to know God as He is, we must understand that He is good.

God's goodness can be defined as the collective perfections of His nature and the benevolence of His acts. In other words, God is good by nature and good in what He does.

When we go home to my parents' house every year, my mother cooks this big meal. Inevitably she will cook some unholy vegetable like squash or one of its cousins. You know, something that seems to have no purpose in creation. Anyway, when that vegetable bowl comes around, I just pass it right on. But my mother will say, "Boy, what do you think you're doing?"

Then I do my George Bush imitation. Remember when Bush said, "I'm the president, and I don't have to eat broccoli"? Well, I say to my mother, "Mama, I don't want any squash. I'm a grown man. I don't have to eat squash."

But she says, "You are in my house. You didn't see a hotel sign outside that front door, did you?" She will take the bowl and start putting the squash on my plate. And she will always put more squash on my plate than I would have if I had just gone ahead and taken it.

Then she says, "And you'd better eat it all. It's good for you." You know, she's right. Squash is good for you. Now I'd rather have German chocolate cake a la mode. I can get excited about that. But it's not good for me. Everything that's good does not necessarily taste good, look good, or give you a pleasant emotional experience. The issue of goodness is its source, not its experience.

The Bible declares in James 1:17: "Every good thing bestowed and every perfect gift is from above, coming down from the Father of lights." Anything that is authentically good has its source in God, because He is a good God who can only produce that which is good.

--------- **Think About It** ---------
If something is not good, it did not come from God.
Don't let anyone tell you God is the source of evil.

"Our God is a consuming fire." Hebrews 12:29

A TOUGH SUBJECT
Read It: Nahum 1:2-6

The story is told of a little boy whose mother got upset when he refused to eat his prunes. She told him that if he didn't eat, God was going to get mad at him. But the boy said no and took off to his room. As soon as he got there, a huge thunderstorm broke out with lots of thunder and lightning.

Thinking her son might be afraid, his mother rushed into his room and saw him staring out the window. "Mama, all this fuss over some prunes?"

God's wrath is a lot more serious than that. It's not an easy subject to talk about, but it's as integral to God's nature as His other perfections, so we need to acquaint ourselves well with this divine attribute if we want to know Him. The wrath of God is His necessary, just, and righteous retribution against sin.

The Bible has more to say about God's wrath than it does about His love. Of course God is good, kind, loving, and forgiving. But if you put a period there, you've got an incomplete story.

God is a God of wrath too. I want to give you the straight scoop because it's better to have a headache now than a "hell ache" later. The Bible's words for *wrath* indicate God's intense displeasure at sin and His judgment against it. God does not throw temper tantrums or pitch fits, but His anger against sin is intense.

In fact, God takes torrid displeasure at sin—big sin, little sin, medium-sized sin. Because He is holy, all sin is repulsive to Him. Romans 1:18 is the most concise statement of God's wrath in the Bible, and we do well to pay close attention to it: "The wrath of God is revealed from heaven against all ungodliness."

Notice that God is not hiding His wrath. He's not putting it under a bushel. It's part of His character. That's why I can't skip preaching about it as a pastor. He's telling us in advance that this is part of who He is. Aren't you glad God told us the truth about His wrath so we could escape it by running to Christ? I am!

——— **Think About It** ———

We have to adjust to God's wrath because He doesn't change (Malachi 3:6). This is God's universe, run by His rules.

"God demonstrates His own love toward us, in that while we were yet sinners, Christ died for us." Romans 5:8

HE LOVES YOU
Read It: 1 John 4:16-19

The concept of love has been so used, abused, and misused today that you can hide almost anything behind it. That's because most people are looking for love in all the wrong places. They know they need it; they know they've got to have it. But where to find it and how to know if it's authentic is another question.

If you feel like that, I have good news for you: God is love! I know you've heard that before, but I hope that little phrase will take on some new meaning for you today. Let me start with a definition: The love of God is His joyful self-determination to reflect the goodness of His will and glory by meeting our needs.

The Bible is absolutely clear on this: There is *no* definition of love that means anything unless it is rooted in God. No matter how you define love, if it doesn't begin with God, it is flawed. It will either be incomplete or imbalanced, but either way it will be incorrect because God's character defines love.

Love is not just saying words. That's rap. True love is always expressed. God expressed His love in creation. You can look around you and see proof of God's love. But His greatest demonstration of love is in redemption— Jesus Christ hanging on the cross for all to see.

Once you see that, you see why true love is willing to pay a price for the one loved. It does not ask, "What am I going to get out of this," but, "What am I going to put into this so that the one I love can get something out of it?" God's love is not tied to the worth of the person being loved. That's good news because the only thing you and I are worthy of is judgment!

But don't misunderstand. The fact that God's love is unconditional doesn't make it weak and accepting of everything. Here's a major difference between divine love and what so often passes for love. Much of what people call love is just mush. God's love always makes judgment calls.

--------- **Think About It** ---------
If you have experienced God's love, you've got the real thing.
Don't settle for a weak imitation.

"For the grace of God has appeared,
bringing salvation to all men." Titus 2:11

CAN'T DO IT OURSELVES
Read It: Titus 2:11-13

What would you think if you went to buy a car, and the salesperson told you that you either had to push it everywhere you went or pay extra for an engine? You'd know something was wrong because that's not how it works. The engine is part of the purchase price of the car.

When I look at Christians who are living defeated lives, I see people who are "pushing" their Christian lives. They don't realize that the power they need is already under the hood.

That power is the grace of God, which is the inexhaustible supply of goodness by which He does for us what we could never do for ourselves. Some of us have the misconception that we have the power to pull off the Christian life. But if that were true, we would be no different than a non-Christian who keeps the Ten Commandments. It's all human effort.

But God has endowed every true believer with an abundant supply of His grace. Grace is not well understood today because it's used so flippantly or without a proper understanding of what's involved in it.

That's sad, because there's a lot involved. The grace of God is possible because of the sacrifice His Son made for our salvation. The only reason we are alive today and not consumed is because of what Jesus did. And the only reason we are going to heaven is because of what Jesus did (Ephesians 2:8-9). The "appearance" of God's grace is the coming of Jesus Christ to earth to die for us and bring us salvation.

Most of us have suffered the embarrassment of bouncing a check because of insufficient funds. But there is no such thing as insufficient grace. God's got some grace for every need you have. And Paul tells us in today's reading that God's grace also trains us in how to live the victorious Christian life.

Grace will give you victory where you didn't have victory. Grace will give you power where you didn't have power. Grace will give you the ability to keep on keeping on when you want to give up. Do you need more grace? God's got it (James 4:6).

——————— **Think About It** ———————
Since God is full of grace, you and I can keep coming back for more.
That's worth praising Him for today!

REFLECTION

D o you feel that you know God a little better this weekend than you did last weekend? That's my prayer, because as I said at the beginning, it's the most important adventure you could ever take.

This week we've considered five more facets of God's perfect and glorious character. Can you name them without looking? I'll tell you what. I'll name the five attributes or traits for you. Then I want to suggest a fun exercise you can do to help in your reflection this weekend.

First, the five attributes: God's Word, His goodness, His wrath, His love, and His grace.

Now the exercise. Take a piece of paper and write down each of these five things, leaving plenty of space between each. For each item, write out your own definition and then add what this attribute or trait means to you personally, the difference it has made in your life.

Since we're only in the third week of the year, it's most likely cold where you are. Why not do this one in front of a warm fire—and when you're done, share your stuff with your mate or someone else in your family.

"The Word became flesh, and dwelt among us,
and we beheld His glory." John 1:14

GOD WITH US
Read It: Matthew 1:18-25

You may have taken all your Christmas decorations down by now, but these verses from the Christmas story describe the incarnation of God as well as any in the Scriptures. They tell us of Jesus Christ, who is one of a kind. He never wrote a book, yet the book that tells His story, the Bible, has outsold every other book in history. He never wrote a song, but there have been more songs written about Jesus than about anyone else. He never traveled more than a few miles from home, yet there are few places you can go where His name is not known.

Jesus is called the Son of God and the Son of Man because in His incarnation, He has the essence of both. Some groups who come knocking on your door will tell you that Jesus Christ is less than God. Don't believe it. He is fully God, co-equal with the Father. The title "Son of Man" does not involve any denial of deity.

When the Bible calls Jesus the "Son of Man," it means that He bears the true essence of humanity, apart from sin. When the Bible declares that Jesus is the "Son of God," it does not mean He's less than God. On the contrary, all of the characteristics that make God who He is are present in Jesus. He is God too.

In Jesus we have the perfect wedding of deity and humanity, coexisting in one Person without being confused or mixed. Theologians call this the "hypostatic union" of Christ, the nature of God and the nature of man located in one Person.

The glory of the Incarnation is that all of God was in Christ, and all of man was in Jesus. *Jesus* is the name that recognizes His humanity. *Christ* is the name, or actually the title, that recognizes His appointment for salvation.

What it all adds up to is a glorious Savior who is worthy of your complete trust and worship. Is Jesus Christ your "all in all" today?

-------- **Think About It** --------

The Incarnation solved our biggest problem: the need
for a Savior who had to be sinless and yet fully human
so He could die a real death for us.

*"Can you discover the depths of God? Can you discover
the limits of the Almighty?" Job 11:7*

CAN'T GET ENOUGH
Read It: Philippians 3:8-10

I hope you get the idea by now that we are on the adventure of a life-time when we pursue the knowledge of God. What we've learned about God should give us greater hunger to know Him more. If we're satisfied with what we know about Him already, we're of all people most miserable.

Did you know we're going to spend eternity getting to know God? The essence of heaven is the uninterrupted knowledge of God. What will make heaven so wonderful is that there will always be something new to know about God. And we have so much to learn, and this knowledge will come at such supersonic speed that we will not have time to sleep.

Let me mention four practical benefits of knowing God. The first is *obedience*. Because you know God, you obey Him. You follow Him. You submit to Him. It's obedient Christians who are blessed, not just smart ones.

Second, knowing God brings *peace*. "Grace and peace be multiplied to you in the knowledge of God" (2 Peter 1:2). The more you know God, the more at peace you should be. Yes, negative circumstances do come, but even in these times you can have a growing sense of inner peace if your knowledge of God is growing.

Third, knowing God gives us *wisdom*. Paul prayed that God would give the Ephesians "a spirit of wisdom and of revelation in the knowledge of Him" (1:17). The better you know God, the better the decisions you make.

Fourth, the knowledge of God brings *freedom*. In Galatians 4:8, Paul writes, "When you did not know God, you were slaves to those which by nature are no gods." When you lack the assurance and confidence that comes from knowing Him and from knowing who you are in Him, you can become a slave to what people think, to circumstances, to your emotions, to other people's rules and expectations—to almost anything.

Search your heart today and make sure that you have a healthy and growing desire to know God.

——— **Think About It** ———
If you really want to know God, no power on earth can stop you!
And God has promised to reveal Himself to those who seek Him.
What are you waiting for?

"Whether, then, you eat or drink or whatever you do, do all to the glory of God." 1 Corinthians 10:31

A PASSION FOR GOD
Read It: John 17:1-3

An airplane is meant to fly, a car is built to be driven, and clothes are designed to be worn. You would have very little use for a plane that would not fly, a car that would not move, or clothes that can no longer be worn.

Why? Because their purpose is not being realized. It's a great frustration to have things that are no longer useful. God must feel that way about us sometimes.

You were designed to know Him, not simply to have a comfortable life. You were not created just to get married, have children and a successful career, then grow old and enjoy retirement. These are some of life's benefits, its side dishes, not its purpose.

The tragedy today is that we have taken life's benefits and tried to make them our purpose. We're trying to make the side dishes the main course. The result is that we often find the benefits very unsatisfactory. No wonder.

So if the purpose of life is not marriage, success, happiness, or any of that, what is it? What were we created for? Answer: we were created to know and worship God with an all-consuming passion. That's it. That's why Paul tells us to do everything to God's glory.

Bringing glory to something means to put it on the mantel where it can be admired. A woman seeks glory when she decorates her home in such a way that guests say, "Wow, where do you get that?" She puts a special treasure on display so that when people see it, they are in awe.

That's what we're supposed to do for God. We're supposed to display Him in such a way that people are awed by Him. Glorifying God means to make Him look good, to place Him on display so that when others see our lives, they are in awe of our God.

Even in the everyday stuff, your goal should be to make God look good. But I can tell you, it takes real passion to live like that.

———— Think About It ————
To anyone who is trying to know and serve God halfheartedly without passion, I think Paul would say, "Why bother?"
If you're going to seek God, go for it like you mean it!

"You shall worship the Lord your God." Matthew 4:10

ARE WE WORSHIPING YET?
Read It: John 4:21-24

Worship is one of those activities we as Christians know we ought to be doing. But we're not always sure how to go about it. Like the puzzled party-goer who asks, "Are we having fun yet?" Christians sometimes try hard to worship but feel like asking, "Are we worshiping yet?"

One reason we get confused is because we tend to limit worship to one hour on Sunday. But what Jesus was teaching in John 4 is that God's presence is no longer confined to any temple or any mountain. He now lives inside His people.

This means that worship is not so much where you are—it's who you are. If you are a Christian, you are a temple of the living God. He lives within you. Does this mean we don't have to go to church anymore to worship God? Not at all.

What I am saying is that if you go to church thinking you are now going to *the* place of worship for *the* hour of worship, you've missed the message. If you limit worship to where you are, the minute you leave that place, you will leave your attitude of worship behind like a crumpled-up church bulletin.

That's why we have people who can worship on Sunday and do their thing on Monday. They do not understand that they carry worship around inside of them. Is the church a place of worship? Of course. But worshiping in church is not the sole extent of our worship.

The Bible does not leave this topic on the individual level only. We are not only temples of God individually, but the corporate fellowship is also His temple. This is the answer to the question, "Do I have to go to church to worship God?" People who ask that aren't really interested in worship.

See, people who balk at worshiping collectively are not worshiping privately. Private temple worship, *me*, always leads to corporate temple worship, *the body*. If you are worshiping privately, you can't wait to worship publicly. If you don't care about private worship, you'll debate whether you need public worship. What's your attitude toward worship?

──────── **Think About It** ────────
Show me a person who debates going to church
for corporate worship, and I will show you a person who
is debating whether to have devotions for private worship.

*"Whoever will call upon the name of the Lord
will be saved." Romans 10:13*

GUILTY BUT FREE
Read It: Romans 3:9-20

A young woman was caught going one hundred miles an hour in a fifty-five-mile-per-hour zone outside one of those small towns. The policeman brought her into court where the judge fined her one hundred dollars. "But I don't have one hundred dollars," she wailed.

"I'm sorry, but you will have to spend the weekend in jail," the judge told her. "You owe the court one hundred dollars. You may not have the money, but the law is the law."

She began to cry. "Please, your honor, I don't have one hundred dollars, but I don't want to spend the weekend in jail."

The judge said, "I can't change the law." But the young woman begged for mercy again—and to the surprise of the bailiff and the policeman, the judge did something very interesting. He pushed his chair back from the bench, took off his robe, walked around to where the woman was standing, pulled out his wallet, and gave the bailiff a one-hundred-dollar bill, went back to the bench, put his robe back on, and sat down.

Then the judge picked up his gavel and said, "Young lady, I see someone has paid your fine. Case dismissed. You're free to go."

That's what God did for you and me. We stood before the bench of His justice, and He said, "You've been found guilty of sinning against My holy character. You've either got to pay the price of perfection or spend eternity in the prison called hell."

But God the Judge also heard us cry out for mercy. He knew we had nothing to pay our debt with. So in the Person of Jesus Christ He stepped out of heaven, "zipped down" His deity, put on the robe of humanity, and paid the price Himself on the cross. Three days later, He put His robe of deity back on and ascended back to the bench of heaven.

Now He looks down and says to anyone who comes to Him and begs for mercy, "I can't change the law, but I can pay the price." You will never have to worry about heaven again if you know Jesus Christ.

——— Think About It ———
The Judge who pronounced sentence against you also paid your fine.
He'll do it for anyone who comes to Him. Do you know
someone who needs good news like that?

REFLECTION

We've packed a lot into these last four weeks. But you notice I haven't passed along any shortcuts or "tricks of the trade" to knowing God, because there aren't any. If you see a book with the title, *Getting to Know God in Four Easy Steps*, be suspicious!

The fact is that knowing God intimately takes the same kind of dedication and sweat and attention and time that it takes to know anyone really well. But just ask anybody who has a rich, growing, and satisfying marriage. The payoff for the effort is tremendous.

I think half the battle in this business of knowing God is learning to focus your heart and mind on Him and eliminating as many distractions as possible. There are a number of things you can do to help yourself here. Make it a regular habit to look at your daily schedule and figure out what you're spending your time on.

Try turning the TV off twenty minutes early, set your alarm twenty minutes early, and get in the habit of spending some quiet time with God. Start saying no to some things, maybe even to some good things, so you can say yes to something better, intimacy with God.

We still have a long way to go this year and a lot of good stuff to share, so I hope this opening series will give you a good foundation for a terrific year of spiritual growth and blessing.

TWO

FAITH

Gotta Have It!

Is faith a leap into the dark or a gift only a few people possess? Maybe it's "believing something you know isn't true," as a child once said. The answer is none of the above. Faith is your birthright as a Christian. Let's talk about how to tend and increase it by looking at the necessity, the anticipation, the confidence, and the conflicts of faith.

"We walk by faith, not by sight." 2 Corinthians 5:7

SIGHT UNSEEN
Read It: Romans 8:24-25; 2 Corinthians 4:16-18; Hebrews 11:1

Someone has said you don't have to be blind to have faith, but it helps. For some people, *blind* is a synonym for faith.

Do you buy that? I don't. Faith isn't blind, and God never asked you to close your eyes and leap into anything ignorantly. Where did we get the idea faith is blind? People confuse that idea with the fact that faith involves the unseen. But there's a world of difference between blindness and "things not seen."

Take the Hebrews. These Jewish Christians were wavering between their new faith and returning to Judaism. The writer of Hebrews is telling them that they must move on and not go back. But if they are going to move on, they are going to do it by faith.

That's the setting for Hebrews 11, God's "Hall of Faith." The writer is saying, "Look, the fact that you need to live by faith is nothing new. God's people have always lived by faith."

Hebrews 11:1 says faith takes things God has spoken about in the future and brings them to the present: "the assurance of things hoped for." It makes visible the invisible: "the conviction of things not seen." So if you don't see it, if it is tomorrow and not today, then it is a candidate for faith.

The world says, "Seeing is believing." I don't think so. You've got to take a blind leap of faith to believe that. Look at those grocery store tabloids with the phony photos made up to look like a ten-year-old gave birth to an alien. If you believe everything you see, I'd advise you not to watch too much television!

Committed Christians say, "Believing is seeing. Faith precedes sight." Now this is a fundamental distinction that tells you why many Christians are living defeated lives. If you are waiting to see before you believe, if you are saying, "I've got to see it before I move on it," you are living a defeated Christian life.

Faith is not just a nice idea; it's a necessity. If you're a Christian, you are by definition a person of faith. And Colossians 2:6-7 says you never outgrow your need for faith. So walk it and live it today.

──────── **Think About It** ────────
If God tested your "faith quotient" today,
what kind of reading would He get?

"The righteous will live by his faith." Habakkuk 2:4

APPROVED BY FAITH
Read It: Hebrews 11:2-3

How many times have you been showing your child how to do some task the right way when he stops you in the middle and says, "Dad, do we really have to do it this way?" What he's asking is, "Isn't there some quick lazy-man's way to get the same result?" That's when you say the same thing your parents said to you: "You have to do it this way if you want to get the job done right." What you're saying is, "If you want my approval, and my approval is what counts, you've got to do it this way."

That's what verse 2 of today's text is saying. If you want God's approval, you live by faith. This is how "the men of old" were approved. The people who were recognized by God were people who understood the necessity of faith.

Well, what did these people know and believe? One answer is in verse 3. They knew where they came from and where the world around them came from. God spoke, and the visible was created out of the invisible. As poet Elizabeth Barrett Browning wrote:

> *Earth is crammed with heaven*
> *And every common bush aflame with God.*
> *But only those who see will take off their shoes.*
> *The rest sit around and pluck blackberries.*

A person has to be a fool to be an atheist when he sees the creative genius of God. But a Christian has to be a fool to be a practical atheist, to live as though God is not there.

Because the believers of old, the men and women of Hebrews 11, were people of faith who knew who made them and whom they belonged to, they had a tremendous sense of God's presence even in tough times. They couldn't always see the answer, but they believed God.

So if you cannot see the solution to your problem or need or burden, but still you keep on believing God—if you live by faith—you are a great candidate for God's presence. Faith is confidence in the trustworthiness of God—the foundation of the house. Everything else stands on it. Stand on God's trustworthy Word. Build your hope on things eternal.

———— Think About It ————
Only Christians who live by faith enjoy the benefits of God's approval.

*"You received from us instruction as to how you ought
to walk and please God." 1 Thessalonians 4:1*

FAITH'S BEST
Read It: Genesis 4:1-4; Hebrews 11:4

When the author of Hebrews says he's going to talk about the "men of old," he isn't kidding. He goes back almost to the very beginning, to the second child born into this world—Abel, the son of Adam and Eve.

We learn real quick that Abel was a man of faith, while his older brother Cain was a man of sight. We see that from their offerings because Abel brought what God required. Cain brought what would look good in a fruit basket. Of course, the primary way we know these things is that God accepted Abel's sacrifice and rejected Cain's.

What we have here is an issue of faith and obedience. God had revealed to Adam's family that worship was important. We know that because they worshiped. They must have had a place for worship because the sons brought their offerings to a place. We also know that they had a time for worship—"in the course of time" or at the appointed time (v. 3).

So both Cain and Abel went to the appointed place at the appointed time. But only one offering was acceptable to God. Abel brought the kind of offering God wanted. He brought a blood offering. Abel sacrificed a sheep from his flock.

That means the boys had learned from their mother and father "how [they] ought to walk and please God." They knew blood was the only way by which God would forgive sin. "Without shedding of blood there is no forgiveness" (Hebrews 9:22).

But only Abel acted in faith on what he had learned. A blood sacrifice would be costly, but Abel knew it was what God wanted, and he was willing to give his best. Cain simply went out into his field, found some of his produce, picked it, and brought it. It was really leftovers. Didn't cost him much. A couple of apples out of a bushel don't amount to much.

Abel brought the best of his flock. He brought the choicest. He offered God a sacrifice of faith, and because of it God is still talking about Abel!

———— Think About It ————
Wouldn't it be great to have the kind of faith
God bragged about? You can have it—but only by giving Him
your best, not your leftovers.

*"Enoch walked with God; and he was not,
for God took him." Genesis 5:24*

MISSING PERSON
Read It: Genesis 5:18-24; Hebrews 11:5; Jude 14-15

Yesterday we learned that faith is necessary to please God in our worship. Abel worshiped in faith by bringing the proper sacrifice, and it gained him his plaque in God's Hall of Faith.

Today we learn that faith is necessary to please God in our walk—our life. Enoch must have been a man of remarkable faith when you realize the honor that God bestowed on him. Like the little boy said, "Enoch was walking with God, and one day they walked so far that God said, 'Enoch, we're closer to My house than to yours. Why don't you just come home with Me?'"

Now that's the kind of story you hear and say, "That's cute, but let's go on." No, let's stop. Let me tell you something about living by faith. Living by faith means you submit to the will of God over the long haul. For three hundred years after the birth of Methuselah, Enoch walked with God.

What does it mean to walk with God? It means that you live in light of the future so that you live to please God rather than living to please yourself. And that may mean pleasing God even when it's at a distinct disadvantage to your self-interests.

Walking by faith means giving up what you want because you would rather have what God wants. See, too many of us don't want to walk with God. We want to walk with ourselves or our friends—that is, live to please ourselves and others. But that doesn't require faith. Living by faith means I submit my will to God's will. I submit *myself* to God.

What gave Enoch the strength to go three hundred years? That's a long time to be walking with God. I think the answer is in Jude. Enoch looked ahead as a prophet and saw the coming of the Lord. And because he saw that, he proclaimed the coming of the Lord and walked with God.

So because Enoch saw the future, he could live in the present by faith. You have God's Word on the future lying open before you right now. Are you living today in light of it?

─────── **Think About It** ───────
Faith says, "This is what God says about tomorrow,
so I'd better adjust today."

"Without faith it is impossible to please [God]." Hebrews 11:6

THAT'S RIDICULOUS!
Read It: Genesis 6:13-14, 22; Hebrews 11:6-7

This week we've been dealing with the necessity of faith. Next week we'll consider faith's anticipation as we continue learning to tend and grow our faith.

Abel showed us the necessity of faith in our worship, Enoch in our walk. Today, through the eyes of Noah, we see the necessity of faith in our work. Notice that Noah acted after "being warned by God about things not yet seen" (v. 7). Remember what faith is? "The conviction of things not seen" (v. 1).

This dimension of faith takes on added meaning in Noah's case. Noah had never seen rain because it had never rained before. He's living in an area where in all probability he's never even seen a seagoing vessel. Yet God said, "I'm going to destroy the world. Build a boat."

Now if there was ever a time when it would be hard to act in faith, this was it. Noah was the only saint around. You think you've got it tough being a Christian. Well, at least there is another one next to you. In Noah's day, it was him and his household—that's it.

If there was ever a man who had a reason to complain, it was Noah. "God, it's too wicked out here to be righteous!" But Noah doesn't complain, doesn't whimper. He obeys. He does what God tells him even though it seems ridiculous. We can only imagine the ridicule he endured.

All Noah had going for him was a four-word sermon: "It's going to rain." All he had going for him was the prophecy of God: "One day the sky's going to open up, and it's going to rain. Now, Noah, you only have one question to answer. You don't need to go to meteorology school. You don't need to analyze the weather. What you need to decide is, am I trustworthy?"

Here's what I want to ask you today. What "ark" has God called you to build? What ridiculous thing has He called you to do? What crazy command has He asked you to follow through on? What seemingly imbecilic instruction does He want you to carry out faithfully? And what ridiculous ridicule are you undergoing?

——— **Think About It** ———

If you're going to live by faith, you'd better learn to discount other people's opinions and mark up the value of God's Word.

REFLECTION

Yesterday I didn't say much about Hebrews 11:6 because I wanted to save it for some more extended reflection. The verse is absolutely clear: "Without faith it is impossible to please Him, for he who comes to God must believe that He is, and that He is a rewarder of those who seek Him."

Please underline the word *impossible*. Without faith you are not experiencing God in your life. It's possible for us as Christians to live by sight and not by faith. When that happens, we are not pleasing to God, and we will not be rewarded by Him.

Faith is necessary for anyone who wants to "come" to God —which means to draw near to God, see God, know God, experience God, sense God, know God's power, know God's presence, know God's character. Anyone who really wants to see God work, anyone who wants to come near to God, must first believe that He is.

Now what does this mean? If you are a Christian, you already believe and know that God exists. The idea here is that we must first believe He is there. See, many of us who are saved really don't believe that God is there.

How do I know that? Because we think we have to pull off the Christian life on our own, in our strength and under our own power. We think that if we don't do it, it won't get done. So we go around in circles trying to pull off in the flesh what God wants to do in the Spirit if we'll believe He is there and available.

This weekend why not take a new step of faith and tell God you believe He's there, and you want to do things His way.

*"Abraham believed God, and it was reckoned
to him as righteousness." Romans 4:3*

LOOKING FOR A CITY
Read It: Genesis 11:27–12:4; Hebrews 11:8-10

Today begins the second week of our series on faith. This week we'll see that people of faith live in *anticipation* of God's promises.

Suppose the doctor told you you had an incurable disease and had only twelve months to live. I suspect your anticipation of death would greatly alter your life, beginning today.

You might start rebuilding broken relationships. You would probably start going places you'd always wanted to see and doing important things you had put off. You would get your personal and financial affairs in order, because there's something about the knowledge of the future that has great impact on the present.

That's how people of faith live. They are able to see God in their tomorrow and live in light of that in their today. In fact, the anticipation of faith was enough to cause a resident of a sophisticated city to slap a For Sale sign in the yard and head to a desert for a sweaty existence in a hot tent!

I want to show you something about this man called Abraham, the "father of the faithful." Notice that Abraham immediately obeys God's Word when it is revealed. Hebrews 11:8 literally reads, "While he was being called, he obeyed."

To put it another way, as soon as Abraham hears God's voice, he begins packing. And remember, Abraham doesn't find out where he's going until he obeys the command to go. Until you do the little that God has told you to do, He won't show you the more you are praying about.

Many people want to know the back end result before they do the little thing God has commanded them to do on the front end. But God only hits a moving target, and if you are not moving, you will never know where you are supposed to be going.

Abraham obeyed. God was calling him to a new world and a new way of life, and Abraham got up and went. You have been called out of an old way of living, thinking, and acting into a new way of living, thinking, and acting called the walk of faith. How is yours going today?

——— **Think About It** ———
It's only when we faithfully obey what God has clearly
revealed to us that He reveals the unclear areas.

*"The things impossible with men are possible
with God." Luke 18:27*

DON'T LAUGH
Read It: Hebrews 11:11-12

Probably no event in life is anticipated with more eagerness than the birth of a baby. Once a pregnancy is confirmed, you've got about eight months to look forward to the big day. And if it's your first child, those are the longest months of your life.

Well, when it comes to anticipation, you haven't seen anything like Abraham and Sarah. They had twenty-five *years* to anticipate Isaac. That's how long it was between God's promise and Isaac's birth. In fact, it was so long that by the time God announced He was going to fulfill His promise, Sarah laughed (Genesis 18:12). Now everyone knows that, but did you know old Abe laughed too (see 17:15-17)?

Hebrews 11:11 makes it sound like a simple deal, but that's just a summary statement. The full story is that Sarah is ninety, and Abraham is one hundred. Sarah has never been able to have children, and Abraham is far past the age for producing children.

When God says, "I am going to give you a baby," Sarah falls down laughing. Why? It was beyond human possibility. Sarah knows she has three problems. She's barren; Abraham is "as good as dead" (Hebrews 11:12) when it comes to fathering a child, and both of them are hitting the century mark. Three excellent reasons not to take God seriously.

Faith kicked in somewhere. Hebrews says that Sarah's ability to conceive didn't take place until she engaged her faith. When she took God at His word, things happened. The anticipation of faith got serious.

See, faith has a unique perspective. It looks at God's power, not at people's limitations. The exercise of faith gave Sarah and Abraham power they didn't have before. Some of us are anemic because we listen to people and not to God. We let people control us.

Is a lack of faith holding you back? Are you living so much to please people and fit their limitations that you're not tapping into the power of God? Maybe it's time to stop looking around and start looking up today.

——— **Think About It** ———
If Sarah didn't receive the power to conceive until she
exercised faith, then Abraham didn't get the power to do anything
until she exercised faith. That's the key.

"All these, having gained approval through their faith, did not receive what was promised." Hebrews 11:39

UNFULFILLED PROMISES
Read It: Hebrews 11:13a, 39-40

Today's lesson packs a wallop. It shows us that people of faith antici- pate receiving what God has promised whether they ever experience that fulfillment or not.

We would say, "Wait a minute. How can you believe in a promise you never see fulfilled?" But that's exactly what verse 13 says. People like Enoch and Noah and Abraham did not live to see the ultimate fulfillment of God's promise, yet they still died believing it.

In other words, to trust God is to bank on His Word even when there is nothing visible to demonstrate that what He says is going to come true. Trusting God means that when you are on your deathbed, and it still doesn't happen, you trust Him. That's living the life of faith.

We get some help in the preposition translated "in" (v. 13). It's a dif- ferent word than the one used in the preceding phrases, "by faith." The word here reads "through faith" or "according to faith." That is, these peo- ple lived in accordance with the faith rule. Faith was the ruling principle on which they built their lives.

So even though they went to their graves without seeing the full real- ization of the promises of God, they closed their eyes in death saying, "God still told the truth." They knew that fulfillment was coming, and they lived in the anticipation of it.

That's what God is asking you and me to do today. He wants us to live before Him in such a way that we anticipate His promises even when every circumstance is going opposite to what those promises say.

This is a revealing section. For instance, it kills the teachings of "pros- perity theology," the concept of faith as a means of manipulating God to do what I want Him to do. The Bible tells me that some of His people live and die, and it doesn't happen, and yet they live and die in faith. If you're still anticipating something you are asking God to do in your life, don't try to manipulate Him or your circumstances. Let Him bring it about— and be prepared to keep trusting Him if it doesn't happen.

——— **Think About It** ———
Faith is trusting God when He's not doing what I want
and when He's not conforming at all to my desires.

*"By faith [Abraham] lived as an alien in the
land of promise." Hebrews 11:9*

TALK IT UP
Read It: Philippians 3:20; Hebrews 11:13b-14

If you have the kind of faith we've been talking about here in Hebrews 11, it's worth talking about! Today's verses tell us that people of faith verbalize the promises of God to others.

Notice what the writer of Hebrews says. Both of these verses have to do with what these people said. They didn't mind admitting they were "strangers and exiles" on earth. In fact, that's what they called themselves, because they were anticipating a better place.

Then verse 14 broadens it: "Those who say such things." One of the ways you validate and illuminate your faith, and strengthen it somewhat, is to learn the talk of faith while you're learning the walk of faith.

Many of us are self-defeating in our conversation. We confess doubt. Now this is very different from the "name it, claim it" crowd that wants to conjure up things by sheer force of their confession. I'm not talking about conjuring up new things. I'm talking about verbalizing old things.

I'm talking about communicating what God has said rather than conjuring up just what I want. See, there are some people who say, "I need a new car. I believe God wants to give me a new car. So in faith I speak it into my garage by confessing it and claiming it. If I just talk about this new car the right way, it's going to appear in my garage."

Well, you may be disappointed. You won't find any basis to talk that way in these verses. What Abraham and his pals did when they confessed was to verbalize and visualize the Word of God applied to their situation.

The Bible is so sufficient, so complete that when you take the principles of the Word and verbalize them in your situation, they become real to you where you are. That's why you don't need magic to live the Christian life.

The Word of God is so comprehensive that when you apply the truth of Scripture to your circumstance, it will address that circumstance and sustain you while you have to wait. Practice talking the talk of faith today.

--- **Think About It** ---
Someone has said you should never doubt in the dark what
God told you in the light. That's a good word.

"They desire a better country, that is a heavenly one."
Hebrews 11:16

NO GOING BACK
Read It: Genesis 24:1-9; Hebrews 11:15-16

What a great passage to finish up the work week! These verses show us that the person of faith focuses on the future rather than the past.

See, Abraham could have gone back to Ur. He could have called his realtor and canceled the closing on the house. But he didn't go back because he wasn't thinking back. Neither were these other people of faith.

If you are going from Ur to Canaan but you are thinking only about Ur, you are either not going to get to Canaan, or you are not going to enjoy being in Canaan because your mind isn't there. Fundamentally, living by faith is a matter of the mind.

It's very clear from Genesis 24 what Abraham was thinking about and where his heart and mind were. He made his servant swear an oath that he would never take Isaac back to the land of Ur. Better to have him be a single man in Canaan than find a wife and settle down in Ur.

Much later Israel got stuck in the wilderness because they kept reflecting on Egypt. Every time God said, "Go to Canaan," they said, "Oh, but back there in Egypt . . ."

Many of us can't enjoy the Christian life because we are thinking about how much fun the world used to be. We're thinking about the garlic and the leeks back in Egypt, and we are stuck out here in the wilderness with manna.

Well, I'm here to tell you that if you start thinking like that, you're looking at about forty years of aimless wandering in your Christian pilgrimage.

The person of faith is looking to tomorrow, as hard and as far away as it may look. Biblical faith says, "God, I am looking at Your tomorrow." Now what's back there may be enticing. Back there may be a lot of fun and old friends. But God isn't back there. God left Ur, God left Egypt, and you'll find Him in Canaan. God is in your future.

Are you being tempted to look back or even go back today? Claim the promises of God, anticipate them, look ahead to God's future for you. Look ahead to where He is taking you.

--- **Think About It** ---

A person of faith distinguishes between time and eternity (v. 16).

REFLECTION

You know, true faith brings with it a lot of wonderful rewards, but here's one I bet you haven't thought about for a while. It's sort of hidden in the middle of Hebrews 11:16: "Therefore God is not ashamed to be called their God."

This is not talking about salvation. The picture here is the flip side of 1 John 2:28, where the Apostle John tells us to abide in Christ so that when He comes, we won't be "ashamed" (KJV) before Him. The writer of Hebrews says God is not ashamed of these folk because they believed Him and lived in anticipation of His promises.

Think about this. People you are ashamed of, you don't hang around much. If I'm ashamed to be with you, I'm either going to avoid you, or we are going to be very uncomfortable with each other. Now hold onto your seat. The reason many Christians are living unhappy lives is because God is ashamed of them. He doesn't want people to know that they know Him. And since He's not happy to be walking and talking with them, they are not living lives of real joy, peace, purpose, or direction.

I realize that's a heavy concept for a weekend reflection, but give it some thought. For a practical step of application and a fascinating Bible study, take your concordance (and if you don't have one, put this book down, go get one, and put it next to your Bible) and look up the references for "ashamed." They're a real eye-opener.

"By faith Abraham, when he was tested, offered up Isaac."
Hebrews 11:17

RIGHT, LORD!
Read It: Genesis 22:1-2; Hebrews 11:17; James 2:14

So far in our study of faith we've considered the necessity and the anticipation of faith. This week let's talk about the *confidence* of faith. Faith has about it a sense of confidence that's embedded in its definition: "assurance of things hoped for, the conviction of things not seen" (v. 1).

The message I want to plant in your heart this week is this: Christians who live by faith exercise confidence in God's promises. The essence of the faith life is that you believe what God says enough to stake a claim on it and obey it.

Now you knew we weren't going to get far into any discussion of faith without running into Abraham. And the Abraham story we've got this week is one that the Bible recognizes as one of the greatest expressions of faith ever recorded: Abraham's offering of Isaac. It's a rich saga of faith, because Abraham shows us here what it means to live by faith.

It's important to remember that Genesis 22 is not when Abraham gets saved, to use New Testament terminology. He expressed his faith back in Genesis 12, many years earlier. So what we have here is a way of life—a living, decision-making kind of faith in motion. It is not enough to rest on what you did with God ten years ago.

Some of us have great *deja vu* stories. We're still talking about how things used to be. But we need an "I Am" kind of God, a God who works in the present tense. That's why you ought to underline the word *tested* in today's verse. Abraham's faith was a present reality that would stand by him in the great test God was about to send his way.

Think about it. There's one sure way you can know whether you really believe what you think you believe, say you believe, and ought to believe. Let God put your faith to the test. And don't worry—He will.

How will God test you this week? I don't know, but that's not the issue. The issue is, how will you respond? Pray that God will enable you to pass His faith test.

--- **Think About It** ---

True faith demonstrates confidence in God in the time of testing.
It's easy to trust when everything is cool.

"Blessed is a man who perseveres under trial." James 1:12

TAKING THE TEST
Read It: Genesis 22:3; James 1:2-4

Many of us are great faith-talkers. We talk about trusting God very smoothly, and unfortunately sometimes very glibly.

But trust in God is not a static statement. It is active obedience. That's why you don't know the stuff your faith is made of until it's tested. So what God does is design tests for us—not to wipe us out, but to show us where we stand and teach us how to put some muscle on our faith. The confidence comes from passing the test.

God does not test you for His information. He already knows whether you are going to pass and graduate to a new level of spiritual maturity. As I said yesterday, God's purpose for testing you is to let you know whether you really believe what you think you believe.

I used to tell my teachers in school, "I know that stuff." They would say, "We'll see. We'll see." They were saying, "Okay, Anthony, what you think you know will be demonstrated by a test."

Testing is not unusual in life. James even tells you to get excited when you come up against all kinds of tests because they give you the opportunity to strut your stuff. Here's the chance to put into practice the things you have learned.

To get a driver's license, you have to take a test. Never mind that you've been driving since you were thirteen. The driver's test is still the standard you have to attain. And didn't it feel great to pass and get that license? When God gives you a test, He does it with joy because He knows it's going to bring you joy to pass it.

So Abraham is going to be tested. Now this is a great test because this is a great man who has received a great promise. And the New Testament says that you and I, as members of the Church of Jesus Christ, have received many "precious and magnificent promises" (2 Peter 1:4), marvelous things that God has supplied for us in time and in eternity. Are they worth the effort it takes to pass the test? You know it!

--------- **Think About It** ---------
A product that has never even been tested
to see if it can do what it claims it can do isn't worth
a whole lot. It's the same with our faith.

"Take now your son, your only son . . . Isaac." Genesis 22:2

ONLY ONE LIKE HIM
Read It: Genesis 22:4-6; Hebrews 11:18

I still get chills when I read Genesis 22. See, I have two sons. Anthony, Jr., is my firstborn son, although he's not my oldest child.

God has never asked me to sacrifice Anthony. From the human standpoint, from father to son, Abraham is being asked to make a horrific sacrifice.

But there's more here. Isaac is the son of promise. Through Isaac God's promise that Abraham will become the "father of a great nation" is going to be fulfilled. So if you're with me here, you know the question: How can Abraham kill Isaac and still be the father of a great nation? Abraham not only has to kill his son, but it also looks as if he will lose the promise.

That's because Isaac was Abraham's "only son" (Genesis 22:2, 12, 16). Now Abraham already had a son named Ishmael. But Isaac was Abraham's "only begotten" son—his unique, one-of-a-kind son.

Does that sound familiar? Who else is called the "only begotten Son"? It's Jesus Christ. We are sons of God, but Jesus Christ is *the* unique Son of God because He's deity.

Isaac is a type of Christ, so it's not as if Abraham can say, "Well, I'm going to kill Isaac, but I still have Ishmael." No, the promises were only through Isaac. Just like if Jesus is not the Savior, we are in trouble because God doesn't have another unique Son.

So this is an awesome test. I doubt if any of us will ever face one of this magnitude in our lives. How was Abraham able to do it? His faith gave him confidence in God's love and wisdom.

Let me make an observation. Some of us measure our spirituality by how much we give to God of our time, energy, money, whatever. But spirituality is really measured by how much you keep for yourself.

Jesus said the widow gave more with her two coins than the rich gave, because they were just tossing God a tip (Mark 12:41-44). They kept the big wads in their wallets. But the widow kept nothing back. Neither did Abraham. You can't "sort of" kill your son!

——————— **Think About It** ———————
What's the dearest thing you have? What if God asked for it?
That's the test He asks some of His kids to pass.

> *"Abraham called the name of that place*
> *The LORD Will Provide." Genesis 22:14*

DO SOMETHING, LORD
Read It: Genesis 22:7-13

So many of us see so little of God's power in action because we believe so little of God. Too many Christians have a midget God, and so they get midget blessings, midget joy, midget peace, and midget power. If you want to experience God, you've got to put confidence in His Word even when that Word appears to be contradictory.

That brings us back to Abraham. We're slowly getting him and Isaac up that mountain this week. So they are on their way up when Isaac says, "Hey, Dad, I'm a little confused."

"What's the problem, son?"

"Well, we've made this trip plenty of times. Every time we've come before we've brought something to sacrifice. Where's the sacrifice?"

Abraham says, "Isaac, the Lord is going to come up with something. I don't have the slightest idea what, but He will provide."

That, my friend, is the confidence of faith! There are some things in life only God can take care of, some things you don't have the answer for. But faith is confidence the Lord is going to come up with something.

You say, "I don't see anything." But you are not the Lord, so therefore you are not supposed to come up with something. You are supposed to get on your knees and say, "Lord, I know You are going to come up with something. I don't know when or how, but I am going to hold my ground because I am confident You are going to honor Your Word."

So they finally get to the top of the mountain, and Abraham lays Isaac on the altar. Now here's where most of us would have said, "Okay, God, you're cutting it close here. I did my part. I got up. I got him dressed. I brought him to the mountain. I answered his questions. I got him on the altar. The party's over. I'm through!"

Have you ever done that with God? Have you ever said, "Come on, Lord, You should have done something by now"? Don't cave in at the moment of truth, because that's when the test is passed.

——————— **Think About It** ———————
You've got to love Abraham's response because,
remember, he didn't have Genesis 22 or Hebrews 11 to read!
All he had was pure, even raw faith.

*"[Abraham] considered that God is able to raise men
even from the dead." Hebrews 11:19a*

A RISK-TAKER
Read It: Genesis 22:14-18; Hebrews 11:19

We've been saying all along that the life of faith elevates the power of God over circumstances. That's a theological statement, by the way. Your ability to have confidence during the trials of your life is wrapped up in your theology, which is simply what you believe about God.

Faith is asking you to take a risk. You are being asked to step out there on stuff you don't know and you haven't seen simply because someone told you to do it. So you are taking a risk.

Now what determines whether you take the risk of faith—or any risk? The level of confidence you have in the person asking you to take the risk. So the higher your view of God, the stronger your theology, the more risks you will be willing to take. Abraham was willing to take the ultimate risk because he was confident of God's power.

What power? Well, Abraham believed in God's power to create life out of death. Go all the way back to Hebrews 11:3 and you'll recall that faith says that the things we see around us were created by the invisible God, not out of visible stuff.

Faith says, "I wasn't there when it happened, but I stake my claim on God and His Word regardless of what I see or don't see, because of my understanding of who God is."

See, it's not how much faith you have. When you hear people telling you that you need more faith, that's an incorrect analysis. You don't need a lot of faith. You don't need a blessed handkerchief or a bottle of water from the Jordan River to give you more faith. The issue of faith is not the amount but the object of your faith.

If you trust a rowboat to get you across the Pacific Ocean, we will have a good time at your memorial service, because I don't care how confident your faith is, you are going to die in the ocean. The issue is the object you put your faith in. Abraham was confident because he knew whom he trusted.

─────── **Think About It** ───────
We sometimes think Abraham's faith wasn't tested
to the ultimate because he never killed Isaac. Forget it. God
Himself said Isaac was as good as dead (v. 16).

REFLECTION

If you're like most good Christian adults, your weekend probably starts with a good, hot cup of coffee or tea—especially if it's a cold winter weekend where you are.

So imagine this scene for a minute. It's still real early, but the light's on in the back of the tent. Abraham is brewing up a fresh pot, saying to himself, "I've got to sacrifice Isaac today because God told me to. But God also told me He was going to make me into a great nation through Isaac."

The man should have an insurmountable problem. But he says, "The how of all this is God's problem. If I could answer that, I would be God. I'll just obey and see what God does. I'm confident that both Isaac and I are coming back, because I know God's going to keep His promise. But I also know I've got to kill my son. How God's going to figure all this out isn't up to me. I'll let Him do it His way."

You know why so many of us don't get anywhere with God? Because we're still trying to figure it all out. "Now, Lord, if You'll let me know how You are going to do this, if You'll just show me Your timetable, I'll trust You."

But that's not faith. Faith is confidence in God, *period*. Tell you what. While you're enjoying that first weekend cup of brew, bow your head and ask God to give you the kind of confident faith that can't be shaken when the wind starts to blow a little heavy. That's a prayer He'd love to answer.

"We must obey God rather than men." Acts 5:29

CHOICES, CHOICES
Read It: Exodus 1:15–2:2; Hebrews 11:23

For three weeks we've been looking at the saga of faith in Hebrews 11. We could spend another month in this incredible chapter, but we're going to wrap up this week by talking about the *conflicts* of faith.

Now I'm not saying there are conflicts *within* our faith. I'm talking about the conflicts that come up when we decide to live by faith. We've got a great example before us this week, the man Moses, and we're going to learn some powerful lessons from his life. Let's start with this one from Hebrews 11:23—the life of faith chooses the plans of God rather than the plans of this world.

This is critical because whether you decide to follow God or the world will determine how fruitful, how victorious, and how successful your life is. If you are a defeated Christian today, one reason may be that you've made the wrong choices.

Moses' life was determined by choices even when he was too young to choose for himself. The Pharaoh was worried about the birth rate of Jewish males. Can't have the slaves outnumbering the home folk.

So Egypt instituted a program of Jewish baby boy genocide. Moses' parents looked at their baby and said, "We are not going to submit to the king's plan. We are not going to sit here and do nothing while this government comes and destroys this baby."

So in an act of sovereign faith, they placed baby Moses in a basket and put it behind the bulrushes in the Nile River. They did not allow the king's edict to become the final word. They decided that even though the government had a plan, God had a better plan.

Many of us think that because someone in authority gives the plan, it's the plan we have to follow. But unless that plan agrees with God's plan, it's the wrong plan. What God wants you to understand is that your ultimate allegiance is not to this world and its system. It's not to the popular trends in society, and it's not to what everyone else wants for your life. The issue for you as a Christian is, what does God want?

——— **Think About It** ———

Even if you've made some wrong choices, the beautiful thing about the grace of God is that you can change your choices.

"You cannot serve God and mammon." Luke 16:13

A LOT TO GIVE UP
Read It: Exodus 2:11-15; Hebrews 11:24

We're talking about the conflicts of faith from the life of Moses. Today I want you to see that living by faith means rejecting the world's identity.

Moses' faith got him into conflict right off. The writer of Hebrews says that when the time came to make a choice, Moses rejected his adopted identity. Now this is very significant. We know from Exodus that he is forty years old. He's in the full bloom of his manhood, ready to take over.

Plus, Pharaoh has let Moses know he wants him to be his successor. Basically, Moses is a prince who's going to be king. So now he is faced with a cataclysmic decision: "Am I willing to give up incredible prestige?"

He also has to ask, "Am I willing to give up incredible power?" As the next Pharaoh, Moses would be the most powerful man in the world.

A third question Moses has to ask is, "Am I willing to give up incredible money, honey?" He's living in the king's palace. He's got servants waiting on him, but he has a conflict on his hands, because what they want from him is a total commitment to Egypt.

So now Moses is facing the choice you and I face every day of our lives—if not on the same grand scale—which is, will we sell our souls to this world order because it offers us prestige, power, and money? Today we have a generation of people who have said yes to that proposition.

You must understand, if you choose to be called the son of Pharaoh's daughter, God then chooses not to identify with you as His son. When Moses refused to be called the son of Pharaoh's daughter, it wasn't just that he didn't want anyone calling him Junior. It meant he was renouncing all association and identification with Pharaoh and his rule.

What does this mean for you today? Just this: if you are going to gain God, you must give up allegiance to this world order. You cannot be Pharaoh's child and God's child at the same time. You must make a choice.

——— Think About It ———
When prestige, power, and money become
the driving force in your life, you've become a child of Pharaoh,
and you've negated being a child of God.

"God called to him from the midst of the bush, and said, 'Moses, Moses!' And he said, 'Here I am.'" Exodus 3:4

SOMETHING WRONG WITH YOU?
Read It: Exodus 2:23–3:4; Hebrews 11:25

The Bible says Moses chose God and His people over Pharaoh and his family who were symbolic of the world. That's how Moses settled the conflict of faith.

How do you know whether you've chosen the world or God? One answer is the treatment you got with your choice. It cost Moses "ill-treatment" to identify with Israel. He knew that when he became publicly identified as a Jew, the Egyptians were going to treat him like they treated all other Jews—as a despised slave and outcast.

Let me say something straight to you today. If no one ever puts you down because you are a Christian, if no one ever calls you a fanatic, if no one ever says to you, "You're crazy. You're carrying this stuff too far," you are still living in Egypt. You haven't faced the conflict of faith.

See, once you reject Egypt, they are going to know something is wrong with you. You will become identified with this group of people called Christians, who are believed to be on the lunatic fringe of acceptable society.

Now when you're a prince, certain pleasures are always available to you. So one of the things Moses had to decide was whether he wanted to endure ill-treatment with God's people more than he wanted to dip into the passing pleasures of sin.

This phrase at the end of verse 25 says two important things about sin. First, it says sin is fun. Sin has to be fun, or no one would do it. In fact, the more sinful people can make it, the more fun it seems to be.

But sin's fun is short. It's "passing." And the sting lasts a long time. Every day we have to choose between the momentary pleasures of sin and lasting joy with God.

Doesn't sound like much of a choice when you put it that way. But some of us are still sitting on the fence. We want hell and heaven. We want God and Satan to work us a split deal. But God will not do it (James 4:4). How goes the battle with you today when it comes to the conflict of faith?

———— **Think About It** ————
When you stop identifying *with* the world, you are going
to receive some level of rejection *from* the world.

"Whatever things were gain to me, those things I have counted as loss for the sake of Christ." Philippians 3:7

HE DOESN'T SCARE ME
Read It: Hebrews 11:13, 26-27

One time my wife and I were visiting with a new couple in our church in Dallas. The sister told us, "Since I've begun growing in my faith, I've noticed my friends don't invite me to their affairs like they used to."

Want to guess why? Probably because her presence was becoming a reproach to them—not because she was being overbearing or self-righteous, but because she was a living reminder of Christ to them. And they didn't want her around anymore.

That's a small example of what today's text calls "the reproach of Christ." Reproach has to do with ridicule and persecution. You have to choose it, because nobody seeks it naturally. Moses looked things over in Egypt and said, "I'll take the reproach of Christ."

But he did it "looking to the reward" (v. 26). When you win a contest, in this case the conflict of faith, you get a reward. If you're willing to go with Christ outside the camp, "bearing His reproach" (Hebrews 13:13), no longer identifying with this world, you will reap a reward. Part of it you get in this life, and part of it you will get in eternity, but you will get it.

Notice also that to be a winner in the conflict of faith, you must choose the power of God over the power of this world. Moses wasn't afraid of Pharaoh. The reason many of us won't live for God is that we are too afraid of what people will say or think. Well, you might as well decide that some people are going to talk about you and even reject you. Recognize that now, and you won't have to fear it later.

See, Moses didn't fear Pharaoh, even though he was a visible threat, because Moses saw someone who motivated him far more: "Him who is unseen" (v. 27). Moses saw God.

I like that phrase! It's a paradox. How can you see someone who can't be seen? With the eyes of faith—that's how. You cannot see God with 20/20 vision, but you can see Him clearly. Is God in your line of sight today?

─────── **Think About It** ───────
Pharaoh wasn't any big deal after Moses saw God.
Who or what are you afraid of today? Look to Jesus!

*"When He sees the blood on the lintel and on the two doorposts, the
LORD will pass over the door." Exodus 12:23*

GOT TO BE THE BLOOD
Read It: Exodus 12:1-3, 21-28; Hebrews 11:28

L et me hang the key to today's study right here at the front door: The
conflict of faith means choosing the provisions of God over the provisions of this world.

You are probably familiar with the term Passover. It was the tenth and
final plague God inflicted on Egypt through Moses, sending His death
angel to kill the firstborn in every Egyptian home.

But God said, "Israel, when I come over to kill Egypt, I don't want to
kill your firstborn. So I want you to kill a lamb and put its blood on your
doorpost. And when I see the blood, I will pass over you. I won't judge
you. Only the firstborn of those who don't have the blood will die."

Now what did it take for the average Israelite to survive that awful
night? Faith. That's all—just believing what God said and accepting His
provision.

Notice God didn't pass over these people because of their good works.
His death angel wasn't looking for people who were hard-working, honest, nice to the neighbors, faithful at synagogue. He was looking for the
blood. None of that other stuff mattered.

That's the only way you get to heaven. When God sees the blood, His
wrath passes over you. The blood of Jesus Christ, shed on the cross for
you and me, is the only thing that satisfies God. The Egyptians were in
trouble on the Passover because they had no God and no blood.

Now here's where the conflict of faith comes in. Suppose a Jewish person said, "I want to be like the Egyptians. I don't want to smear blood on
my door. What if they come after everyone tomorrow who put up blood?
I trust in the power of the Egyptian empire to keep me safe tonight."

Any Jew who did that would have been subject to the same judgment
as the Egyptians. Are you counting on your good works, your reputation,
your standing—your own provisions—to get you to heaven? Then you'd
better face up to the conflict of faith and accept God's provision!

————— **Think About It** —————
God's provision isn't any harder to come by than the world's
provision. It's easier, in fact. He's already done the work.
All you have to do is believe.

REFLECTION

"Anything that's worth something costs something." You've probably heard this adage, or a variation thereof, all your life. So have I. But people are still saying it because it's true.

Is your faith worth something? You bet it is. It cost God His only Son to bring you into a faith relationship with Him. But faith has a price for you to pay too.

That's what we've been talking about this week. I call it the conflict of faith—the everyday choices and decisions you make for Christ that involve a cost on your part. Now you may say, "Aw, Tony, my stuff is no big deal compared to what Moses had to choose." No, in your world your faith choices are just as significant as Moses' choices were in his world.

Here's a weekend exercise to show you what I mean. Divide a piece of paper into three columns. In the left column, list the faith choices you made this week. Be generous; give yourself credit for even the smallest incident where your faith brought you into conflict with the world, and you made the right choice.

Okay, now beside each one list in the middle column what it cost you to make that choice. Maybe a decision to read your Bible or pray cost you the pleasure of propping your feet up and vegging in front of the TV for twenty minutes.

Now in the right column, put down the way you think God blessed you, or will bless you, for these choices. When you're done, hang onto that paper. It will make for some interesting reflections someday.

THREE

MARRIAGE & FAMILY

Doing It God's Way

Marriage and family are in! Everybody's talking about what makes a family, what makes a home. This is a hot topic even in Washington, but we who know God have the real scoop. This thing of marriage and family was an item in Eden long before it came to D.C. We've got the Owner's Manual on this stuff, so let's get into it. I want to talk about the foundations for marriage, Christian parenting, and then how to rekindle the flame.

*"He who created them from the beginning made them
male and female." Matthew 19:4*

WE CAN!
Read It: Genesis 2:15-17

There's something wrong when Christians say, "I can't," about some-thing when God has already said, "You can."

See, if you are a Christian who says, "I can't," you don't understand who your God is and who you are. If the resurrection power of Christ in you means anything, it means that you now have the power resident within you to do things you couldn't normally do.

As Christians our job description is to demonstrate the power of Christ in everyday situations—and there's no place where the resurrection power of Jesus Christ needs to be seen more graphically today than in this area of marriage and family life. That's what we want to focus on for the next four weeks.

We've got a problem here, no question, because too many Christian husbands and wives say they can't work it out. Too many fathers are bail-ing out on their families. Too many mothers are trying to carry unnatural loads laid on them by their culture and the expectations of others.

My goal for this section is to help you avoid the pitfalls and patch up any potholes that may have already developed in the course of daily liv-ing. I want these days together to be a joyful celebration of the good things God built into us as men and women.

Besides, it's an embarrassment to the kingdom and to our awesome God when people who name the name Jesus Christ keep winding up in someone's divorce court. That's when the world sits back and says, "Is that all your God can do for you?"

So we're going back to the beginning on this thing. And we're start-ing with the man, because that's where God started. You may have read today's verses and said to yourself, "These don't have anything to do with marriage." Well, I said we were going to dig down to the foundations.

So here is today's scoop. Ladies, before God ever gave Adam a wife, he gave him a job (v. 15) and instructions to obey (vv. 16-17). Don't mess with a man who isn't interested in working and obeying God!

--------- **Think About It** ---------
Manhood is more than the ability to wear pants. It's the ability
to take divine truth and make it work in the home.

"She shall be called Woman, because she was
taken out of Man." Genesis 2:23

WHAT A HELPER
Read It: Genesis 2:18; 1 Corinthians 11:8-9

You've heard this before, but it needs to be said again. Whose idea was it to make Eve—and Adam, for that matter? Whose idea was it to bring these two people together? This was all God's idea.

We need to keep that in the front of our thinking, because God's never had a bad idea yet. Marriage is a terrific idea! We just need to do it God's way. I want to concentrate on Genesis 2:18 today because it's absolutely basic to the male/female relationship, and yet it's often where we start getting off track.

Notice that God calls the woman a helper—and that's before she's even around. This wasn't an afterthought on His part. Okay?

This word *helper* means one brought alongside to assist. My male friend, God has given a woman one basic responsibility in marriage—to help. You bear the primary responsibility for the home. When Eve ate the forbidden fruit, what did God say? "Adam, where are you?" (see 3:9). Adam had to answer for the breakdown.

See, a woman was never meant to bear the burden. She was meant to help the man bear the burden. You say, "Come on, Tony. Tell me something new." Yes, this is foundational stuff, but evidently it's not getting off the page and into Christian marriages very well.

I happen to believe that one of the major problems we have today is that we men are overloading our wives' circuits. That's a cataclysmic mistake, because when that happens, ain't no one havin' any fun! A woman is the best helper God ever designed, but you can't go messing with His plan and hope to pull it off.

I thank God for the way Christian men are starting to come forward and accept the responsibility—and find the *joy*—of being a lover and leader to their wives, of affirming and supporting and providing for them. When we do it God's way, let me tell you, something wonderful happens. Why? Because the woman was made to be a helper "suitable" to the man, someone necessary to complete and fulfill him. I give that one a big amen!

————— **Think About It** —————
Whenever a man says, "I have achieved this," he ought to add,
"because I have someone at home who has helped me."

"He who loves his own wife loves himself." Ephesians 5:28

NAME THAT CREATURE
Read It: Genesis 2:19-20; Ephesians 5:28-30

So Adam's already got a full-time job tending the Garden of Eden (v. 15). Then God says, "Adam, I want you to do something else. I want you to name all the animals."

Now it doesn't look as if naming the animals has anything to do with getting Adam a wife, but he hasn't heard about woman yet anyway, so he says, "Fine. I'll give it my best."

So the parade starts, and Adam gives everything a name. That's good. Got to call those animals something. But God is preparing Adam for something bigger than a degree in zoology.

As Adam is doing his thing, he notices that when the gorilla comes by for his name, there's another gorilla on his arm, laughing at his jokes and smiling pretty. When Adam names the bull and the cow, he notices that old bull looking cross-eyed at the cow. For the he zebra, there was a she zebra.

You get the idea. Every creature had a suitable partner. Except Adam. He didn't see anyone who could fulfill his need for a helper. The gorilla didn't do anything for him. He knew the zebra had nothing he needed. Adam knew he needed a suitable partner, and he knew he wouldn't find such a creature in the animal kingdom.

Young lady, if you're dating a guy who says to you, "I don't need you," watch it! Think twice about marrying him, because the whole point of creating Eve was that Adam *needed* her. He couldn't make it by himself.

My man, do you know what that means? It means a woman is not a nice addition to your life. She's not an adornment on your arm when you go out, someone to make you look and feel good.

Until a man can say to a woman, "I love you, and I need you. I can't make it without you. I don't even want to try to make it without you," he's not ready to get married.

A woman needs the security of knowing that she's marrying a man who needs her, who cherishes her, who has no intention of ever living without her again, till death do them part. That's doing marriage God's way.

--- **Think About It** ---

Once Adam realized there was no one around for him,
he was ready to sign the divine "surgery consent" form!

*"The LORD God fashioned into a woman the rib
which He had taken from the man." Genesis 2:22*

DIVINE MATCHMAKER
Read It: Genesis 2:21-22

It's said that God didn't take woman from man's head to rule over him, or from his feet to be beneath him, but from his side to be beside him.

That says it pretty well. But the part I want to underline today is that it's God who's doing the operating and the closing up of Adam's flesh and the fashioning of the woman and the bringing together.

In other words, it looks like God is in the matchmaking business! We'll see tomorrow that when Adam got his first glimpse of Eve, he knew something good was cooking. That's what the Hebrew says. It was God who shaped the woman, both externally and internally, so that she and the man would correspond.

Now I realize the body of Christ also includes many brothers and sisters who have not yet found God's partner for them. So let me say a word here to Christian single people.

When Eve woke up, I can assure you the first thing she said wasn't, "I'm twenty-five (or whatever age), and I'm not married yet." No, she didn't know about Adam. God hadn't brought her to Adam yet. The formal introductions hadn't been made.

I think the first thing Eve did was make herself available to the Lord. What do I mean? I believe that Eve enjoyed fellowship with the Lord as a person before she enjoyed His provision in matchmaking. And she didn't have to surrender that fellowship when God brought her to Adam.

This is crucial, because I know we have a big numbers problem when it comes to marriage. I see it in my church in Dallas. There are simply far fewer single men than single women out there.

Numbers aren't the point, however. Single people have several options before them. The first two are bad. Either try to find satisfaction in an immoral lifestyle, or lower the standards and marry a non-Christian.

But in both cases, you lose your fellowship with God. The Bible is clear that until the Lord does the matchmaking, He wants you to do what Eve did—make yourself available to Him.

——— Think About It ———
If you are cultivating your fellowship and your walk with
Christ today, that frees Him up to cultivate your future.

"This is now bone of my bones, and flesh of my flesh." Genesis 2:23

―――――――

THIS IS . . . WOW!
Read It: Genesis 2:23-24

I'm not a Bible translator, but I know that when Adam first saw Eve, the man wasn't saying, "This is now." Something got lost between the Hebrew and the English on that one!

Finally, this was the suitable helper he had been looking for. So he called her *ishah*, Hebrew for woman, because she came from *ish*, Hebrew for man. In other words, when Adam woke up, all of him was not there. A rib was missing. And when Eve woke up, all of her was not brand-new, because she had something that had once belonged to Adam.

So what God did in marriage was give Adam back what he had lost and give Eve the rest of what she needed. Now the man and the woman are different. One of the dumbest things a couple can say is, "We're not compatible. We're as different as night and day." Of course you're different. If you were just alike, one of you would be unnecessary! That's why you need each other.

So Adam meets Eve, and it's true love. Now comes the wedding ceremony in verse 24. This verse gets read at almost every Christian wedding, but the problem is that a lot of couples don't know what they're promising when they stand before the altar.

Leaving father and mother means a man must be willing to break all other human ties to give himself totally to his mate. But most men aren't saying, "I'm ready to give up anyone and anything that would keep me from loving and cherishing you above all else." They're saying, "I'll marry you, and I'll work you into my schedule, television watching, friendships."

But marriage is not working your partner into the game. It's realizing he or she *is* the game!

Now the man is also called to cleave to his wife—to stick like glue. Men usually interpret this to mean physical cleaving. But a wife needs emotional cleaving too. She needs a sense of security. She needs to know that her husband has her best interest at heart, that she's safe in his love and care. Anybody for taking a shot at a marriage like that?

――――― **Think About It** ―――――

Notice the change to the plural pronoun in verse 24. Both parties are responsible to maintain their one-flesh relationship.

REFLECTION

Ileft Genesis 2:25 for our reflection this weekend because I didn't want to just dismiss it with the obvious note that Adam and Eve were naked before each other. The word means more than physical nakedness. It means they were transparent. They were open to one another. They had become best friends.

Is your wife or your husband your best friend? Is he or she the person you share your total being with? That's important, because the reason God created marriage was so that you and I could experience the Trinity.

What is the Trinity? Three coequal persons who are one. What is marriage? Three persons who become one—a man, a woman, and the Lord. That's marriage. It's a picture of a higher unity, a symbol on earth standing for the reality in heaven. The marriage relationship is the closest we'll get in this life to the oneness and unity of the Trinity.

And by the way, one reason we've got to get this marriage deal right on earth is that the Bible tells us there is no marriage in heaven. Why? Because we won't need the earthly symbol anymore when we have the heavenly reality.

But until we reach heaven, let's make the most of this wonderful God-given union called Christian marriage. Will you join me in praying that God will enable us to make our marriages everything He meant them to be . . . and will you join me in committing yourself to this goal?

"Although He was a Son, He learned obedience from the things which He suffered." Hebrews 5:8

LEARNING TO OBEY
Read It: John 8:29b; Ephesians 6:1

Time for a Monday pop quiz. Question one: Who was the only perfect Child? Right, Jesus Christ. Question two, true or false: Jesus never had to learn to obey because He never disobeyed. False? Got it.

Luke 2:51 says Jesus lived in "subjection" to His earthly parents. Think about that one and it's pretty staggering. He was Joseph's and Mary's Creator! But He was obedient to them. And in His ministry He was obedient to His heavenly Father.

So when Paul tells children to obey their parents "in the Lord," he's on real solid biblical ground. And there's no place I'd rather be to begin two weeks of studies on the topic of Christian parenting than on real solid biblical ground.

Now if you're a Christian parent today, you may be saying, "Amen, brother, preach it. I want my kids to read this stuff." But as we're going to see over the next two weeks, *you've* got the big job. It starts right here in Ephesians 6:1, because your instruction must be "in the Lord."

Sometimes we expect our kids to do things that even the Lord Himself wouldn't ask them to do. No, our task as parents is to instruct our children in how they ought to live under God's authority. That's key because, remember, even though they will move out from under our authority someday, they will always need to be under God's authority.

In fact, this is the first problem we face as parents right here: authority. No one wants to be under anyone's authority. "You ain't my mama. Don't tell me what to do." Problem is, in today's world kids don't want their mamas telling them anything either.

We are living in a world of rebellion. The Bible teaches that God is the ultimate authority. But we don't want Him telling us what to do.

You say, "That's right. This thing really bothers me. But what can I do to counter this influence with my children?" Well, in these devotional studies we're going to talk about a lot of things you can do. But recognizing the trend and committing yourself to counter it is half the battle.

--------- **Think About It** ---------
You cannot be neutral in raising children. They must learn to obey.
You must be dedicated to their instruction in godly living.

"God said, 'Honor your father and mother.'" Matthew 15:4

———

YES, SIR
Read It: Exodus 20:12; Matthew 15:4-6; Ephesians 6:2

There isn't much mystery about the word *honor*. It means to hold in high esteem, to treat with reverence and respect.

In the course of this year I'm sure I'll be telling you about my father, Arthur Evans. He has always commanded my respect. Today, even though I'm a grandfather too, I do *not* go to his home and greet him, "Say, Arthur, what's happening?" I just can't do it. The man would only stare at me. It's "Dad" or "Sir" or some other term that tells him I respect his position.

See, kids need their parents to help them understand that you are the adult and they are the child, and that children are to respect adults. In time, they are going to get that right. But what we need to do as parents in the meantime is be consistent, teach it, expect it, and encourage it.

And by the way, today's verse from the lips of Jesus, along with the other verses in today's reading, remind us that honor isn't just some nice little concept we teach to help polish our kids' manners and keep them from being rude. It has the power of life and death in it.

But let's turn this around for a minute, because if we're going to be worthy of honor as parents, we'd better take a reading of our "honor quotient" toward *our* parents.

For us, honor means two basic things. We've already mentioned the first one, to hold our parents in high esteem and treat them with reverence. So we have no right to speak to them any way we want, no matter what age we are. That doesn't mean you have to agree with them, but you disagree in honor.

The second thing honor can mean is financial help and/or personal care. I believe we as Christian children are responsible to support our parents. It will be our turn soon enough.

So as parents we must teach our children to honor us and ultimately to honor God. Why? There are several good reasons for it, according to the Scriptures. We'll talk about them tomorrow.

——— **Think About It** ———

Honor is meant to move in a cycle through each generation.
Today's parents have their chance to pass on the blessing.

"Children, be obedient to your parents in all things."
Colossians 3:20

DOING WHAT MAMA SAID
Read It: Deuteronomy 5:16; Ephesians 6:3

Why should you teach your kids to obey and honor you, other authorities in their lives, and God Himself? That's a very good question, and the Bible has some even better answers.

First, "because it is right" (Ephesians 6:1). Do you want what's right for your kids? I sure hope so. God says, "I'm not telling you something wrong. When you teach your children according to My ways, it pleases Me. And when I am pleased, I will bless you." Since God Himself is the standard of what's right, it's right to teach our children His ways because He commands us to do it.

Second, there's a promise attached to this. Now of course Paul is going back to Exodus 20 where the Ten Commandments were given. Read the list, and you'll see that the first four commandments deal with our relationship to God: "Don't have any other gods before Me. Don't make any graven image," and so on.

Then, the fifth commandment becomes a transition commandment because it doesn't deal with God, but with family: "Honor your father and your mother" (Exodus 20:12). Then the promise is stated, and the rest of the commandments deal with personal relationships.

Why did God make a special promise to children who obeyed their parents? The reason, I think, is this: God knew that the children in a home would become the fiber in society. If respect for authority, if reverence and honor, did not start in the home, it would never get to the street.

And if it never hit the street, it would never hit the community. And if it didn't hit the community, it wouldn't touch the city. And if didn't touch the city, it would never move on to the state.

You get the idea. Eventually a whole country undergoes a collapse that started because some kid didn't want to do what mama said. Now we don't look at it that way. That's because we are like the frogs in the pot, not knowing the water is slowly being brought to a boil under us.

We say, "Well, one kid not obeying his parents ain't going to bring down the United States of America." Maybe, but try fifteen or twenty million!

--------- **Think About It** ---------
You want to change the world? Teach your child the ways of the Lord.

"Teach [these things] diligently to your sons."
Deuteronomy 6:7

EVERYWHERE, IN EVERY WAY
Read It: Deuteronomy 6:4-9; Matthew 22:34-37

Deuteronomy 6:4 may be the single most important statement of truth in the entire Old Testament. It's the declaration of the utter unique-ness of Israel's God, and it's at the heart of all our theology. Verse 5 is absolutely indispensable too, according to Jesus.

But notice the very next thing God said: "Now, fathers, go home and train your children in My truth. I want you to train them when they wake up. I want you to train them when they lie down. I want you to train them in between their waking up and lying down. I want you to train them for-mally. I want you to train them informally. I want the words wrapped around their foreheads. I want them to bump into My truth when they come into the house and when they leave the house."

Why? Because God wanted Israel to be different from all the other nations. He wanted Israel to be a people built on truth and righteousness, love and respect, worshiping God as opposed to the world around them.

That's not what we have today. We have Christian kids acting like all the other kids in the neighborhood and parents saying, "I love Johnnie, so I don't spank him."

Excuse me, but you hate him then. Do you know what the Bible says about God? "Whom the Lord loveth, He skins alive." That's a pretty good rendering of Hebrews 12:6.

My father would tell me, "I want you home at 10:00 P.M. That's not 10:01. You be in here at 10:00, or it's fire!" I would be upset and say, "Why do I have to be in here at 10:00? My friends are making fun of me. They can stay out until 2:00 and 3:00 in the morning." And Dad would say, "Well, maybe their parents don't care. But I care. Be in here at 10:00."

Now when I go back to Baltimore, guess where those guys are? Still hanging out on the corner until 2:00 and 3:00 in the morning. I can trace where I am today back to a father and mother who had a hold on me, who disciplined me, who would not let me have my way all the time. I'm in love with Jesus Christ today because of it!

——— **Think About It** ———
Too many parents today are worried about upsetting their kids
when they should be worried about upsetting God.

"Fathers, do not exasperate your children,
that they may not lose heart." Colossians 3:21

TRAINING AND TEACHING
Read It: Ephesians 6:4

Look at the last line of yesterday's study again. Today is the balance to that. Good parents don't let their kids run things, but they also know you can't provoke children and expect them to come out right.

As a father, I think I know why Paul spoke to fathers. All things being equal, Dad's the first one to get mad and the one most likely to react by coming down hard. But this isn't limited to fathers. All of us parents need to ask, what are some ways we can provoke or anger our kids?

One way is by smothering them, overparenting them. Favoritism is another spirit-killer: "Why can't you be more like your sister?"

You can anger children by forcing your unfulfilled dreams on them. "I didn't get to be a doctor, son, but you are going to be a doctor."

Son's reply: "But, Dad, I don't like doctoring."

Discouragement, criticism, and the withholding of approval are several other prime ways we can exasperate our children. A lot of it has to do with the need for us as parents to guard our tongues. The kid messes up and we say, "You dummy! Why are you so clumsy?"

I've got to mention one more because it's a biggie in the 1990s: failure to sacrifice. By that I mean parents who send this message to their kids: "I need fulfillment now. You're in my way." For a lot of modern parents, their kids are in their way. They stop Dad and Mom from doing what they want to do. This one is convicting, so we'd better move on.

Thankfully, Ephesians 6:4 has a flip side. If you're not to anger your children, what do you do? You do two things: You train and discipline them (same idea), and you instruct them.

Train means you give them the rules with rewards and punishment. The expectations are clear, and you create an environment where the kids are helped to succeed, not set up to fail. *Instruct* is the inculcation of God's Word. Of course, this means we have to be in the Word and living the Word ourselves!

───── Think About It ─────
Remember what Jesus said about bringing kids to Him?
He said, "Don't hinder them." Kids will be drawn to Jesus
if they see Jesus in their folks.

REFLECTION

What sincere Christian parent doesn't want to build a good Christian home? You know, like the ones you read about in the magazines—the family altar and all that.

Every time I think of this, I remember the story Dr. Howard Hendricks, my prof at Dallas Seminary, always told about the guy who heard him talk about having family devotions and a family altar. This guy decided that's what his family needed, and he asked Prof. Hendricks if they sold those altars at the bookstore.

Well, at least this dad was willing to invest some bucks in building a Christian home. Listen, you'll never have a Christian home if you are not willing to invest in the children.

You can't have it if all you want to do is watch television. You can't have it if you don't want to learn God's Word and find out how to teach them. You cannot have it if you don't want to invest time and energy in your children and in the ministry of your church where your efforts are supported and enhanced by the work of God's people.

But if you're willing, you've got a staggering promise. It will be well with your children and well with you. Every now and then Anthony, Jr., will say, "Dad, I think I want to be a preacher too."

And I say, "It's well with me."

Is it well with you and your family this weekend? If it is, keep at it! If not, ask God to help you start turning it around today. He's ready, waiting for you to ask.

"For this boy I prayed, and the LORD has given me my petition
which I asked of Him." 1 Samuel 1:27

GOOD BOY, BAD BOYS
Read It: 1 Samuel 1:1-3, 9-18; 2:11-12

I love the way God's Word lays stuff out straight, no sugarcoating. That's what today's Bible reading does, especially 1 Samuel 2:11-12. It's sort of a Monday morning splash of cold water to get us going this week as we continue talking about Christian parenting.

What a contrast. Here was Samuel, just a little boy, serving the Lord in Shiloh. His mother Hannah was what we would call a layperson. She didn't spend all of her time studying God's Law. She just lived it, and she loved God.

But right down the hall from Samuel were the bedrooms of Hophni and Phinehas, the no-good, grown-up sons of Eli who didn't even know the Lord. They should have. They were the preacher's kids, messing around while Dad faithfully served the Lord. Ouch!

In case you haven't figured it out by now, Eli was your classic poor parent. By the time we meet the family, his boys were assisting him in the ministry of the temple. They were going to church with him every Sunday. They were wearing the veneer because Dad was the holy man of Israel.

But these brothers had a racket going (2:13b-16). They were dipping their hands in the offering plate—only it wasn't money. They were taking more of the sacrifices than the priest's rightful share. And if anyone called them on the scam, they threatened him.

By now you're probably saying, "Please, tell me what Eli did or didn't do as a parent so I can run as far and as fast the other way as possible." Okay, we'll do that this week. But we'll also look at a lot of positive parenting instruction from the Word of God.

Let me close today with a couple of observations to set the context for the week. Eli was a man of God. No question about that. The sons of Eli dishonored the Lord, but Samuel, only a child, honored the Lord. The contrast is between these two grown men, the sons of Eli, and this young boy who had been dedicated to the Lord, Samuel, who ministered to the Lord.

--- **Think About It** ---

The two sons of Eli ministered for themselves. Samuel
ministered before the Lord. That says a lot.

"Prove yourselves doers of the word, and not merely hearers who delude themselves." James 1:22

ENFORCING THE TRUTH
Read It: 1 Samuel 2:22-25

How many times have you been in the grocery store or mall and heard a parent say to a screaming, obnoxious two-year-old who's hitting him or her and pitching a fit, "Now, now, don't do that, dear. Here, let's stop that"? Meanwhile, the kid is wreaking havoc.

Well, I don't know if that's how Eli got started with little Hophni and Phinehas. We're not given any details of their childhood. What we have in 1 Samuel is the bottom line, which is this: Eli's sons were vile before the Lord, and he did absolutely nothing about it.

Now it's true that he did speak to them. You probably just read it. Eli heard about the terrible things his sons were doing and said, "Now, boys, you ought not to do that. The Lord don't like ugly. No, no. Bad, bad."

And the boys said, "Yes, Daddy," and then went right back to robbing the people who came to the temple and misusing the women. And from all indications, Eli just turned away from it.

The issue was not that Eli didn't tell his children the right things. It's that he didn't *enforce* the right things he was telling them. I don't know any parents who go out and tell their kids, "Go rob a bank. Go find someone to kill. Ten or twenty years in prison will do you good." I suspect you don't know any parents like that either.

No, the parents we know probably say the right things. A lot of prison inmates' parents said the right things too. But what is missing in so much well-intentioned parenting is enforcement.

Eli was not enforcing the truth. He was only stating it. He didn't pull his boys from their posts and strip them of their privileged access to the temple and the people of Israel. He knew what they were doing, but he let them keep on doing it while telling them they ought not to do it.

Discipline includes more than telling your children what they ought to do. You do not leave sinners to decide things for themselves because they will inevitably decide on sin!

--------- **Think About It** ---------
Parents have to be consistent in following through.
Does it take more effort? Of course. Is it necessary? Ask Eli.

"Those whom the Lord loves He disciplines." Hebrews 12:6

HOW DOES GOD LOVE US?
Read It: Hebrews 12:3-8

By now I hope we've made the point that it takes more than saying the right thing to get the job done. If we are going to get the results God wants, we must lovingly discipline our children.

In fact, according to Hebrews 12 discipline is one test of God's love. One way you know God loves you is that He doesn't just let you go on in your sin without doing anything about it.

Now I can't stop all the neighbors' kids from messing up because they are not part of my family. But my kids—that's a whole different story because I love them. If you want to love your children the way God loves His children, chastening has to be part of that love.

See, love means you'd better say something. And if that doesn't take care of the problem, you'd better do something. If you love me, and you see that I'm destroying myself, yet you keep quiet, you're killing me. The most loving thing a parent or any spiritual leader can do is chastise in love.

Why? Because that's what God does (v. 6). The writer of Hebrews asks us fathers a question: "What kind of father is it who doesn't correct his son?"

Answer: "Not much of a father at all. That's not being a dad. Without discipline, you are treating your children just like everyone else does."

Then the writer drives his point home in verse 8. Have you ever had kids in the neighborhood who come to your house and act like they live there? Your kids bring some kids home to play, and it's fine at first. You know, they come in, and all they want is a little glass of water.

But after a while it gets out of hand, and you have to make it known that this is not a hotel, and you're not a bellhop. The reason you do that is because the neighbors' kids don't have legitimate rights to that freedom. Your children have the right to partake of your home because they are part of your family. But then they also get to partake of your discipline.

——————— **Think About It** ———————

The thing that makes you unique to your children
is that you are the unique one bringing correction in their lives.
That's also what makes God unique to us.

"Shall we not . . . be subject to the Father of spirits, and live?"
Hebrews 12:9

GETTING THE MESSAGE
Read It: 1 Samuel 2:27-35; 4:10-11

One of the Bible's inescapable principles is that when you walk away from the will and the Word of God, you walk toward death. Now I don't necessarily mean you are going to die and go to the grave. That's a possibility, but what I'm talking about is spiritual death. That is, the "Father of spirits" is responsible for spiritual life. When you walk away from Him, then you move toward the realm of spiritual death.

One thing that can bring you closer to God or push you away is His discipline. Like a loving parent, He chastens His children. Now when that happens, we have two options. We can say, "I'm not serving You anymore." Or we can say, "I get the message."

If we choose option one, God has some work to do. There comes a time when He has to say like a good Father, "If you don't want to abide by My rules, you cannot live in My house." That's the decision He had to make with Eli's sons, although it was even more harsh than that.

They went too far, and God said it was time to get rid of them. Their deaths were prophesied, and that's exactly what happened. Unfortunately, they took Eli with them. His failure as a parent brought destruction to the whole family.

Read 1 Samuel 4 and you'll see that this became much more than the saga of one family. It became a case of national disaster for Israel, which shows how when sin enters a house, it can destroy everything.

So what do we do as parents in light of this today? We enforce the truth in love; we discipline, we chasten. We do our best under God to be consistent, not like the mother who kept calling her son, and he kept ignoring her. His friend looked at him and said, "Your mother's calling you. Aren't you going home?"

"Not yet."

This mother trained her son to know she didn't mean for him to come in on the first "Come in." She meant, "I am starting a process that will lead to your coming in sometime in the future." Wrong message!

--- **Think About It** ---

The outcome of discipline is blessing. God does you a favor
when He disciplines you. Return the favor with your kids.

"Our struggle is not against flesh and blood." Ephesians 6:12

THE GLORY IS GONE
Read It: 1 Samuel 4:12-22; Ephesians 6:10-18

The last chapter in the life of a failed father often isn't pretty, and Eli is no exception. He lived to see his sons die and the ark of the covenant captured by the Philistines—and that's the last thing he lived to see.

As we wrap up our study on Christian parenting, I want to step back from the story and draw a spiritual parallel that I hope will encourage you today. The world is still doing the same thing the Philistines were successful in doing to Israel.

The world is trying to take the ark of God—His glory, His presence, His power—out of our homes. The weapons are not swords and spears, but the battle is just as intense. Using weapons such as the media and popular entertainment, the forces of darkness are seeking to make our kids just like them.

Your children and mine are being taught values and behavioral patterns that do not belong to Christ. They are being taught a selfishness and a self-orientation that would make them live for themselves. We cannot allow that to happen.

The good news is, it doesn't have to happen. You may not be able to change Hollywood, but you can do something just as effective. You can turn off Hollywood in your home!

What Christians like you and me need to do is to step forward in our homes and claim that ground for Jesus Christ. We need to write over our houses, not "The glory has departed," but "As for me and my house, we will serve the Lord." As they tell the men at Promise Keepers rallies, "You're in a war, but a lot of you have not been *at* war."

You read Ephesians 6 and you say, "We've got the right weapons, and we're on the side that's *already* won. Let's get after it."

Now if we're going to fight a good fight for and with our kids, we need to get our own act together. Children don't mind following someone who's showing by example how it's done and who's doing it with them. Christian parent, are you ready to lead the way? Let's get after it!

--- **Think About It** ---

Don't settle for letting your kids feed off *your* Christian experience.
Help them learn to walk with God themselves.
He doesn't have any grandchildren.

REFLECTION

I thought it would be refreshing this weekend to flip back to the beginning of 1 Samuel and take a closer look at Hannah.

The woman is barren and has been for years. So she takes her problem to the Lord. This is a seemingly impossible situation, and there is nothing human that can be done about it. Yet Hannah comes to God with a vow.

That is, she not only takes her problem to the Lord, but she argues for the benefit He will receive by answering her prayer and giving her a child (see 1:11). Her vow is total: "If you will give me a son, I will give him back to You that he might be available to You all the days of his life."

God answers her prayer with Samuel, and she fulfills her vow. Later God gives Hannah five more children in answer to Eli's prayer (2:21).

What's the point? God knew that He could safely answer Hannah's deepest prayer desire and that it wouldn't make her selfish. Why? Because she was as interested in His glory and benefit as she was in her own.

You know, I have to wonder if God can trust me like that.

"How beautiful is your love, my sister, my bride!"
Song of Solomon 4:10

GETTING REAL
Read It: 1 Corinthians 7:28

One of the questions married couples often ask themselves is: "What happened? What went wrong?" What they mean is: "How did we go from the excitement of those early days to what we have now?" And the second part of the question is: "Can we recapture what we once had?"

Well, we're going to try to answer that question this week as we talk about rekindling the flame of marriage. The basic answer to the question of what happened in a marriage is this: the honeymoon ended. That early period of euphoria where you felt like you were never going to land came to an end as you and your mate encountered the realities of daily life.

But that's okay because the early euphoria of marriage isn't supposed to last. However, what a lot of married couples do is fail to go to the next step and build on that honeymoon feeling. What they do is let their marriages slide into sameness and boredom.

But there's a lot you can do even if your marriage has reached that point. First, it helps to recognize what Paul says in today's reading. The rough spots that can make a marriage go bump in the night are natural, normal, and to be expected.

Once you begin to live together and become comfortable around each other, you dispense with the party behavior. Husband, you are no longer trying to win her. You have now won her. You have papers on her. So you stop trying to woo her.

And, wife, you no longer have to pretend you don't mind the stupid things he does. Before, you'd act like it didn't matter because you wanted to marry him. But now it matters. The masks are off.

That's when marriage gets fun, because both of you feel comfortable being who you really are. It can be exciting to discover that the wonderful person you thought you married really is wonderful—in ways you never imagined.

If that sounds too ideal for your marriage, stay with me this week—and ask God to help you rekindle the flame.

--- **Think About It** ---

You'll both get a lot further and be a lot happier if you concentrate on fulfilling each other instead of trying to perfect each other.

"Many waters cannot quench love, nor will rivers overflow it."
Song of Solomon 8:7a

WRONG DISTRACTION
Read It: 1 Corinthians 7:32-33

For Paul the benefit of singleness was undistracted devotion to the Lord (see v. 35). But don't misunderstand what the apostle is saying in today's verses. He's not saying single people are more devoted to Christ than married people. What he's saying is that if you are married, you have a distraction—a wonderful distraction but a distraction nonetheless.

But that's okay because you are supposed to be distracted if you are married. By that Paul means you are supposed to be concerned about pleasing your spouse. It comes with the marriage license, and there's nothing wrong with it.

In fact, one of the things that will douse the flame of a marriage in a hurry is that one party stops trying to please the other and focuses totally on pleasing self. The great problem of marital breakup is selfishness.

The problem with selfishness is that selfish people don't want to lose. They want to win. So whenever two people get married and then forget that they are supposed to be focused on pleasing each other, you've got a mess on your hands.

A marriage will start to hurt when the partners are too distracted with their own wants and needs to meet each other's needs. When two selfish people lock up, someone is going to lose. You cannot have two distractions at work in a marriage and expect to build a winner. There are plenty of things in life to distract you. The question is, what are you going to allow to distract you?

Let me show you what I mean. Men have a tendency to focus their energy and attention on their jobs. When that happens over a long period of time, a wife comes to resent her husband's job, viewing it almost like another woman vying for her husband's attention and emotional energy. As the lady sits at home feeling this way, this stuff accumulates in her emotional system, and the flame flickers. That's why it's a good idea for married people to take a periodic reading on what's occupying their time and energy. The answer can be the first step toward rekindling the marriage.

--- **Think About It** ---

Have you been giving too much attention to the wrong distraction lately? Make an extra effort to meet your mate's needs today.

"Husbands, love your wives, just as Christ also loved the church and gave Himself up for her." Ephesians 5:25

A PROTECTIVE COATING
Read It: 1 Corinthians 7:34-35

Listen, just give me three more months. In three months, I'll have this project behind me, and things will get back to normal at work."

I wonder how many wives have heard this or something similar from their husbands when they try to let him know they need more of his time and attention. What often happens is that the three extra months come and go with no change.

Or the project gets finished, but the husband gets focused on something else just as demanding. See, a man is built so that if he's excited about something, he's going to need those extra three months. Then it's six months. The result is that he's always putting off getting to his wife's needs, and in the meantime her spirit forms a protective coating.

She doesn't want to be let down again, so she provides her own protection. What this does is produce an emotionally cold woman—and a husband who is clueless as to why. He says, "I work hard. I bring my money home. I'm not running around." And then the big one: "I'm doing all this for you."

But his wife didn't marry a business or a paycheck. She married a person. And there is absolutely nothing a husband can do to replace himself in her life, no matter what he gives her. That's why when many couples had nothing, they had everything because they had each other. Now they have everything, but they have nothing.

Now once a woman's emotional shell gets hard, it's a whopper to soften. It would be a lot better if a husband could keep that shell from getting hard like that. Not only is that emotional protective coating hard to soften, very few men have the patience to do it. That's when men get attracted to other women and pursue adulterous affairs.

But you know what? A warm flame can soften that hard shell. Husband, if you commit to start where you are and love your wife all over again, God will meet you in your commitment and rekindle the flame.

———— Think About It ————
An affair may seem attractive, but it is a sin and will pay
its own consequences. Recommit yourself to faithfulness to your
mate and watch love start to glow again.

"I can do all things through Him who strengthens me."
Philippians 4:13

———————

"CAN-DO" SPIRIT
Read It: Ecclesiastes 4:9-12; 5:4

I serve as chaplain for the Dallas Mavericks, our National Basketball Association team. One time I was there doing some shooting by myself, and I was making everything. Then one of the Mavericks started guarding me, and suddenly I wasn't making anything.

The difference was a six-foot-five obstacle in my face, keeping me from achieving my goal. I think you get the point. The test of a marriage is not the honeymoon. It's not the times when the house is nice, the money is coming in, and the kids are bringing home all A's.

It doesn't take much to be happy under those conditions. But when the winds of opposition blow, and the flame starts to flicker, our tendency is to back off. It's when your mate has grown a little cold and the passion has died that your commitment to your marriage needs to be at its strongest.

When you got married, you made a vow to the Lord. You may not have understood that when you got married, but if you're a Christian, I hope you have come to that understanding. Now you may be looking at your marriage and saying, "This isn't what I thought it would be. It's getting tough in here. I'm not sure I want to continue with the game."

If this describes you, I have good news. You can not only stay in there, you can turn the game around. How? By deciding that you will apply to your marriage the same commitment and "can-do" spirit you put forth in areas such as your work.

For instance, it's amazing to me how many men will go for it at work, do whatever it takes to succeed, but won't bring that spirit home. I'm talking about a spirit that says, "I'm going to make my marriage better. I'm going to take God's principles and put them to work and love my wife with His kind of love and light a new flame in my marriage."

I don't mean just working up enthusiasm or doing "self-talk." A Christian marriage has a third Partner in it, Jesus Christ. He's for you and your mate, and He can help you rekindle the flame. Just ask Him and see.

——————— **Think About It** ———————
Anyone can look good when there's no opposition.
That's not the test of what you're made of.

"Love never fails." 1 Corinthians 13:8a

CHOOSING TO LOVE
Read It: 1 Corinthians 13:4-8a

You've probably noticed by now that I haven't talked about the flowers, candlelight dinners, weekend getaways, and other romantic things people think about when the subject is rekindling a marriage.

Hey, don't get me wrong. These things are great. I'm all for them. They'll help to relight the flame, but my main concern is keeping the flame lit once you get back home and Monday morning hits. So I'm trying to deal with the foundational stuff that you build a strong marriage on.

So I began on Monday by reminding you that rough spots in marriage are normal. What else would you expect when two sinful people get together? The issue is not that you have trouble, but what you do when trouble comes.

That's why I talked about commitment, about deciding to rekindle this thing as an act of commitment. You decide, "I'm going to win him or her again. I'm going to do it." It starts with a decision of the will, not a feeling in the stomach.

Love is saying, "I will do what I need to do for the highest good of my spouse, even though right now I don't feel what I want to feel."

You say, "But how long do I determine to do that?" You'd expect me to say as long as it takes. I know it's tough when only one partner makes the commitment to relight the fire. But if you will make that commitment, that's one more person on board in this thing than you had last month or last year. And when you get on track with the Lord, that frees Him up to deal with your mate.

The encouraging thing is, any marriage will work when the people in it say to God, "You tell us what to do, and we'll do it. We are ready to obey You no matter what. We know the Holy Spirit can make a difference in our marriage."

What I'm saying is it takes work to rebuild a marriage. The feelings will come back, but feelings can't be the determining factor in your decision.

I hope you'll decide with God's help to rekindle the flame, because your marriage is worth it.

——— **Think About It** ———
A great place to start is to agree that the word *divorce*
will be eliminated from your vocabulary.

REFLECTION

I didn't want to close out this week without giving you some ideas you can start using this weekend to put new life and new warmth into your marriage. Here we go.

1. *Renew your commitment.* Lots of people do this in a public ceremony, but that's not necessary. This would be a good time for that candlelight dinner where you express your love for your partner and your commitment to make your marriage sizzle.

2. *Start dating one another again.* Nobody likes being taken for granted. Adopt the attitude, "I'm going to keep wooing and winning my mate."

3. *Give up something for your mate.* I'm not sure what that may mean in your situation, but I know the positive signal it sends to your partner when you say, "Yeah, I was supposed to do that. But I'd just rather be with you."

4. *Start doing the little kindnesses again.* You know, the little stuff that gets forgotten too easily in marriage, like opening the car door and taking your wife's hand to help her out. For a wife, surprising her husband one night by wearing his favorite dress to the dinner table.

5. *Accentuate the positive.* Anybody can be a critic. If you look hard enough, you will never run out of things that aren't perfect about your mate. Try looking that hard for something good, and let him or her know what you find.

FOUR

STEWARDSHIP

Giving Until It Feels Great

Everybody knows that real giving is when you give until it hurts, right? Not in God's kingdom it doesn't! He's looking for "cheerful giver[s]" (2 Corinthians 9:7)— believers who smile when they give, whether it's their money, their time, or their abilities, because they know that faithful giving makes God smile. Read on and discover how to make God happy and how to experience the secret of real contentment.

"We look not at the things which are seen,
but at the things which are not seen." 2 Corinthians 4:18

LOOKING AHEAD
Read It: Romans 8:24; 1 Peter 1:8

Your view of heaven and eternity will go a long way toward determining what you do on earth. This is true in a number of areas, nowhere more than in our stewardship. Everything we talk about over the next four weeks is built on the premise that being a good steward on earth is vitally and irrevocably linked with your view of heaven.

Now it may seem unusual to link so closely together the unseen world with that part of our world that is probably the most easily seen: the things we have around us, particularly our material possessions.

But we'll see that this is exactly what the Bible does. And besides, people actually do this in the secular world all the time. We call it investing. An investment is putting away something today for tomorrow because you believe tomorrow is coming, and you need to be ready for it even though you can't see tomorrow.

People who make investments believe that the future is significant to the present, and they act accordingly. The biblical concept of stewardship has to do with how you and I handle what we have now in light of what is to come.

A smart investor has to look way beyond what is happening around him now. So does a good steward. A smart investor can't be influenced or sidetracked by those who are blowing everything they have on immediate pleasures, living just for the moment. Nor can a good steward.

A smart investor has to be disciplined and patient, knowing that all the accounts aren't going to be settled now. Same thing with us believers who are only stewards or managers of what God has entrusted to us.

Finally, an investor has to take risks. Even if he has a solid investment plan from the best people on Wall Street, no investor can be totally sure his financial future won't go crashing down if something drastic happens.

God's stewards take risks too, but with one big difference. When we follow God's plan, even if we lose it all here on earth, we can still gain it all in heaven!

--- **Think About It** ---
The question in stewardship is not
what I get out of it, but what God gets out of it.

"What do you have that you did not receive?" 1 Corinthians 4:7

JUST LOOKING AFTER IT
Read It: Luke 16:1-2

One reason I know you'll enjoy these devotional studies on steward-ship is that we'll be looking at some of the most intriguing passages in the New Testament. When the Lord Jesus Christ is your Teacher, you know you're in for something good.

That's the case with the parable of the unjust steward. Since we haven't defined our terms yet, let's do that. A steward is a manager of someone else's property and business affairs. A stewardship is the realm of respon-sibility given to the steward.

Stewards in New Testament times often had a great deal of responsi-bility. A wealthy person might turn his affairs over completely to a trusted steward. That's the case in Jesus' story.

The issue of ownership is a key point in understanding biblical stew-ardship. The steward did not own the property he managed. Therefore, he needed to handle things with an eye to pleasing his boss, the owner.

That rubs against our grain right away. We Westerners are taught to say, "My time is my own. My abilities and gifts are mine to use in the advancement of my career, because I'm the one who worked hard to develop them. And all this stuff here, this is my stuff, bought and paid for. My life is mine."

Is that what the Bible says? The correct answer to the question Paul poses in today's verse is, "Nothing." If you look at the verse you see that Paul follows with another question. If everything we have, even the next breath we draw, is a gift, what right do we have to brag about anything?

So here in Luke 16 we see the basic elements of New Testament stew-ardship. It involves two parties, the owner and the steward.

The second element is a specific responsibility. We can assume that the steward in Jesus' story was to manage his property well, which meant pay-ing the bills, seeing that the work got done, and making the owner a profit.

The third element of stewardship, as suggested above, is accountability. A steward had to be ready to answer to the owner. If Jesus called for an accounting from you today, how would you fare?

——————— **Think About It** ———————
A good steward never forgets that it's not his money
or his property he's foolin' with. It belongs to another.

*"The sons of this age are more shrewd in relation to their
own kind than the sons of light." Luke 16:8*

SHREWD MOVE
Read It: Luke 16:3-8

Y ou have to hand it to the unrighteous steward. He may not have been
a good manager, but he was excellent at conniving. He figured out
an unemployment insurance plan right on the spot after his master fired
him from his stewardship.

Actually, you have to hand it to Jesus here, since it's His story. In just
a few verses He illustrated and drove home a principle that would have
taken most of us a whole book to explain. Even though he was no longer
employed by his master, the steward was still using the master's property
to make friends for himself.

If he cut these debtors' bills, he could knock on their doors later to say,
"I'm unemployed. My family is hungry. Remember when I helped you?"

While the disciples were still shaking their heads at the steward's
actions, Jesus delivered the punch line in verse 8. When the master found
out what the steward had done, he didn't have him arrested for being dis-
honest. He praised him for being shrewd enough to secure his future in
light of his present.

What Jesus is saying is that the children of this world often make the
children of God, people like you and me, look bad when it comes to stewardship. They're often more future-oriented than we are. And they know
how to protect their future through wise investments.

There's a real irony when you consider that Jesus calls His children the
"sons of light." It implies that the other guys are sons of darkness.

In other words, we have a clear view of things as they really are
because we are in the light. We have an eternal perspective. Worldly people don't see things as they really are because they are in darkness. They
may be future-oriented, but they don't have an eternal perspective.

Yet in spite of this, they make us look bad because we don't use our
heavenly shrewdness to lay up heavenly investments the way they use
their earthly shrewdness to lay up earthly investments. Does that sound
like you? We'll see tomorrow.

────── **Think About It** ──────
Lots of people are busy putting something away for retirement.
What are you storing up for eternity?

"Make yourselves . . . an unfailing treasure in heaven." Luke 12:33

MAKING FRIENDS
Read It: Matthew 19:21; Luke 16:9; 1 Timothy 6:17-19

If there's one thing the world knows how to do, it's using money to make friends. In fact, all you have to do to acquire a whole lot of friends is get some money. Ask any celebrity, someone who is constantly surrounded by an entourage of hangers-on, fun-seekers, and other types looking for a ride on a rich and famous person's coattail. Trouble is, when the money disappears and the bright lights fade, so do the friends.

In applying the parable of the unrighteous steward, Jesus tells us to use our earthly goods to make friends for ourselves. But He's not talking about doing it the world's way. Let's see what He means.

One reason Jesus calls money and material possessions "unrighteous mammon" is because the world uses money primarily for unrighteous purposes. Also, money has an unrighteous, all-controlling nature about it that lures people into doing all kinds of unrighteous deeds. That's why Paul told us not to love money.

Jesus is telling us to invest what we have here on earth in eternal things so that when our material possessions "fail" or run out, and they will, we will still have a solid investment in eternity.

In other words, make sure you are investing in the Gospel and the work of Christ so that when you get to heaven, there will be a whole crowd of people there who are glad to see you.

Who are they? People who are in heaven because you were faithful to give. People who heard the Gospel and trusted Christ because you invested your time, talents, and treasure in your church.

I suspect that what will happen in heaven is that people who used their earthly goods to win people to Christ will get a gold-engraved invitation to the heavenly home of someone they helped get there. And at the party will be all of those who made it to heaven, thanks to these people's faithfulness as stewards.

My friend, I hope someone throws a party like that for me, because I want to take as many people to heaven with me as I can. How about you?

———— Think About It ————
Your faithfulness in "a very little thing" (v. 10) can actually make an eternal difference for someone. That's awesome!

"It is required of stewards that one be found trustworthy."
1 Corinthians 4:2

———————

IT'S ALL HIS
Read It: Luke 16:10-12

When was the last time you took the premium due notice on your life insurance policy and tossed it, figuring you'd let this one ride and catch the next one?

Never, right? Why? Because if you're unfaithful in paying the premium, you know they are going to cancel your policy. So you're faithful to pay.

That's all God wants: your faithfulness. He's saying, "If you can't do anything for Me with the little bit of unrighteous mammon I entrust to you, if I can't trust you with that junk that's going to burn up someday, how can I trust you with the real stuff—My heavenly riches?"

How many of us parents would reward our kids for squandering a ten-dollar allowance by upping it to twenty dollars? See, what matters to God is how you are doing with what He's entrusted to you, not how you might do if things were different.

On Monday we talked about the key element of stewardship: The steward doesn't own anything. He's the manager of someone else's property. The Bible teaches that everything we have, we hold as God's stewards.

That beautiful house you cherish? In God's mind, that's His house on loan to you. How do I know it's on loan? Because someday you're going to leave it. That's the test of whether you really own something or not. If you have to give it up, you don't really own it.

So everything we have is on loan from God. For many people, that should not be a hard principle to understand since they are so deeply in debt that the paycheck already belongs to someone else anyway.

How complete is God's ownership? We don't even own ourselves (1 Corinthians 6:19-20). We have been bought with a price, the blood of Christ, and we are His.

Therefore, the issue in stewardship is not that 10 percent of what you have goes to God. He owns *100* percent of what you have, and He's just as concerned about how you use the other 90 percent as He is about the part you give back to Him.

——————— **Think About It** ———————
If it all belongs to God, then He's responsible to meet my needs
if I'm a faithful steward of what He entrusts to me.

REFLECTION

Luke 16:13 is one of those truths that is so obvious and so widely accepted it's become a truism. Jesus said, "No servant can serve two masters; for either he will hate the one, and love the other, or else he will hold to one, and despise the other."

He's talking about God and "mammon," of course. You can't have it both ways. You've got to choose.

My friend, I'm wondering if you've made that choice. Now I know that in some sense it's not a once-for-all decision. We're tempted regularly to chase after material things.

But until you've made the basic decision that God is first in your life, you won't have the context and the foundation you need to evaluate the daily stuff. It's sort of like marriage. I don't have to debate whether the next woman I see is for me.

I settled that issue a long time ago when I married Lois. Ever since then I've had a wonderful, unambiguous platform on which to base decisions about relationships.

That's why I always tell my people not to wait until the trial or temptation hits to make their commitments. That's especially true about the issue of our stewardship, because money and material things have a very seductive power.

So how do you know whether you love God or money? Answer: Which one is telling you what to do? Jesus says, "If you love Me, you will obey Me." Obedience is the test of love. So the question on the floor this weekend is, who or what are you obeying?

"He who is faithful in a very little thing is faithful also in much."
Luke 16:10

HE KNOWS YOU
Read It: Matthew 25:14-18

We're beginning our second week talking about stewardship, and we've got another fascinating passage of Scripture before us.

Jesus' parable of the talents is a classic picture of New Testament stewardship. All the elements we talked about last week are here. We have the two parties, the master or owner and the steward or manager; a specific responsibility, the management of the owner's possessions; and the steward's accountability to the owner for how well he did the job.

Now let me remind you that a talent was a measure of weight used to weigh precious metals. Suffice it to say that one talent of silver (that's what the word *money* in verse 18 means) was a tremendous amount of wealth.

So for this man to have eight talents to distribute means he was awesomely wealthy. This is serious stuff. These three servants have very legitimate responsibilities to carry out, but notice that the master gives to them "each according to his own ability" (v. 15).

What Jesus is saying is that this man knew his servants very well. He knew exactly what each of them could handle, the amount of pressure they could withstand, the level of their business savvy, and so forth. We know that this master stands for Jesus Himself, because Jesus says this story is a picture of His kingdom (see v. 1).

As a modern-day steward or manager of God's possessions, this fact ought to bring you some comfort today. The master in the parable didn't burden the one-talent guy with five talents. Now I'm not saying that all the people who have lots of stuff are the best stewards and that all those who have little must be the worst stewards. Some people acquire wealth by choosing gold over God.

God knows us intimately and perfectly and deals with us according to that knowledge. That's comforting for two reasons: first, because you won't have to answer for what God has given another brother or sister; and second, you don't have to fret if God chooses to entrust more to another steward than He entrusts to you. You are responsible only for you.

--- **Think About It** ---

Whatever God has entrusted to you to manage, He has done so
in the knowledge that you are capable of handling it.

"We must all appear before the judgment seat of Christ."
2 Corinthians 5:10

OPEN THE BOOKS
Read It: Matthew 25:19; Luke 12:42-46

Do you believe the Master's coming back? I don't want you to skip over verse 19 of Jesus' parable of the talents because it's one of the keys to the story. Remember, this is a picture of the kingdom. As the Master, Jesus has gone away on a long journey. In His absence, He has entrusted us with His business on earth. That's what it means to be a steward.

But He's coming back, and He will call for an accounting of our stewardship. That's why as God's managers, we need to remind ourselves that we don't own the things God has left with us, whether it's our time, our bodies, or our bank accounts.

Remember, I said yesterday that if God has given—actually, I should say loaned—you something, He does so with the knowledge that you can handle it. If God has loaned you a house, for instance, the assumption is that you can manage a house and use it for the good of His kingdom.

Therefore, when Christ comes back, He will want to know how well you handled His house. He'll be very interested in how well I handled my pastoral calling. The same holds true for our jobs, our cars, our money, our abilities and spiritual gifts, and anything else that comes under our stewardship.

But if we become like the steward in Luke 12 who really didn't believe his master would come back, our outlook will change. See, if the Master isn't coming back, then there's nothing to get excited about.

If the Master isn't coming back, it's *my* house to use any way I want. If the Master isn't coming back, it's my car to drive, my money to spend. I worked and sweated for it. If the Master isn't coming back, it's all mine, mine, mine.

Ah, but don't stop reading too soon. Verse 19 says the master of that estate did return. Yes, he was gone a long time. But he came back, and he wanted to see the books. Don't allow yourself to forget that you're just the manager of God's possessions. Ask Him right now to make you faithful so that at His appearing you will be commended.

——— **Think About It** ———
Imagine the Master saying to you someday, "Well done!"
That's what I want to hear. Don't you?

*"Well done, good and faithful slave . . . enter into
the joy of your master." Matthew 25:21, 23*

WELL DONE
Read It: Matthew 25:20-23

Did you notice something interesting about the two faithful servants in the parable we're studying this week? Check out the personal pronouns in today's verses. Each servant says the same thing. "Master, *you* entrusted to me . . . *I* have gained" (emphasis added). This tells us something very important we need to know as Christians and God's stewards.

I think what Jesus is illustrating here is that when God entrusts something to us, He doesn't sit up in heaven pulling all the strings to directly control how you handle your stewardship. I believe we have a certain freedom in the way we carry out the responsibility of handling God's affairs.

In other words, we have the freedom either to mess up His affairs or to maximize them. These servants said to the master, "You entrusted, and we gained." The divine and human element are brought together here. These servants met their human obligation to do with their master's money what he desired and expected them to do with it.

God must give it. I must handle it right. If I don't, God's not going to handle it right for me. That's obvious from the fate of the third servant, which we'll talk about tomorrow.

It's also obvious from the end of the story that these servants knew their master's expectations. That's what being a good steward is all about.

We certainly know what our Master's expectations are for us. He's put them in a Book for us. We know from God's Word that if He has given us children, we have the responsibility of training those children in His ways.

If God has given us a job, we know from His Word that we are responsible to be honest and hard-working employees, working for our employer as if he or she were Jesus Christ. God has given us our bodies, but we are responsible to take care of them.

The reason the master's commendation meant something is that the servants' work meant something. They had authentic responsibility, and they carried it out faithfully. Where do you rank on the faithfulness charts today? If you're not sure, better check yourself out.

———— Think About It ————
God isn't holding a beauty contest or talent show here. Stewards are measured by faithfulness, not by looks, personality, or poise!

"Whatever you do, do your work heartily, as for the Lord."
Colossians 3:23

DON'T BREAK YOUR NECK
Read It: Matthew 25:24-25

At first glance, this third servant in Jesus' parable doesn't look so bad. He didn't lose his master's money. He deposited it, even if it was in the ground.

But what was this guy really doing? And what was so bad about it that, as we'll see tomorrow, his master lowered the boom on him?

What this man was doing is what we call playing the ends against the middle. Here's how it works. He digs a hole and hides his master's money. Now when the master comes back, he will at least have his money back with no loss.

But if something happens to the master and he never returns, this guy doesn't have to worry about the fact that he never went out and worked and invested his master's money wisely. Besides, the money wasn't in his name anyway. So even if he does make a big profit, he won't see it.

Do you get the idea? The reason this is important for stewardship is that this is exactly what a lot of Christians do today. They are just spiritual enough that when Christ does come back, they can say, "Look what I did for You. I went to church most of the time; I threw in a few bucks; I was on this committee."

If for some reason the Master doesn't come back, they haven't broken their necks for Him. They play the ends against the middle, trying to have it both ways. But you can't play it safe and expect a big payoff in the end.

Notice that this servant even tried to turn the focus of blame from himself to his master. He says that if the master weren't so demanding, he wouldn't have done what he did.

Do you know people who say that about God? "God's standards are too high. He expects too much. I'm afraid that if I come to Christ, He'll demand too much of me. I'll just stay here on the sidelines where it's safe."

That's bad stewardship and even worse theology. Don't let anyone convince you that you can't do what God expects of you. In His power, you can!

──────── **Think About It** ────────
There are no sidelines in life. You're either
in the game for Christ or for the Devil.

"To everyone who has shall more be given, and he shall have an abundance." Matthew 25:29

A BIG LOSS
Read It: Matthew 25:26-30

As I said yesterday, this third servant did what many Christians do today. They bury gifts, abilities, and money God has given them. They may use these things for their own gain, but God gets nothing out of it.

The master wasn't buying his servant's excuse. We said Monday that this parable is a picture of Christ's kingdom. I believe the story pictures us believers at His judgment seat as our earthly stewardship is evaluated.

This is serious stuff. Notice the three ways this man lost any reward he might have had as a steward.

The first was the master's stinging rebuke (vv. 26-27). When you stand before Christ, when He shows you the price He paid so you could enjoy heaven, and when you see what you could have had, it will sting to know you have incurred His displeasure.

The second loss was kingdom disinheritance (vv. 28-29). Christ will show you what you could have had and what you could have been in His thousand-year kingdom that follows immediately after His judgment seat.

Imagine going to work next Monday and having your boss give your paycheck to someone else in your presence. That's something of what's going on in verse 28. This man lost even what he thought he had to take into the kingdom with him.

The third judgment was exclusion from Christ's kingdom wedding feast (v. 30). I believe some of His children will be excluded from the banquet because of unfaithfulness.

The Bible teaches that there are degrees of punishment in hell (Matthew 11:21-24). By the same principle, there are degrees of blessing in heaven. So when some Christians show up at Christ's judgment seat, all their stuff will burn up, and they will be sent to the penalty box, like an ice hockey player who has broken the rules and has to miss the action.

What a tragedy to know what we could have had. Sometimes we can do something to fix our regrets. At the judgment seat, there'll be no fixing of anything. That's why we must be faithful stewards today. Amen?

--- **Think About It** ---

We don't know all the loss this faithless steward suffered. But it's something you don't want to experience as a child of God. And neither do I.

REFLECTION

There's a saying that goes, "It's not what you would do with a million if a million were your lot, but rather what you are going to do with the dollar twenty-five you've got."

Every time I think of that saying, my mind goes to the widow of Mark 12:41-44. Jesus saw her give and called her to the disciples' attention as a model of what God wants in stewardship.

There were some rich people tossing in their fat checks too, but Jesus wasn't impressed. They were just giving God a tip—a big tip, to be sure—but a tip nonetheless. They didn't even feel the loss of their money. But the widow gave everything she had.

I'd like to talk to that woman. I'd like to ask her where she learned the principle we've been reviewing this week, that God owns it all anyway.

How do I know she believed that? By the way she gave. I don't think it was a death wish that made her give all she had. I think she was saying, "Lord, I don't know where dinner is coming from tonight, but that's Your responsibility now."

I'm convinced that too many of us are saying, "God, if You'll just let me hit it big, the first check's going to You, and it's going to be for $10,000." And God is saying, "Really? What about the money I'm enabling you to earn now?"

My friend, once you become convinced that God can do more with the 85 or 90 or whatever percent you have left over after your giving than you can do by keeping 100 percent, you won't have any problem being a faithful steward.

"Where your treasure is, there will your heart be also."
Matthew 6:21

CHECK YOUR BALANCE
Read It: Matthew 6:19-21

How big is your bank account today? You probably have a pretty accurate idea of how much you have in savings and investments. But my question doesn't have to do with the funds you may have on deposit at First National or First Federal or wherever. I'm talking about the vaults of heaven, your spiritual bank account.

We've come halfway through our series on biblical stewardship, and we're learning that God is intensely interested in how you and I handle His resources. He wants us to invest our earthly goods in building His kingdom, thus accruing glory to Him and spiritual wealth for ourselves.

The key word here is *invest*. No bank is going to put money into your account for you if you fail to do so. You have to deposit or invest your money in that account before you will draw any interest on it.

Many Christians are like the poor country preacher. As he came to church one day with his little boy, he stopped and dropped two quarters into the collection box, hoping to stimulate church members to give. After the service the preacher went to the box, opened it, and found only his two quarters. He was fussing about the poor offering when his son piped up, "Well, Dad, looks like if you'd put more in, you'd have got more out!"

That's where many of God's people are. We aren't putting that much into our heavenly accounts. Then we wonder why God doesn't give us a better return. In Matthew 6:19-21, Jesus says the problem with money—and the solution—is in the heart.

What Jesus is saying in this crucial passage is that your heart always follows your money. Now we would have said it the other way, because it seems as if your money would follow your heart. That is, what you love you'll spend your money on.

But Jesus reversed it because He understood the power of money. He said what you spend money on or invest money in, you will come to love.

That one takes a minute to sink in, so think about it today. How much kingdom investing have you been doing lately?

-------- **Think About It** --------
The reason God doesn't have some people's wallets
is because He doesn't have their hearts.

*"A man with an evil eye hastens after wealth, and does not know
that want will come upon him." Proverbs 28:22*

THE EYES HAVE IT
Read It: Matthew 6:22-24

I was taking a shower one day when I suddenly got soap in my eyes. I grabbed for the towel, but because I couldn't tell where I was, I cracked my head on the soap dish.

Now I couldn't see, and I had a knot on my head. I also didn't know that the soap had slipped out of the dish. So as I groped for the door or something to grab hold of, my foot hit the soap. Suddenly I did my James Brown impression, slipping and sliding all over the place. Why? Because when my eyes went dark, I was in trouble.

What does that have to do with stewardship? Well, Jesus cautions us to use our money with our eyes set on heaven and eternal values, not just on the earthly bottom line. Why? Because when your eyes go, the rest of you goes.

The hands don't know where to touch if the eyes go. The feet don't know where to walk if the eyes go. If the eyes go, the rest of you is in darkness. If you lose divine perspective, if gold replaces God as the trust and guide of your life, you are not only messed up financially, the rest of you goes too.

Jesus says that if you lose heaven's perspective on your earthly possessions, your stewardship will soon get off track, and you will wind up forfeiting God's joy and blessing. If all you can see is the earthly side of your resources, you'll get real guarded and protective of what you've got.

In other words, you get a bad case of "mine" disease, and now no one can touch your stuff because it's yours. You can't use that house and that car God gave you to reach out to other people because it costs too much. Your time is too valuable to use up serving at your church.

When the eyes go out, you lose focus. You can't see the eternal side of things quite as clearly because eternal things are not visible to the naked eye. Is it time for an eye exam? Ask the Holy Spirit to check your spiritual vision today.

--- **Think About It** ---
Unless your spiritual eyesight is 20/20, spiritual
things are going to look fuzzy to you.

*"I have not seen the righteous forsaken, or his
descendants begging bread." Psalm 37:25*

STOP FRETTING
Read It: Matthew 6:25-34

If you've been reading along with us so far this week, you can imagine the looks on the faces of the disciples and the others listening to Jesus teach about true wealth and not loving two masters.

Remember, the verses we're studying in Matthew 6 are right in the heart of the Sermon on the Mount. Jesus is teaching about the way His kingdom operates as opposed to the way the world operates. And what He has just said about money turns the world's view of money on its head.

Jesus knew that what He said would cause some people to worry. He knew there were people standing on the edge of the crowd saying, "Doesn't He know how tough times are? Doesn't He know how hard it is just to keep the bills paid? Doesn't He know I have real needs? Is He in touch with the real world?"

Jesus knew the anxious thoughts that must have been swirling all around Him. So He said, "For this reason I say to you, do not be anxious for your life" (v. 25). For what reason? For the reason He has just given in verse 24: You can't serve and love two masters.

See, Jesus knows that if we start loving material stuff, we'll start fretting about our stuff and give all our attention to it. So He says, "Don't worry about what you're going to eat or wear."

Jesus is saying, "Look, if God has the power to keep your heart ticking and put air in your lungs so you can keep on breathing, then He is going to take care of the other things you need. If God has the power to keep you alive and wake you up tomorrow, then He will see to it that you have something to eat and something to wear tomorrow."

Do you see what Jesus is telling us? First, most of us are worried about the wrong things. Second, not worrying about our material needs frees us up to focus our hearts and minds where God wants them—on Him and His kingdom. And third, if God is supplying what we need, then giving a portion of it back to Him as His stewards should be no problem.

--------- **Think About It** ---------
Providing you your daily bread
doesn't run God low on resources at all!

*"We have brought nothing into the world, so we
cannot take anything out of it either." 1 Timothy 6:7*

NO U-HAULS TO HEAVEN
Read It: Job 1:21; Proverbs 30:8-9; Ecclesiastes 5:13-15

When my wife and I were in seminary, we used to house-sit for income. People who were going on vacation would call Dallas Seminary for the name of a seminary student or couple who would stay in their home and keep an eye on things.

We got the full run of the home. We could eat the food and sleep in the bed. Sometimes we would stay in a home in the posh section of Dallas. I knew I would never get there again, so I "maxed" that baby out. Sometimes we would invite people over.

It was magnificent, but Lois would always remind me that this was not our house. We could use it, but it belonged to someone else. We were merely the stewards.

Today's verse and reading are a powerful reminder that we are merely the stewards of everything we have. The Bible says it's all on loan. We came into this world with nothing, and we are leaving here the same way. Hearses don't pull U-Hauls. The only reason you won't go out naked is because somebody else will dress you.

Over the last few weeks we've learned that the moment we lose sight of the fact that we are only the managers of God's stuff, we are headed for problems. Many of us act as if what we have is "mine, mine, mine."

No, no, no. It is just yours to manage, not to own. If you don't have this view of stewardship, you make God the visitor and you the owner, and God is not into that. He's into ownership.

That's a blessing, because the beautiful thing about having someone else own something is that when it breaks down, the owner has to fix it. If you let God own your life, when it breaks down, He has to fix it. When you let Him own you and own your money, when the money runs out, He has to supply it.

But as long as it is your money and your house and your car, when it breaks, you get to fix it. Which sounds like a better way to go for you?

——— **Think About It** ———
God can do a better job of ownership than
you or I ever thought about doing.

"Let our people also learn to engage in good deeds to meet pressing needs, that they may not be unfruitful." Titus 3:14

GET TO WORK
Read It: Proverbs 6:9-11; Ephesians 4:28; 2 Thessalonians 3:10

When God made Adam, the first charge He gave him was to be productive. Even in a perfect environment, Adam had a job to do. If you want to be an effective and fruitful steward, taking your Master's resources and increasing them to His glory and your benefit, you need to engage in productive work.

In order to have "something to share" (Ephesians 4:28), you have to have something left over. Paul said the way you have something left over to give is by labor.

By the way, that's what's wrong with gambling in the hope that you'll strike it rich and never have to work again. You can't substitute luck for productive labor. That's not what God had in mind.

This is why you never help people who don't want to work. Part of good stewardship is seeking opportunities to be productive instead of waiting for something to be handed to you. The problem with much of our contemporary welfare system is that it is an incentive not to work.

I am not talking about people who can't work. I am talking about people who won't work. According to Paul, if a person who refuses to work comes home saying, "I'm hungry," tell him, "Starve." That's what the Scripture says.

God made us to be productive. He made us for meaningful work and made provision for us to enjoy the fruit of our work. Instead of wondering when he's going to get a slice of a handout pie, a good steward is busy baking pies, enjoying the results, and sharing what he has with others.

Some people question investing, because it doesn't fit their idea of work. But there's nothing wrong with legitimate investments, because they're part of the productivity mechanism. God told Adam to plant seeds. Seed-planting is an investment made in anticipation of a good return.

Ever since the Fall, mankind has been inventing ways to avoid honest, productive labor. Your job is a major part of your stewardship from God. Are you performing it as if He were your employer? Actually, He is!

--- **Think About It** ---
From the very beginning, God prescribed work as part of
His creative order. It's not a punishment for the Fall.

REFLECTION

There's one aspect of stewardship you don't hear much about, but it's appropriate that we reflect on it this weekend. It has to do with the seventh day, which God aside for His and man's enjoyment and which the Bible calls the Sabbath.

After God had worked six days in creation, He sat back and rested—not because He was tired, but that He might enjoy His creation. Then God said, "This is such a good thing to do that I'll share it with My creation."

That's why we celebrate the Lord's day every Sunday. It is a day set aside for us to enjoy God in the context of worship and to enjoy His created order.

Besides providing a day of rest and worship, God honors His children in other ways. Read Ecclesiastes 5:18, and you'll see that God's reward for you as His child is that you might enjoy His goodness. He says, "I want you to enjoy your labor and its fruit."

So you ought to do things well. Work hard and play hard. If you love your job, you should love the fruit of your job. Solomon says that God has given all of this to us to enjoy.

My point is that if you are honoring God with your money, when He gives you a little extra, and you want to do something fun with it in a way that does not dishonor Him, God says He has given you that extra to enjoy. You don't need to feel guilty for enjoying it either. God is not a miserly giver. Determine you'll be faithful in your stewardship, thank Him for His provisions, and enjoy Him!

*"Not even when one has an abundance does his life
consist of his possessions." Luke 12:15*

HOW MUCH IS ENOUGH?
Read It: Luke 12:13-15; 1 Timothy 6:6-8

One Sunday a man came to church looking very sad and despondent. The pastor noticed him and asked, "Why are you so sad?"

"Well, two weeks ago my uncle died and left me $75,000. Then a week ago my aunt died and left me $50,000."

The pastor said, "Wait a minute. Two weeks ago your uncle died and left you $75,000. Last week your aunt died and left you $50,000. Why are you so sad?"

The man answered, "Because nobody died this week."

Greed is an ugly thing. By greed I mean a consistent desire to have more or demand the best without regard to need. The greedy person sees money as an end itself. The greedy person always says, "I want more."

The opposite of greed is contentment. First Timothy 6:6-8 is one of the best statements on greed and contentment in the Bible. One reason we can be content is that, as we've already seen several times during this series, when we leave this place our wallets stay here (v. 7).

I don't mean it's wrong to want to better yourself. But if you cannot be content with where you are until God takes you where you want to be, you are greedy.

As we look around today, we have to wonder why so few even of God's people are truly content. We're knocking ourselves out just like the world to get ahead and pile up the toys. What's missing?

Well, I think what's missing too often is an important part of the formula Paul gives us here. Notice his formula: godliness plus contentment equals gain. We tend to skip over that first part of the equation.

What is godliness anyway? It's focusing my mind and heart so completely on being like Jesus Christ in how I think and what I do that when people look at me, they get a clear picture of what Christ is like. Let me tell you, you can't follow Christ wholeheartedly and also be chasing the pot of gold at the end of the rainbow. Which path will you take this week?

——————— **Think About It** ———————
Greed is not tied to how much you have.
You can be rich and greedy, poor and greedy, or middle class and
greedy, because the heart of greed is the desire for more.

"[God's] commandments are not burdensome." 1 John 5:3

CHUMP CHANGE
Read It: 1 Timothy 6:9-11

Here in our final week on the subject of stewardship, we want to consider at least two more key biblical passages. We started yesterday with 1 Timothy 6 and will spend a couple more days in this chapter.

Verse 9 is where you get into the problem Paul is talking about, the issue of greed versus contentment. This verse and verse 10 need to be read carefully to get at the meaning, because they're often misunderstood.

Notice Paul doesn't say those who *are* rich are in for trouble. He's going to talk to the rich down in verses 17-19, which we'll look at tomorrow.

The people Paul is addressing here are those who "want to get rich." That is, their desire for more of this world's possessions is beginning to possess them. That's the lust for more we've been talking about. Verse 9 is an important verse because some people think God just wants to keep folk poor to keep them under His thumb or something.

That's not it at all. God is looking out for our welfare. He wants to make sure we don't settle for the "chump change" of this world and miss His true riches. Besides, when we decide to pursue gold rather than godliness, we bring upon ourselves a mess of problems.

So God's not just trying to stunt your economic growth. I've said it before: God is *not* against you bettering yourself if you do it without compromising godliness. But look what happens when money is your priority.

First, you "fall into temptation." The original says you keep on falling. That is, you continually expose yourself to compromising situations. You also get caught in a "snare" like an animal lured into a trap. And finally you start doing "foolish and harmful" things you wouldn't do normally.

No wonder the "love of money" leads to all kinds of evil. Verse 10 is often misquoted and misunderstood. Money is not immoral in itself. It's amoral, like your VCR. You can use it for good or for garbage. The only way to handle the temptation of greed is to flee (v. 11), do a 4.4 forty-yard dash in the other direction. If you really want to flee, God will put wings on your feet!

--------- **Think About It** ---------
No matter how much you get, if you have to
leave God behind to do it, it's just chump change.

"Do not love the world, nor the things in the world." 1 John 2:15

DON'T FIXATE ON IT
Read It: 1 Timothy 6:17-19

A few years ago former heavyweight boxing champ Muhammed Ali was interviewed by a major sports magazine. You may know that Ali suffers from Parkinson's disease, and his walk has been reduced to a slow and painful shuffle. His speech is also affected.

The article told how it used to be when Ali was champ. Ali said in the story: "I had the world, and it wasn't nuthin'."

That's the message the Bible wants you and me to get! This world is "nuthin'" compared to what God has in store for us. That's why Paul reminds those who are rich not to get a big head or fall in love with their wealth.

Now Paul is not jumping on rich folk, and neither am I. Some of God's best stewards are wealthy believers who handle their wealth for His glory. And you and I don't need to be getting ulcers because we're jealous over how God is blessing someone else.

But wealth does bring responsibility—and notice Paul doesn't set any monetary amounts here. Compared to the rest of the world, we Americans are wealthy. So don't check out on me here.

Besides avoiding pride, Paul also tells us not to "fix [our] hope" on money. That is, we don't get locked into it, bolted down to it so that it controls us and quenches our desire for godliness. That's good advice for several reasons, one of which is that riches are uncertain. You don't want to be hugging too tight on something that could disappear tomorrow.

Instead, we're to fixate on the God who gives us these things to enjoy. This goes back to what we talked about last weekend. God is not a tight-fisted miser who hoards His blessings. When we are pleasing to Him, He delights in giving us good things to enjoy.

Verses 18-19 ought to sound real familiar by now. They restate the principles we've been studying over the last few weeks. God places His resources in your hands so you might use them to do good, help others, and bring Him glory. And as you do, you are laying up for yourself treasure in heaven. Any questions?

——————— **Think About It** ———————
When you use your time, talents, and treasure to make spiritual investments, you've discovered "life indeed" (v. 19).

*"Be devoted to one another in brotherly love . . . contributing
to the needs of the saints." Romans 12:10, 13*

GOD'S MATH
Read It: Philippians 4:10-16

I want to wrap up our study of stewardship by considering another
potent passage of Scripture that has a lot to teach us.

Philippians 4:19 is one of the most memorized verses in the New
Testament. It would be easy to camp there, but we need to step back and
see the context of this great verse to grasp what Paul is saying to us.

The church at Philippi loved and cared for and supported Paul as did
few other churches, and he felt very close to these believers. They did all
of this for Paul and for the work of Christ despite the fact that they were
persecuted and impoverished and barely had enough to live on themselves (see 2 Corinthians 8:1-6).

So the first thing we need to understand is that Paul is writing about
stewardship to one of the poorest churches around. An accountant might
say you're wasting your time to teach poor people about stewardship.

But not if you buy into God's mathematics. See, the world says one
plus one equals two. But God says zero plus zero can equal a million when
you plug Him into the equation.

So Paul is thanking the Philippians for their recent gifts to his ministry.
But he's not writing to pry another gift out of them. It's not that Paul was
glorifying poverty. It's that he had learned to be content whether he had
a little or a lot. And he says he had times of both need and abundance.

Notice that it's in the context of living contentedly on what God provides that Paul writes verse 13, another verse often quoted, memorized,
and claimed by believers.

This is a powerful truth that reaches beyond just your finances. If you
can be content where you are, then ultimately there's no problem you
can't handle, because God has given you the greatest gift of all, His Son
Jesus Christ, to strengthen you. That means you have all the resources of
Christ to draw on in tackling whatever comes your way.

Could you write your friends and honestly tell them you've found the
secret to a life of contentment and joy? If so, you're a wealthy person!

--------- **Think About It** ---------
On the other hand, if you expect financial success alone
to bring contentment, you're in for a long wait.

"My God shall supply all your needs according to His riches in glory in Christ Jesus." Philippians 4:19

WHO BENEFITS?
Read It: Philippians 4:17-19

Let me ask a question. Who benefits most from a gift to God's work? You might say, "Well, that's obvious. The recipient does." Really? Paul teaches us here in Philippians 4 that the primary beneficiary of your faithful stewardship is *you*. And I don't just mean the warm feeling you get inside when you help someone. What the Bible is talking about here goes far beyond that.

Look at the financial terminology Paul uses in verse 17: "profit which increases to your account." Whenever you invest your time, energy, talents, financial resources—whatever—for the benefit of God's kingdom, God deposits blessing into your heavenly account. It's like accruing interest, gaining profit.

Your gifts are like the sweet savor sacrifices of the Old Testament—offerings the Israelites weren't required to give. They were gifts made to God out of love and devotion. So when those offerings were burned, God smelled the aroma and smiled. It was "well-pleasing" to Him (v. 18).

Now lest you think Paul is just talking about "pie in the sky by and by," we're now ready for verse 19. It's to people who give to God freely, out of a heart of love without concern for the bottom line, that the promise of needs met is addressed. You're not ready for verse 19 until you come to grips with verses 10-18.

There are two ways this promise can be abused. One is called prosperity theology: "I'll give so I can obligate God to pour out His blessings on me. I'll just pile all my bills on the table, and He has to pay them. I've got God over a barrel." But God will never be in debt to anyone.

Another potential abuse is the idea that my needs include a new house, new car, new wardrobe, etc. The Philippians themselves help to fix that notion. They were poor, but God was giving them life's necessities.

God calls the shots on this, not us. The only thing you and I need to know is that you can't outgive God. So we can give freely, knowing that God honors faithful stewardship.

--- **Think About It** ---

God is not limited by our accounting methods. When He does the math, a little can equal a lot!

REFLECTION

If a millionaire offered to give you a gift either "out of" his riches or "according to" his riches, which would you choose?

Well, if you're smart, you'd take the "according to" gift. See, a millionaire could give you $10 out of his riches. But it would not even begin to reflect what he is capable of giving, which is what "according to" means.

Philippians 4:19 says our God is an "according to" God when it comes to meeting the needs of His faithful stewards. Supplying your needs "according to His riches in glory in Christ Jesus" really means that God gives you access to all the riches of heaven.

When you have a need, God lines you up alongside His supply and determines what aspect of His riches your situation requires. There's a thought to brighten your weekend.

Now someone may say, "Tony, you ought not to be telling folk stuff like that. It'll make them get greedy." No, like I said yesterday, any thought like that is an abuse of God's promise. There is the potential for abuse here, of course, but that's true with any of God's promises. Besides, people who try to take God for all He's worth are doomed to serious disappointment anyway!

What I'm saying is that you can't discount this tremendous promise just because someone might try to misuse it. In fact, I would never even think about making a promise this bold. Only our gracious God would do that for His faithful ones! Are you in that band? If not, sign on today!

FIVE

◇

SPIRITUAL REBOUNDING

Bouncing Back from Life's Failures

*In basketball, rebounding is such a valuable
skill because there are so many missed shots. That's
also true in life. We miss a lot of shots. The reasons may
be different, but we all miss. In fact, if you haven't missed
yet, just keep playing. After a missed shot, the thing to do
is get that rebound and get back into the game. We're going
to see how Joseph, David, Jonah, and Peter did just
that—and how you can rebound too!*

"I will never desert you, nor will I ever forsake you." Hebrews 13:5

A ROUGH START
Read It: Genesis 37:1-11

There aren't many of us who don't get broken sometime, somehow. If it hasn't happened to you yet, simply keep living, and your turn will come. Whether you become the breaker or the one broken, life has a way of catching up with us all.

That's why we need to learn the art of spiritual rebounding, the ability to recover from a missed shot and get back into the game.

One area where all of us have experienced pain is in broken relationships. Because we're all sinners, when we start relating to one another, things get broken. It may go back to your childhood when you were rejected by your father or mother. You may have a history of abuse, betrayal, and divorce. Or you may have friends or loved ones you don't talk to anymore.

Broken relationships come in all shapes, sizes, and degrees. They can last a long time. But this problem is not new to God. He's aware of any broken relationship you may be suffering from today, and He has a word of hope and healing for you. To find that word we want to look at the life of Joseph this week. The last fourteen chapters of Genesis record his remarkable life, and as we study the Bible together, we'll see that it tells the whole truth about relationships.

Joseph didn't come from an ideal family, to say the least. He was the eleventh son of Jacob, the master deceiver. By this time Jacob had gotten his spiritual act together, but his ten older sons took after Dad.

They once deceived and killed an entire city of men because one of the men had raped their sister (see Genesis 34, especially v. 13). And they are about to commit their worst deed of treachery against Joseph. This was not what you would call a well-adjusted family.

Joseph had a lot going against him, yet the Bible presents him to us as a man of greatness and dignity. I say this to let you know that just because your mama is bad and your daddy is bad and your brothers or sisters are bad, you don't have to be messed up too. With God's help, you can rise above your circumstances.

--------- **Think About It** ---------
There's no denying that your past has influenced you.
But it need not control you.

"If God is for us, who is against us?" Romans 8:31

SOLD!
Read It: Genesis 37:12-28; 39:1-6

Let's see. One of Joseph's brothers makes a motion that they kill him, and the motion carries nine to one. Reuben saves Joseph, but the boys throw him into a pit and then sell him to traders on their way to Egypt where Joseph becomes a slave (v. 36). I would call that rejection.

Perhaps you have been rejected for one reason or another. Maybe you discovered that people you thought loved you don't really love you at all. Well, that's Joseph's story. He has been sold like an animal by his own brothers and finds himself in a hostile land.

But don't miss Genesis 39:2: "The LORD was with Joseph." This is the covenant name for God. The God who keeps His promises kept His eye on Joseph in Egypt.

You say, "Joseph had a bad family background." But the Lord was with Joseph. You say, "His brothers hated him, got rid of him." But the Lord was with Joseph. You say, "Joseph was just a teenager many miles from home." But the Lord was with Joseph. Because the Lord was with him, Joseph became successful.

The first principle of rebounding from broken relationships is that even when the people you love don't want you, if you stay with the Lord, you can still get somewhere. Joseph was rejected by his loved ones, but he was accepted by the Lord. Regardless of what happened to you yesterday, if you will remain faithful to the Lord today, He can control your tomorrow. Many people who have been mistreated are still focusing on the people who hurt them, waiting for them to make things right. That isn't going to happen in a lot of cases. Those who are wronged need to turn to the One who won't hurt them and who is there to help them.

The fact is that some broken relationships are not going to get fixed. You may never get your parents to accept you. You may never be able to completely heal some relationships. You may not be able to get around that problem you have been living with all these years.

But the Lord can take you where you are and still make you a success. Broken relationships don't have to control you.

――――― **Think About It** ―――――
If the Lord is with you, in the final analysis
it doesn't matter who's against you.

"The Lord was with Joseph." Genesis 39:21

GO DIRECTLY TO JAIL
Read It: Genesis 39:7-23

Did you ever wonder why Joseph turned out so much better than his ten older brothers? I have an idea. Joseph's daddy, Jacob, was a spiritual mess for a long time. But when he got older, he had a wrestling match with God and received His blessing (Genesis 32:22-29).

So Jacob made a decision for God that Joseph was able to benefit from because he was still at home. I hope this is an encouragement for you if you feel like you've blown it with your kids and you think it's too late to fix those broken relationships. If you get right with God, He can help you get right with your kids, especially those who may still be at home.

Jacob was now committed to God. He could not undo the past, but he could walk with God in the present and see God bless his present in spite of what had happened in his past. So he did. And he raised Joseph to be committed to a holy life.

This was evident when Joseph resisted the sexual advances of his master's wife (vv. 7-9). He saw clearly that his situation could only be explained by the hand of God working in his life. So he said to Mrs. Potiphar, "How can I be in the midst of what God is doing and be unfaithful to Him?" Mrs. Potiphar cried rape, and Joseph was dragged away to prison.

Come on. The man is living right, and he's already been through a broken relationship at home. Now he's got a broken relationship at work even though he has done nothing wrong.

Is that right? Talk about damaged relationships. I mean, I could see some of us walking around in that jail saying, "Lord, have mercy. I try to do right and I get fired. Shucks, I should have had some fun and kept my job too. Now I have nothing but a prison term."

But Joseph had a lot more than that. "The Lord was with Joseph" (v. 21). We've heard that one before. When the Lord decides to take you somewhere and be with you there, you're going to be all right.

——— **Think About It** ———
If you are willing to go all the way with God, then even being
in jail in His will is better than being at home out of His will.

"Forgetting what lies behind and reaching forward to what lies ahead, I press on toward the goal." Philippians 3:13-14

FROM PRISON TO PALACE
Read It: Genesis 40:1-23

We said it yesterday, but somehow it still seems to go against what we think of as right and fair. For Joseph at this point in his life, there was no better place to be than in jail because he was right where God wanted him to be.

By now the principle ought to be obvious: Even when you walk with God, human relationships can still get broken. Everywhere Joseph turned, people were either turning on him or turning away from him.

Here's another principle of spiritual rebounding we're learning: Sometimes God must take you to the bottom in order to take you to the top. The hard part is remembering when you hit bottom that it's not the end of the trip.

Don't get me wrong. I'm not saying the scars are not real or that people don't ever need help in healing the past. I'm saying that lasting hope for rebounding from broken relationships is found in commitment to Christ.

Let's go back and visit Joseph in jail. Genesis 40 relates still another problem for him. He helped one of Pharaoh's officials, but the man forgot about Joseph, and our boy served two more years in prison.

Here was a young man leaving a mile-long trail of broken relationships. And not one of them was his fault. Joseph could have been saying by now, "You know, life would be good if it weren't for people."

But his faith in God told him different, so he waited out his time. And Joe's time was definitely coming. Pharaoh was about to have a dream, and Joseph was about to go from zero to hero, from prison stripes to Pharaoh's main man (Genesis 41).

No one can do that kind of miracle but God. See, if you and I were in jail, we would settle for release, a suit of clothes, and a hundred bucks to get back home. But God says, "Trust Me, and I'll take you from prison to the governor's house—not so you can show off for yourself, but so you can show off My power and glory."

--- **Think About It** ---

God knows where He's taking you. And He knows the lessons you need to learn on the way so that when you get there, you can do the job.

"You meant evil against me, but God meant it for good."
Genesis 50:20

GOOD OUT OF BAD
Read It: Genesis 45:1-15

What would you do if you were the second most powerful person in Egypt, holding the power of life and death, and had the guys who caused all your pain standing in front of you?

It would make a great movie script, but for Joseph it was real life as we jump ahead to his reunion with his brothers in today's study. Once again we see that all you have to do is be successful, and people will call!

Joseph was on top now. He was alone with his brothers. Would he kill them himself, make them suffer first, or just throw them in prison and let them rot?

Of course, Joseph chose none of the above. He didn't forget what they did (vv. 4-5). He just saw what God was doing with what they did.

See, God knew what you were going to go through at five years old. He knew how people were going to mess you over at twenty-five. None of that can keep Him from taking you where He wants to take you today.

Joseph was about thirty years old by this time. We can figure out that he was seventeen when he was sold into slavery. That means he had thirteen years of a confused life, not knowing whether he was up or down, in or out. Yet he maintained his commitment, so God was able to use his negative circumstances to produce good.

God can do the same for you. Maybe your mother or father took part of your life away, but God can give it back to you. You don't have an excuse for not doing anything.

Joseph didn't forget what happened. Anyone who tells you, "Just forget it," is not living in the real world. It happened, but God can do something about it. Later we read that God gave Joseph his own family. He had new relationships to replace the old ones.

One reason old relationships may be destroying you is that you haven't replaced them with new relationships. You are hanging out with the wrong reminders. God helped Joseph to forget the pain of what happened. He still had the memory, but it no longer hurt.

--- **Think About It** ---
You may not be able to forget your past. But it doesn't
have to control or dominate you anymore.

REFLECTION

Maybe you can identify in a special way with Joseph. Maybe you can honestly say right now, "My life is a lemon."

Well, I have good news. God can make lemonade out of it! He can take a mess and turn it into a miracle. He can transform either your circumstances or your relationship to your circumstances if His sovereignty is allowed to work in your life.

That's what God is after. He wants to take the "lemons" of your life—broken relationships, broken past, broken circumstances—and mix them together until He comes out with something that you can taste and say, "That's good." Here are some things to keep in mind while He's doing the mixing:

1. Don't try to ignore the past or pretend it never happened.

2. Ask God in His time and in His way to "make up to you" the time or relationships or whatever it is you have lost (Joel 2:25).

3. Make a list of the people who have wronged you and then consciously release those people to God in prayer (Romans 12:19).

4. Tell God you are ready to start over right where you are this weekend.

"Flee immorality. . . . The immoral man sins against his own body."
1 Corinthians 6:18

A POWERFUL GIFT
Read It: 2 Samuel 11:1-5

One of the most devastating sins any person can commit is sexual immorality. Many a man and woman have bitten the spiritual dust because of failure to bring this area of their lives under God's control.

Those who have fallen morally need to know there is forgiveness for their sin. They can rebound. But my prayer is that as we consider the life of David, you will commit yourself to moral purity so you won't have to.

God's gift of sex is a powerful passion that brings joy and fulfillment when used correctly, but when used incorrectly, leads to devastation. We might liken sex to a fire. In the fireplace, it's warm and delightful; but if it ever gets out of that fireplace, it can burn the house down. So we'd better learn how to handle this powerful gift.

God isn't embarrassed about sex. He created sexuality. It shouldn't surprise us that the Bible doesn't hesitate to talk about it. The Song of Solomon celebrates marital intimacy in explicit detail without shame.

God's Word is also honest and unblinking when relating the story of David, who committed immorality and suffered the consequences. This week we are going to watch David's life crumble, and then we'll see how he rebounded through the grace of God.

I doubt if there's anyone who hasn't messed up on some level when it comes to sexual sin, whether through lust, pornography, or physical immorality. We've all felt the flame. We need to constantly be on guard.

David's problem began when he let down his guard. "Then it happened" (v. 1). What an opening line. It was springtime, the time for love and for war. A king usually went to battle at the head of his army. But David had solidified his kingdom. There were just a few skirmishes to take care of, so he decided to stay home.

David is about fifty years old here. Maybe he looked in the mirror and noticed some gray. Maybe like a lot of middle-aged men, he began to wonder, "Do I still have it?" Whatever he thought, he wasn't on his guard—and the enemy knew it.

——— **Think About It** ———
The fire of sex is meant for the fireplace of marriage. Once it leaves there, someone is going to get burned.

"Let him who thinks he stands take heed lest he fall."
1 Corinthians 10:12

——

NOT ME
Read It: 2 Samuel 11:6-17

As you read 2 Samuel 11, realize that David is coming off of about twenty years of spiritual success. Yes, he blew it a lot as a young man, but he's had two decades of spiritual strength. We are talking about the David who killed Goliath, the "sweet singer of Israel" who wrote many of the psalms, the man after God's own heart.

But on this evening, a woman captivated David. We are not seeing a man who was carnal, trying to be immoral, or looking to fall into sin. We are seeing a man who was tempted and yielded.

David saw Bathsheba that night, but it's what he didn't see that would change the rest of his life. He didn't see that his sin would cause four of his children to die (the baby, Amnon, Absalom, and Adonijah). He didn't see that this one night would split his kingdom in half. He didn't see that he would become a murderer.

That's the problem with sin. My friend, if you are looking at things you ought not to look at, imagining things you ought not to imagine, or planning things you ought not to do, remember that you are not seeing the whole picture. And it's what you don't see that will get you.

So David commits sin with Bathsheba; she gets pregnant, and now he's got to cover this mess up somehow. He can't let anyone know what happened. It's always bad when it's a king in this situation, because a king can do whatever he wants to get rid of problems. So David devised Plan A, Plan B, and Plan C.

Plan A was to bring Bathsheba's husband Uriah home from the front, have him relax, and spend the weekend with her so the baby would appear to be his. But Uriah was too loyal a soldier. Getting him drunk and then trying to send him home, Plan B, didn't work either.

Plan C wasn't so tame. It was murder. Put Uriah on the front line unprotected so the enemy would kill him. Tragically, Plan C worked.

Many of us would say, "I could never do that." Better watch out. You can do anything when Satan gets hold of you.

——— **Think About It** ———

Twenty years of spiritual success didn't mean David would never fall. What you did yesterday doesn't guarantee you spiritual success today.

"Do not grieve the Holy Spirit of God." Ephesians 4:30

THE HARDNESS OF SIN
Read It: 2 Samuel 11:26–12:1-14

The hardening effect of sin is amazing. You feel real bad at first. You feel kind of bad a little bit later, and a little bad after that. Then particularly in the case of moral sin, before long you hear, "Everybody's doing it." And finally, "I'm only human."

Look how David reacted to Uriah's death (v. 25). David had become so cold and so hard by this time that he said, "Well, you win some, you lose some. That's the way it is. Don't be upset about it."

The cover-up was now complete. Uriah was dead, and David was married to Bathsheba, so the child was legitimate. Plan C (see yesterday's study) seemed to work to perfection. David had covered all of his tracks . . . except one (v. 27c).

Things would have been fine if the Lord hadn't seen it. The plan would have worked if the Lord hadn't seen it. David would have gotten away clean. Uriah was killed in action. Play taps for him, fold the flag. Give him a hero's burial.

But the Lord saw everything. Husband, if you are running around on your wife, the Lord sees it. Single person, if you are sleeping around, the Lord sees it. The Lord saw David, so chapter 12 opens the same way chapter 11 opened: "Then . . ." Only it's a different story now. David is going to be called out.

It's about one year later by now. But time is no problem for the Lord when He is ready to expose sin. How many people know is no problem either. Nathan the prophet came to David and told him a sad story. David's anger flared against the culprit in the story, and then came the crusher from Nathan: "You are the man!" (v. 7).

What God was telling David is: "Your problem is Me! Look at all I've done for you. How could you pull a number like this on Me after all I've done for you? You've made My name look bad. You have soiled My reputation. You have been an affront to Me."

Believer, if you think moral sin is a private affair, better think again. The Holy Spirit is in that bedroom or that adult bookstore with you.

——— **Think About It** ———
At its heart, moral sin is an affront to our holy God.
That's the real issue.

"Be sure your sin will find you out." Numbers 32:23

TRUE REPENTANCE
Read It: Psalm 32:1-7; 51:1-3

The result of David's moral sin was loss of life, the devastation of his own family, and the division of the kingdom of Israel. A one-night stand? Hardly. It was a lifetime wipeout.

In Psalm 32 we read about the effects of his sin on David. During that year, his life was empty. He felt guilt and shame and even physical symptoms because he wouldn't come clean with God.

Well, the good news is that this is not the end of the story. We're talking about spiritual rebounding, and David is about to start his journey back. As we saw yesterday, when he was confronted by Nathan the prophet, David did finally admit his sin.

After a year of trying to hide sin, David came to his senses and sought God in repentance and brokenness of spirit. His prayer of confession is recorded in Psalm 51, documenting his rebound from devastating sin.

It's of interest that the man who tried to cover up his sin (2 Samuel 12:12) had it recorded for some thirty centuries worth of people to read. Millions know David's story, underscoring the truth of today's verse.

When Nathan came to David, David turned to God. Read verses 1-2 of Psalm 51, and you will see the heart attitude God accepts from one who has committed moral sin. It's called repentance.

Many people don't know what repentance means. They offer a little prayer something like, "Lord, I'm sorry for the sins I did today. Forgive me in Jesus' name. Amen."

That is not repentance. It begins with confession, which means to agree with. True repentance means agreeing with God that what you did was wrong and needs to be cleansed. True repentance is coming to grips with your rebellion against God so that you see you have been sinful and need to be cleansed.

True repentance makes no excuses. It says, "This is my problem and my sin. I didn't have to yield, but I did. I can't blame it on anyone else."

Do you need to rebound from moral failure, or are you dealing with anyone who does? This is where it starts.

——————— **Think About It** ———————
The only way to bounce back from moral sin is to change your mind
about your sin and confess it before a holy God.

"Wash me, and I shall be whiter than snow." Psalm 51:7

BATHE ME, LORD
Read It: Psalm 51:4-13

David teaches us something very important in Psalm 51:4. Ultimately, all sin is committed against God. That's why we must come to Him with a contrite spirit.

When the Lord calls us out for our sin, He doesn't want excuses. If David had tried to excuse himself, restoration would have halted right there.

The tragedy of moral failure is our failure to own up to moral failure. We write it off to being human or making a mistake, like the guy who once told me, "I'm a man." I said, "I know. That's not the point. The point is that you are a Christian man. Therefore, when you are judged by God, you simply say, 'You've got me. I'm guilty.'"

David pleaded for cleansing with hyssop, a branch that was dipped into the blood sprinkled on the altar. It was a plea for forgiveness. Without it there could be no joy or wholeness (v. 8).

If you are carrying unconfessed moral sin, that's why you have no peace, no power, no sense of God's presence. That's why your prayers are not being answered, because when you don't come clean with God, He doesn't hang out with you.

David wanted a spiritual bath. Some of us need one too. Some of us men are filthy. We wallow in the muck and mire of pornographic literature. We choose our movies based on the amount of sex, and we become defiled. We need cleansing, and the good news is that God is ready to bathe us if we will confess our sin to Him.

Let me give you more good news. Even if you've messed up morally, God can still use you to teach other transgressors His ways (v. 13). You can tell potential homosexuals they don't have to go that way, because you've been there, and it's a dead end. You can tell potential adulterers that adultery is not the way to go, because you know the price you paid.

What does God want from someone who has committed moral sin? He doesn't want denial, excuses, or a cover-up. He wants a broken heart. If your heart is broken over your sin today, you're a candidate for a spiritual rebound.

--------- **Think About It** ---------
God answered David's prayer. David bounced back,
and God used him. God will do the same for you.

REFLECTION

We've talked about some pretty nitty-gritty stuff this week. It's gotten heavy, so let's step back and look at some principles we can take with us to help in this area of moral purity.

1. *Anyone can commit immorality.* I'm not immune to it. You're not immune to it. So never say never. Say, "By God's grace, never." Keep your guard up, especially when you're away from home or feeling spiritually or physically wiped out.

2. *Past spiritual success doesn't guarantee present success.* The fact that you didn't do it over the last twenty years has nothing to do with what you may be tempted to do tomorrow. The Devil is in no particular hurry.

3. *Recognize the power of passion.* St. Augustine said, "There is nothing more powerful in bringing down the spirit of a man than the caress of a woman." Passion is powerful. When you play with it, you will always want more.

4. *God holds you responsible.* Sin is a choice. When you abuse God's grace, you pay a big price.

5. *You are not a helpless slave of your passions.* You may not be able to change what happened last night, but you have a lot to say about what will happen tonight.

6. *If you have sinned, there is hope.* You can rebound. God will forgive you. He can use you again.

7. "Let him who thinks he stands take heed lest he fall" (1 Corinthians 10:12).

"Blessed are those who hear the word of God,
and observe it." Luke 11:28

NO, I WON'T GO
Read It: Jonah 1:1-3

We're beginning our third week of studies in spiritual rebounding. I hope you're getting some bounce back in your walk with Christ.

This week's biblical character not only missed his shot, he had to bounce back about as far as anyone I can think of. Jonah is also the only guy I know who got mad because he made his second shot! It's going to be an interesting week.

Jonah teaches us how to rebound from rebellion. He defied God, so you know he messed up. Some of us are messed up because we have been rebellious. No one is going to tell us what to do—not mama, not daddy, not even God. We want to be our own boss, the captain of our ship, the master of our fate.

The book of Jonah doesn't take long to read, but it's quite a story. I hope that by the time we're finished this week, we'll know more about our big God than we do about the big fish.

Let me set the stage for you. Jonah was a prophet during a rebellious time in Israel. God was angry with His people. Two other prophets who ministered at this time were Amos and Hosea. God dipped down into the school of the prophets and said to Jonah, "I've got a job for you. Go east to Nineveh and deliver My message to those wicked people."

But Jonah said, "No thanks," and headed west.

Why? Because he knew who the Ninevites were. Nineveh was the capital of the bloodthirsty, cruel pagan empire of Assyria. The Assyrians were Israel's enemies, a people who were going to be used by God just a few decades later to punish Israel by taking them into captivity.

You get the picture. Jonah has two problems. First, if he goes to Nineveh and preaches and the people repent, then God will spare them His judgment. Jonah is a loyal Israelite. He doesn't want to see that happen.

Second, if he goes to Nineveh and preaches and they don't repent, he just might get carved up. Jonah is in a classic catch-22, so he decides he won't go. Bad choice.

--------- **Think About It** ---------

If God asked you to reach out to someone you
don't like, what would you tell Him?

"The LORD is compassionate and gracious, slow to anger and
abounding in lovingkindness." Psalm 103:8

TAKING THE LONG WAY
Read It: Jonah 1:4-17

I was talking to a close friend one time who was telling me how defiant his three-year-old son had become. The boy did a horrible thing I can't even mention. His father spanked him, then looked at him, and said, "Don't you ever do that again. Do you want me to have to spank you again?"

The boy looked him in the eye and said, "Yes!"

I told my friend, "You'd better get that boy saved fast, because he's either going to wind up in jail or dead."

That's how seriously I take the problem of rebellion. Jonah developed a rebellious spirit. But he was no dummy. He knew God was everywhere. He knew he couldn't go somewhere that God couldn't find him. What Jonah was trying to escape from was submitting to God's will.

Nineveh is about 550 miles east of Joppa. Tarshish is 2,500 miles west of Joppa. Rather than go 550 miles in God's will, Jonah wanted to go 2,500 miles out of His will. That's exactly the decision many of us have made at one time or another. God says, "Go east, young man," but we go west.

The bad news about rebellion is that if you ever change your mind, you not only have to come back the 2,500 miles you went in the wrong direction, but you still have to go the 550 miles God told you to go in the first place. The trip back is a lot longer than the trip out.

And by the way, whenever you run from the will of God, you get to pay the fare. See, the beautiful thing about going to Nineveh is that God would have paid the fare. The horrible thing about going to Tarshish is that you get to pick up the tab. Many of us are paying a high price for our Tarshish trip when if we had done it God's way, He would have picked up the tab.

Notice also that when you defy God, you not only mess up yourself, but you mess up those in the neighborhood. Those poor sailors didn't ask for Jonah's mess, but they got it. Are you messing other people up by your rebellion?

——— **Think About It** ———
The good news about obeying God instead of rebelling
is that God always supplies that which He demands.

"I will look again toward Thy holy temple." Jonah 2:4

THE HOUND OF HEAVEN
Read It: Jonah 2:1-10

This is quite a situation here with Jonah. The wind, the sea, and the fish all obeyed God. But we've still got problems with the preacher.

Jonah didn't start rebounding until he got swallowed. Some of us are not going to get right with God until we are swallowed either—until God sends us circumstances so adverse, so cataclysmic that running to God is the only thing left.

Remember, Jonah could have repented anywhere along the line, but it took this incredible circumstance to get his attention. He prayed from the stomach of the fish. I guess so.

Chapter 2 is the beginning of Jonah's rebound. It's the start of his turn-around where he looks up after missing the shot and decides to get back in the game.

Jonah prays a wonderful prayer: "Lord, I'm in this fish, but You threw me overboard. Those sailors were doing what You wanted done. You are absolutely sovereign. Everything is under Your control, so I know this is You. I didn't think of it then, but I know it now."

Ever been in the pit? The pit is not a bad place to be if it gets you back in the will of God. It's a bad place to be, but if it took your going to the pit to get you back on the mountaintop, thank God for the pit.

God didn't move until Jonah remembered. God didn't move until Jonah confessed. God didn't move until Jonah got right. Many of us want God to move before we've moved. We want God to act before we act. Jonah acted, and God responded. He commanded the fish, and it vomited Jonah onto dry land, whereupon he asked the way to Nineveh.

Sometimes we don't get it right until the third marriage because of our rebellion. Sometimes in our rebellion we don't get it right until we're fifty. Sometimes we don't overcome that addiction until later, although it could have been overcome sooner. Sometimes we have to hit rock bottom.

But whatever it takes to bring us back, God will do it. He's the "Hound of Heaven" who pursues us until we surrender.

--- **Think About It** ---

You can go to Nineveh yourself, or God can take you there.
It will be a wet ride if God has to take you, but that's what rebellion does. It's easier to obey the first time.

"The word of our God stands forever." Isaiah 40:8

SAME SONG, SECOND VERSE
Read It: Jonah 3:1-10

If you lay Jonah 3:2 on top of Jonah 1:2, you'll notice something. The first seven words of these verses match exactly. God didn't change His mind at all. He told Jonah the same thing the second time.

If God's not going to change, it seems that we ought to do it right the first time. Jonah is now stinky and ugly—and he still had to preach. Since God is not going to change, we might as well do it His way up front. Since He's not going to adjust, His second word (3:1) will be the same as the first.

The beauty of Jonah 3 is that God is the God of the second chance. Even if you have fled to Tarshish, and God has had to bring a storm into your life, even if you have been thrown overboard and you're drowning, God can give you a second chance.

That's the part people love to hear. But here's the part they don't want to hear. The return trip is going to be inconvenient. See, people want to try and escape God's will and then avoid the inconvenience of the return trip.

But you can't do that. You cannot run from God and then expect to have a convenient return trip. It's great to have a second chance, but it still costs something.

Well, Jonah finally got the message. He's now ready to head for Nineveh. The text doesn't say so, but I think God took Jonah back to his port of departure. Jonah left from Joppa, so God said, "I'm going to drop you back off in Joppa, and we'll see which way you go. Would you like another boat to Tarshish?"

God often brings us back to the point at which we messed up so we can get the mess fixed and move on. That's the grace of God. He reinstated Jonah and sent him to Nineveh, and Jonah's preaching sparked one of the greatest revivals in human history.

God can give you a second chance to put your marriage back together. He can give you a second chance to obey Him in whatever He has asked you to do. But you've got to do it His way.

———— Think About It ————
You are messing with unchangeable territory when you deal with God. He's not adjustable. He is unchangeable.

"I knew that Thou art a gracious and compassionate God."
Jonah 4:2

SECOND-CHANCE GRACE
Read It: Jonah 4:1-11

Jonah 4:2 is so full of good news that we could end today's study right here and go away blessed.

I love what this says. When you repent, God's heart will melt because He loves you so much He stands ready to shift His wrath to mercy. All of us need that. We need a God who will relent when we repent (see 3:10).

The problem is that we are so unlike God. The story of Jonah would be a lot easier to understand if it ended here. But Jonah still hated the Ninevites, so when God brought revival, Jonah pouted. Like I said on Monday, Jonah got mad because his second shot hit the mark! He asked God to take him (v. 3).

If I were God, I would have accommodated the boy by now. But our gracious God prepared an object lesson for Jonah. He said, "Jonah, it's a little hot outside today, isn't it? How about a little shade?"

Please notice what we've got here. The wind obeyed God; the sea obeyed God; the sailors obeyed God; the fish obeyed God; the Ninevites obeyed God; this plant obeyed God; and soon a worm is going to obey God. But the preacher . . .

Wait a minute. I want to know how the story ends. I want to know what my man Jonah did. Why does the story end here? Because God is asking us what He asked Jonah: "What are you going to do with My grace and compassion?"

If you have ever strayed from the will of God and come back, if God has ever given you a second chance, what are you going to do with it? And if you see someone else out of God's will, are you going to write that person off or reach out and try to bring him or her back like God brought you back?

See, we don't deserve what we have, but God in His grace has appointed circumstances that have transformed our lives. That means you and I get what Jonah got—which is a second chance and a third chance and a fourth chance and a hundredth chance. Let's not misuse His grace.

--------- **Think About It** ---------
God would love to restore you, to restore your family, to bless you.
All you have to do is turn back to Him.

REFLECTION

L ike I said yesterday, if I were God and Jonah griped to Me, I'd be saying, "Jo' boy, I call you to preach. You try to ditch Me. I have to send the wind and the sea and a fish to get you. I give you a second chance; you deliver your little sermon; I empower it so that a whole city repents, and you get mad and want to die because I'm good! What color coffin do you want, boy?"

But since I'm not God, and neither are you, let's talk about it. The question is not why God shows grace to wicked Ninevites or to pouty prophets or even to us. His nature is to be gracious. The issue is, what are we going to do with His "second-chance" grace?

Here's what I mean. In the 1929 Rose Bowl, a University of California player named Roy Riegels picked up a fumble, got turned around, ran eighty yards the wrong way, and scored a touchdown for Georgia Tech. He became instantly infamous. All his life he was known as "Wrong Way" Riegels.

At halftime there was dead silence in the California locker room. When it came time to go back out, California's coach said, "Gentlemen, the game is only half over. We have another half to play. Roy, go back to your position."

It is said that Roy Riegels played the greatest game of his life after the coach gave him a second chance. You get the idea. When God calls you and me back to the field, when in His grace He gives us another chance, let it be said of us that we played the greatest game of our lives!

"Blessed is he who keeps from stumbling over Me." Matthew 11:6

WHACK!
Read It: John 18:1-11

Peter is one of the most colorful characters in the Bible. Someone has said that Peter must have worn "peppermint socks" since he put his foot in his mouth so much. He was definitely a spur-of-the-moment guy.

Given Peter's nature, it's not surprising that he missed some shots and had some spiritual rebounding to do. As we wrap up our four weeks of devotional studies on spiritual rebounding, we will see Peter's failure and how he bounced back.

Even though Easter is behind us by now, we're going to revisit the Garden of Gethsemane, the events leading up to the Cross, and a very important post-resurrection appearance of Jesus Christ. Peter was a key figure in all these events, so we are going to follow him around this week.

Peter had made it clear he would travel to the cross with Jesus (Matthew 26:33). He was saying, "You can count on Your home boy here."

People are usually hard on Peter for saying this, but I think his intentions were good. A lot of us are like Peter. We have good intentions, we make great promises, we vow great spiritual vows—only to find our lives collapse around us. Almost any believer can find something to identify with in the life of Peter.

In John 18 we find the familiar story of Jesus and the inner circle of disciples in the Garden. When the soldiers came to arrest Jesus, Peter whacked off the ear of a man named Malchus.

On a human level, we might applaud Peter. We might say, "Good for Peter! He doesn't take any stuff. You get close to Peter, you will go earless. This guy doesn't play."

But Jesus rebuked him. "Peter, you have missed the point. This scenario is My Father's will."

Here is a fundamental issue we all face when it comes to walking with God and keeping our lives from collapsing. That is, we need to make sure we are not analyzing events from a worldly point of view, but rather from a spiritual, godly point of view. This was Peter's problem as he assessed the situation in Gethsemane and jumped in with the wrong solution.

--- **Think About It** ---

We are usually quick to adopt the world's methods of addressing
our lives rather than adopting God's methods.

"The weapons of our warfare are not of the flesh."
2 Corinthians 10:4

POOR PETE
Read It: 2 Corinthians 10:3-4

If you ever look for a good illustration of the truth Paul shares in today's reading, I can tell you where *not* to look. Don't look at Peter in the Garden of Gethsemane. He's fighting the wrong battle with the wrong weapon.

If you take out your sword (meaning human methodology) when God wants to give you His cup of suffering (that is, His divine will), when you adopt man's way rather than God's way, then you interfere with the plan of God for your life, and you are about to become a candidate for spiritual rebounding.

As we said yesterday, a fundamental issue that all of us face is whether we are using God's way or man's way of addressing the problems and circumstances and needs in our lives.

Well, Peter used man's way here. Not only that, but we find out from Matthew's gospel (26:36-46) that he was supposed to be praying, and he was sleeping. So Peter had a poor prayer life, and he had a worldly perspective on how to go about this thing of being a disciple.

More than that, Peter was also being disobedient here. Why do I say that? Because when Jesus told the soldiers in John 18:8 to let the disciples "go their way," I believe He was telling Peter and the others, "Leave here now and go back home. You don't need to be a part of this."

In fact, John adds in verse 9 that Jesus said this to fulfill His own prophecy that none of His disciples would be lost. In other words, Jesus was acting to save Peter's neck by trying to get him out of there. But instead of leaving, Peter fought back.

Let's see. Peter is prayerless, worldly, and disobedient. That's a lethal combination. When you have a weak prayer life, when you're thinking like the secular world thinks rather than like God thinks, and when you're not doing what God tells you to do, you're a sitting duck for the forces of hell. You are a big target for Satan. You are ripe fruit ready for the picking. That is exactly what was happening in the life of Peter. No wonder he was about to do what he never thought he would do.

--- **Think About It** ---

If Peter's situation describes you today, it's time to hit your knees.

"The spirit is willing, but the flesh is weak." Matthew 26:41

RAISE YOUR RIGHT HAND
Read It: John 18:12-27

In the early hours after the arrest of Jesus, what was left of Peter's spiritual life came unglued. This is the same guy who said to Jesus, "You can bank on me."

But then a little servant girl said, "Excuse me, but you look a lot like one of those guys who were hanging out with Jesus."

Peter answered, "Me? No, you've got me mixed up with someone else. You've seen one Galilean, you've seen them all."

Then they were all standing around the fire getting warm, kind of rapping, when denial number two occurred (v. 25). Finally, Peter was challenged by a servant who was a relative of Malchus, the man whose ear Peter had cut off (v. 26). This guy was more sure of Peter's identity, so Peter had to make his point very clear. Mark says he denied Christ with a curse (Mark 14:71).

Peter wasn't just swearing like a sailor here. What he did was what you do in a courtroom. He took an oath called a "self-maledictory" oath, which means you take an oath against yourself. That is, you swear that if you are lying, you invite the court to bring down judgment on you.

This is no small thing, because in the Bible, swearing a self-maledictory oath could cost you your life. So Peter did not just deny Christ three times. To convince them he was telling the truth, he said, as we would say today, "If I'm lying, may lightning strike me!"

That thump you just heard was Peter not only hitting the bottom but breaking right on through. He's got a long way to go to get back up.

Now most of us would say, "That's terrible. He denied Christ. I would never do that." But have we ever denied Christ before others by the way we live? If we ever *confessed* Christ, would the people we know be shocked because they see the contradiction in our lives?

Those are tough questions that only you can answer. Peter couldn't remember his promise for even one night. We need to pray that we'll do better when our turn comes.

─────── **Think About It** ───────

Have you ever made a promise to God in the morning that you broke that afternoon? Then you know why we all need His forgiving grace.

"I have prayed for you, that your faith may not fail." Luke 22:32

DON'T GIVE UP
Read It: Luke 22:54-62

No, the verses in today's reading are not a mistake, even though we just read about Peter's denial yesterday. I wanted you to see verses 61-62 in context, because this is where Peter's spiritual rebounding started.

We know that as Peter spoke his third denial, a rooster crowed in fulfillment of Jesus' prophecy. Jesus knows the future because He predicted it before it happened. In fact, He accurately prophesied Peter's three denials. This reminds us that Jesus is sovereign.

What does this have to do with Peter's failure and restoration? Today's verse gives us the connection. Not only did Jesus know ahead of time what Peter's response was going to be, but Jesus also predicted that Peter would rebound from his breakdown and become a leader once again among his fellow disciples.

In other words, Jesus was telling Peter that even though he would fail, his failure would not be terminal. Jesus was saying in effect, "Peter, I won't give up on you even after you deny Me and feel like a total failure."

Jesus wanted Peter to remember this so that he would not give up completely. His tears would then become tears of repentance and healing, not just tears of remorse and despair.

Did you know that Jesus is praying for us too? If He were not, none of us know how low we might go. The fact is, we haven't gone as low as we would have gone if God hadn't kept us from going there.

There probably aren't many of us who have gone as low as Peter, who have sunk to publicly renouncing any association with Christ. But too many of us are two-timing Jesus. We don't renounce Him; we just don't live the life. We're with Him on Sunday; then we step out on Him from Monday to Saturday.

That's why we need to know that Peter was able to rebound spiritually through the grace of God. If there's hope for Peter, there's hope for us. Hardly anyone has messed up like Peter messed up. But Peter bounced back—and if he can bounce back, then there's hope for any broken life.

———— **Think About It** ————

Peter's spiritual healing began at the most painful moment of his life. If you have messed up, don't run from Christ. Bring your pain to Him.

*"You shall love the Lord your God with all your heart, and with all
your soul, and with all your mind." Matthew 22:37*

"DO YOU LOVE ME?"
Read It: John 21:1-17

It's obvious from today's reading that even though Peter hit bottom in denying Christ, the other disciples still followed his lead (v. 3). Peter went fishing. That's what he was doing when he first met Jesus.

Peter was so messed up that he had gone back to doing what he was doing before he became Jesus' disciple. But notice that they caught nothing. When you are out of the will of God, guess what you catch? Nothing. When you are out of the will of God, you cannot produce.

Peter had lost his vision for ministry. He was probably asking himself, "Can God still use me?" The answer was about to come when grace showed up the next morning in the person of Jesus Christ.

Jesus answered Peter's question with the miracle catch of fish. The good news is that when you get right with God, you become productive again. When you get right with God, no matter how low you have gone, no matter far away you've strayed, things begin to happen again.

After breakfast we see one of the greatest demonstrations of God's grace you'll ever see. In this famous exchange Jesus restored Peter three times for his three denials. He invited him back into the fold, back into His service. He told him, "You can leave your fish now and feed My little lambs."

We don't have room here to go into all the details of these verses, but the bottom line is that Peter reaffirmed his devotion to Jesus, and Jesus gave him another chance. Peter was restored to fellowship with his Lord and recommissioned for his apostolic ministry.

People wonder sometimes about Peter. How could Jesus give this guy another shot at such an important ministry after he had failed so miserably? Well, to answer that all we have to do is look in the mirror and say, "Lord Jesus, how can You keep forgiving and using me when I fail You so often?"

What happened on that seashore is that Peter finally told Jesus the absolute truth. He came clean with the Lord. Have you?

———— **Think About It** ————
A lot of us lie to the Lord. We say, "I love You,"
when our lives say, "I don't know if I even like You."

REFLECTION

I really hope you've found some new strength and encouragement for your Christian life this week. As I suggested at the beginning of the week, most people can identify with Peter on some level. He's sort of an Everyman who's all too human: quick to speak, quick to jump in, trying to fix things with worldly wisdom and worldly means.

But I want you to leave this week with much more than just a smile and a knowing shake of the head at how human good old Peter was. I want you to see that for all of his humanness and failure, Peter was authentic on the inside.

Although he denied Christ, Peter got honest with Him on that morning in John 21, and Jesus restored him. This did not minimize Peter's sin. He still hit bottom and needed to rebound spiritually. My point is that if you will be honest with God when you fail, He can still use you and bless you and make your life productive again.

If you will come clean with Him and say, "Lord, I'm not okay. I've failed You, I've rebelled against You, but I love You and want You to forgive and use me," then your "net" can be filled again.

Here was Peter, scared and ashamed, going out to feed Christ's sheep. May God help us to come clean with Him even if we've denied Him, so that He can lift us up and use us for His glory.

SIX

◇

LEARNING HOW TO PRAY

What Happens When We Seek God

We Christians love to study prayer. We write books about it, go to prayer seminars, and love to hear how prayer has changed someone's life. But most of us don't pray as much as we should. Maybe we think of prayer as the exception instead of the rule—something we do on special occasions or when we're in a big mess. Whatever the reason, we stand in need of learning how to pray. So let's open the Word and ask the Spirit to teach us.

"The Helper, the Holy Spirit, whom the Father will send in My name, He will teach you all things." John 14:26

SPEAKING THE LANGUAGE
Read It: Romans 8:26a; 1 Corinthians 2:10-11

Prayer is like the weather: Everybody talks about it, but nobody does anything about it.

Well, we do want to talk about prayer over the next four weeks, but I hope it will be more than talk. If there's any area where most of us are weak, it's prayer. It's not that we don't put a high value on it. It's not that we don't think we should pray. The problem is that we simply don't pray.

If you struggle with prayer, welcome to the family. One reason we struggle is that we don't know how to pray. Prayer isn't natural to us, because our natural state is to run from God's presence, not come before Him.

Some of us have never learned how to pray. Others haven't prayed enough to be comfortable with it. Still others don't understand enough of God's Word to pray biblically and accurately.

Whatever the case, you and I don't have any excuse not to pray. We may have good reasons for not praying well, but we don't have any excuse for not praying.

Paul recognizes our prayer dilemma, and he has some good news. When you don't know how to pray, when you don't know what to say or how to say it, you have a divine Interpreter called the Holy Spirit who can clarify, correct, and focus your prayer so that by the time it leaves you and gets to heaven, it's been fixed.

You don't have to worry that you didn't get that prayer just right. By the time the Holy Spirit took your prayer and carried it into the heavenly throne room, that thing was cooking, because the Spirit's job is to intercede for us. His job is to interpret our prayers and carry them to the Father.

Learning to pray is like learning a foreign language. The best way to learn it is to hang out in an environment where the language is spoken.

So if you want to learn to pray, you need to spend time in an environment where prayer is spoken. You need to pray. The Holy Spirit will help you. He knows the language.

--- **Think About It** ---
Don't worry that you may pray poorly.
Worry if you don't pray at all.

"Pray without ceasing." 1 Thessalonians 5:17

THE GROAN OF PRAYER
Read It: Romans 8:22-23, 26b

Have you ever groaned when you felt something deeply? All of us have had reason to groan, but I suspect few of us know what it is to groan in prayer.

The Holy Spirit does—and He does it on our behalf. This is one of the mysteries of prayer, the work of the Spirit in bringing our prayers before the throne in heaven.

We can see what Paul means by groaning when we look at verse 22. The groaning of a mother in labor is both bad and good news. The bad news is that this is going to hurt. The good news is that something is going to happen. The good news is always worth the bad news. The product of the groan is greater than the pain of the groan. The creation groans as it awaits redemption.

We also groan (v. 23) because, like the creation, we too have been affected by sin. So we groan when we see sin's ravages in our world. We groan when our families don't turn out the way they should. We groan at our own sin and failure.

Paul is saying that the Holy Spirit identifies with us in our pain when we come to God in prayer. But the Spirit does more than just feel with us. He can take our pain and our deepest longings and interpret them to God. What does this say about prayer? It says the Holy Spirit only links with our prayer when it comes from our hearts, not just our lips.

If you say your prayers just because it's bedtime, if you say grace just because it's mealtime, if your prayer never gets deep enough that it enters into Spirit territory, it's not prayer the way Paul is talking about prayer.

So there are times when you may not be able to articulate one word in prayer and yet say a lot. If you've ever come to the point where you are so concerned and so burdened for someone or something that all you can do is sigh, you're learning something important about prayer.

God allows us to groan, because otherwise we would never really pray. We would say the words, but we would never pray from within. And that's where true prayer has to begin.

——— **Think About It** ———
The Holy Spirit only groans when you groan in prayer.
He doesn't groan just with your words.

"O LORD, Thou hast searched me and known me." Psalm 139:1

LOOKING INSIDE US
Read It: Romans 8:27

The Holy Spirit not only groans for and with us in prayer, but He also intercedes for us.

To intercede means to approach someone and make an appeal on behalf of someone else. That's what the Holy Spirit does for us when we pray. He approaches God the Father with our requests and needs when those requests and needs are in line with God's will.

Don't miss that last line in verse 27. The Holy Spirit's ministry in prayer is not to get God to come around to our way of thinking and convince Him to answer all of our requests. The Spirit's job is to get our prayers lined up with the will of God.

That's why the Spirit searches our hearts in prayer. You can't always know what someone is really thinking or really wants just by listening to what he says. But if you could see inside his heart, you would know exactly how to interpret his words. That's what the Spirit does when He searches our hearts and interprets our requests to the Father.

But if the Holy Spirit is only going to intercede for us when our prayers are according to God's will, we had better learn what God's will is. And where do we learn God's will? In His Word, of course.

So before we can pray in the will of God, two things must happen. First, we must have intake from His Word. If your prayers are not based on God's Word, then you are praying out of His will. God's mind is revealed in the Bible, so when you read your Bible, you learn how to pray as you should.

A second thing I believe we must do if our prayers are going to hit the mark of God's will is meditation—the discipline of thinking through and musing over God's Word. It's the idea of a cook simmering the stew to bring out all the flavor. We must meditate on Scripture and allow it to become part of us.

Only then will we see things happen in our prayer lives, because the Spirit's intercession is tied to God's will, which is tied to His Word.

———— Think About It ————
Since we sometimes pray outside of God's will,
part of the Spirit's job in prayer is to change our minds,
not convince God to give us what we want.

"Devote yourselves to prayer." Colossians 4:2

PRAYER AND GOD'S WILL
Read It: Romans 8:28

Did it surprise you today to realize that Romans 8:28, probably the most quoted verse in the Bible, is set in a context of prayer?

Most people who quote verse 28 forget that verses 26-27 precede it. Before you can know that God is causing all things to work together for your good, you have to have a prayer life that is aligned with His will.

In other words, the Spirit has to rearrange your prayers so that you want what God wants for you. The connection between verses 27 and 28 is this: Those for whom God is causing all things to work together for good are the ones for whom the Spirit is interceding according to God's will.

So if the Holy Spirit is aligning your prayer life with the will of God, you will begin to see how God is fitting it all together. The Spirit will help you see the plan of God taking shape in your life.

But you only get the Spirit's help when you are on the Spirit's program. You are only going to enjoy what God is doing when He is free through the Spirit to take what you are expressing and align it with His plan.

See, Romans 8:28 really is a great verse to recall when you're flat on your back in the hospital, because if you love God and are called according to His purpose, He can use even that experience to bring about His will in your life.

But if you have a dynamic, Spirit-directed prayer life, you won't need a friend to come by and drop the verse on you. You'll already be plugged into God's program. That doesn't mean you won't hurt or that everything that happens to you will be pleasant. But you'll have God's peace and perspective on it.

Remember what it's like to fly over a farm and see how orderly the fields are? They were like that all the time. You just couldn't see it from the ground. But now that you are elevated to a whole new level, you can look down and see how orderly things are.

That's what the Spirit does for you when you get your prayer life lined up with God's will. It's the only way to fly!

------- **Think About It** -------
Do you need to take flight today and see things from God's
vantage point? That flight begins on your knees!

"If we ask anything according to His will, He hears us."
1 John 5:14b

PRAYING LIKE CHRIST
Read It: Romans 8:29-30; 1 John 5:14-15

What is God's ultimate purpose for you and me? Paul answers that in Romans 8:29. God's goal for all Christians is that we might be "conformed to the image of His Son." Prayer plays a vital part in making this goal a reality, so let's talk about it today.

God is so passionate about this goal that He foreknew, predestined, called, and justified us so we would become like Christ. And as we have seen in the past few days, God is working according to His will to accomplish His goal, which includes answering our prayers according to His will.

This should be a real encouragement to us to pray. Many times we don't pray because we don't think anything is happening. But with God, something is always happening. We ask, "When is God going to work?" But we don't understand that God is always working.

When it comes to prayer, God is either answering your prayer the way you prayed it, or He is changing your heart through the Spirit's intercession to get your prayer in line with His will.

You say, "But I don't see anything." Well, when you plant a seed in the ground, you don't come out the next day complaining because you don't see the plant. Does the lack of a stem and leaves mean nothing is happening?

No, a lot of necessary things are happening so that you can see the plant when you are supposed to see it. Don't think nothing is happening because you haven't seen anything yet. It's just not harvesttime.

But this doesn't mean God is in the business of being our Santa Claus. He is not up in heaven saying, "Oh, you want that? Let Me run get it. You want Me to do this? Let Me hurry and do it." He only does His will.

So one way God is making us more like Christ is by helping us to pray the way Christ prayed: "Not My will, but Thine be done."

That means if what you are praying for is in God's will, He's doing it even though you haven't seen it yet. But if it isn't, He will work to change your request by changing you.

——————— **Think About It** ———————
Unanswered prayer can be as big a blessing as answered
prayer if it keeps us from violating God's will.

REFLECTION

Our devotional studies for Tuesday and Thursday led off with two verses that tell us how we should feel about prayer. In 1 Thessalonians 5:17 Paul says simply, "Pray without ceasing." And Colossians 4:2 urges, "Devote yourselves to prayer."

You know what that tells me? It should be abnormal for us as Christians not to pray. Prayer should be as normal a part of our daily lives as eating and breathing—not just a hushed, holy exercise we engage in for a few minutes on Sunday morning.

Is it abnormal or normal for you to pray? If you pray abnormally, then don't be surprised if you hear from God abnormally. If you pray every now and then, you are going to hear from God every now and then.

Paul says prayer should be so important to us that it is the rule, not the exception. But we have it backwards, because we see prayer as interrupting our schedule, not our schedule interrupting prayer.

Have you ever tried to sit down and talk with a friend when the kids keep interrupting, the phone starts ringing, and there's someone at the door? You want to deal with those distractions so you can get back to the important stuff, your conversation.

That's how we should be with prayer. The interruptions are what we call our schedule. The real job is prayer. If your days are crowded with too much schedule, look for distractions you can eliminate so you can have time to pray.

"The LORD is a God of knowledge." 1 Samuel 2:3

ONE PROBLEM, ONE GOD
Read It: 1 Samuel 1:1-6

I don't think any devotional study of prayer would be complete without spending some time talking about Hannah, the mother of the Prophet Samuel and one of the great prayer figures of the Old Testament.

When we first meet this woman, she is in great emotional and relational pain. We learn the primary reason for her pain right up front in verse 2. Hannah was childless, a crushing problem for a woman in Old Testament days when the fruit of the womb was a sign of the blessing of God.

But Hannah's problem was compounded by the fact that she was just one of two wives of Elkanah, her husband. And the other wife, Peninnah, was very fruitful in childbearing. Think of the stigma this would have caused Hannah in her hometown in the hill country of Ephraim.

Not only was Hannah unable to have children, but if there was any question that the problem was Elkanah's, the other wife's children answered that. And the fact that Peninnah was able to have children meant that God's disfavor was not on this family in general.

The finger pointed at Hannah as the problem. But there's much more involved here than just the inability to conceive, and we don't have to wait long to find out what else is going on.

First, we learn that Elkanah was a godly man who went faithfully each year to sacrifice to the Lord at Shiloh. By the way, this was in the days before David conquered Jerusalem and a permanent temple was established in Jerusalem. The writer mentions the two sons of the head priest, Eli. We met these rascals back in Part 3, Week 3, so you can turn back there to remind yourself why this detail is important to the overall story.

We also learn that God was intimately involved in the life of this family, because He had closed Hannah's womb (v. 5). And finally, verse 6 tells us that Peninnah made life miserable for Hannah.

The last part of verse 5 is crucial, for Hannah and for you. No matter what you are going through, you cannot simply look at it from the human side, because God is at work. Even in the negative things, God knows what He is doing. Hannah said so herself in the words of today's verse.

——— **Think About It** ———

Hannah had a problem, but she also had the one true God. So do you.

*"In my distress I called upon the LORD, and cried
to my God for help." Psalm 18:6*

WAITING AND WORSHIPING
Read It: 1 Samuel 1:7-8

Now we haven't said anything yet about Hannah's prayer life, but we need to follow the progression of the story the way the writer of Scripture presents it. You'll appreciate the power of her great prayer if you see the context out of which it came.

The context we're talking about here is a bad situation. This routine of Peninnah provoking Hannah became a yearly ritual. We're not told how many years this went on, but that's really not the point. The point is that Hannah's barrenness became the focus of her worship at Shiloh every year, not necessarily because she wanted it that way, but because her situation was thrown into her face by Peninnah.

Verse 7 gives us an important clue about Hannah's character. Although her yearly trip with Elkanah to sacrifice to the Lord was the saddest day of the year for Hannah, she still went to the place of worship every year. Hannah was a faithful woman who worshiped the Lord and sought His presence and His face even though she had a persistent problem.

Now remember that there's more going on here than just Hannah's painful problem and this humiliating routine she went through every year. The Lord was at work, even though it didn't seem that anything was happening. For reasons only He knew, He allowed Hannah to endure this trial to deepen her faith and prepare her for the answer when it came.

I suspect you've been in a position like this more than once. See, the problem wasn't that this thing necessarily got worse. The hard part was that nothing changed for Hannah. Every year she went to Shiloh as a childless woman. Every year she had to listen to the same taunts.

Can you appreciate how Hannah must have felt? You keep trusting and believing and hoping, but nothing happens. People try to say something helpful, as Elkanah did (v. 8), but it only makes things worse. But since God is working, you need to keep waiting and worshiping, because something's going to happen when He's ready.

———— Think About It ————
The more Peninnah provoked Hannah, the more we can assume
Hannah prayed. What do you do when a problem persists,
and it seems that the Lord has forgotten about it?

"Trust in [God] at all times. . . . Pour out your heart before Him."
Psalm 62:8

RUNNING TO THE LORD
Read It: 1 Samuel 1:9-11

Do bitter circumstances drive you to the Lord or away from Him? Hannah was crushed, but she ran in the right direction. Today's reading shows that her childlessness did not keep her from the Lord. This is the secret to the power of her prayer life.

Unfortunately, one of the things we're tempted to do when things fall apart is avoid God's presence, when He's the One we need the most. Sure, it's hard to pray when your heart is breaking.

But if you've never prayed with a broken heart or with a deep sense of your need, if you've never really poured out your heart before God, you haven't really learned what the Bible means by prayer.

See, you may be upset with God because nothing is happening. But if you turn away from Him, where are you going to go for an answer? Hannah had a problem only the Lord could fix, because He's the one who gave her this burden to bear.

Elkanah didn't have any answer for Hannah. He couldn't give her a child. And all Hannah needed to remind her of the mess with Peninnah was having Peninnah's kids running in and out of the house all day. Hannah couldn't do a single thing about her situation . . . except pray!

And this was some prayer (v. 11). We know how serious Hannah was about prayer because she made a vow to the Lord. She put it all on the line. This is not "Now I lay me down to sleep; I pray the Lord my soul to keep." This is serious stuff. She promised to give her child back to God before she ever got pregnant.

When you're willing to make an exchange with God—which is what a vow is—when you're willing to make a promise to God that He can hold you to, then you're getting serious about prayer.

Most of us only pray like this when we have to. We go weeks and months without getting serious about prayer because we don't think we need God that much. When we hit the wall, it all changes. Hannah's pain caused her to run to God. Which direction will your pain make you run?

——— **Think About It** ———
When things get tough, we learn how to really pray.
Maybe that's one reason things get tough.

"My grace is sufficient for you, for power is perfected in weakness."
2 Corinthians 12:9

───────────

IT'S ENOUGH
Read It: 1 Samuel 1:12-18

If there's anything you need to take away from today's study on prayer, it is this: Take your burdens to the Lord. It doesn't matter how painful the load or how pressured you feel, take your need to the Lord.

Someone might say, "I've heard that all my life. Tell me something new." Well, when it comes to the ministry and the discipline of prayer, it's not something new that you and I need. What we need is as old as the answer Hannah sought about three thousand years ago.

Hannah was so intense in her prayer that the priest Eli thought she was drunk. Now you'll remember from our earlier study that Eli didn't have a lot going for him as a father, but he was a man of God, and when Hannah told him what she was doing, he had the right word for her at the right time (v. 17).

Notice what had changed for Hannah. At this point, God had not changed her circumstances. But He had changed her countenance. She had sought the Lord in prayer and emptied her soul before Him, and she went away from the house of worship happy.

I often remind the people in my church in Dallas that I'm not here to make false promises. A lot of people do that. They tell you that if you pray just right, God will come along and set everything just right. I don't know what God is going to do in your case. He doesn't consult me before He acts, and He doesn't share inside information with me. But I can tell you that He can lift your heart. He can take your weakness and supply His strength. God can do that because as He told the Apostle Paul in today's verse, His grace is sufficient. It's enough.

See, Hannah prayed and got her son. Paul prayed about his "thorn in the flesh" three times and got God's no when it came to taking the thorn away. But Paul also got God's grace to bear it, and he said if that's what it takes to get God's power, let it be! Can you say that today? If you can, you're at the graduate level in God's school of prayer.

─────── **Think About It** ───────
Hannah found her peace on her face before the Lord in prayer.
Guess where you'll find your peace.

"The LORD remembered [Hannah]. . . . She gave birth to a son."
1 Samuel 1:19-20

GOD HAS THE LAST WORD
Read It: 1 Samuel 1:19-23

The reason you need to go to the Lord with your burden is that if He's the one responsible for the burden, He's the only one who can release you from it.

That's one of the important lessons we can learn from the experience of Hannah. We know that verse 19 wasn't the first time Elkanah and Hannah had marital relations. It wasn't anything physical that made the difference when Hannah became pregnant. Today's verse and text could not be any clearer that it was the Lord releasing her from her burden.

I also want you to see that this didn't necessarily happen the next day. It may have been months later. The point is, Hannah had no up-front promise. She had Eli's word of encouragement, and that was very important. But I don't think Eli was giving her a guaranteed answer. He was saying, "Hannah, your prayer is a good one, and I'll pray with you that the Lord will answer it." Much like what I might tell one of my church people who shares a prayer burden with me at the door.

But Hannah had prayed. She knew where to turn. She saw her inability to conceive as from the Lord, and she knew that's where the answer would come from. And God remembered her. Everything about Samuel's birth, right down to his name, was a testimony to answered prayer. And notice that Hannah did not forget her vow.

My friend, if she could speak to you today, Hannah would have good news for you. She would tell you that circumstances may be a word, but they are never the last word when you belong to the Lord. Until God speaks, the last word hasn't been spoken.

See, you may have been given a bad word by your boss. Things are tight, and your job had to go. You may have gotten a bad word from the bank or the doctor, but it's never the last word.

The last word hasn't been spoken until God speaks. That may not be tomorrow, but like Hannah you can have God's peace about it today if you'll take your burden to Him.

——————— **Think About It** ———————

If God remembers you—and He has promised never to leave you—
then it doesn't matter if others forget about you.

REFLECTION

I don't know about you, but after reading a story like Hannah's, I sort of sit back and wonder why it took so long.

Couldn't God have given Samuel to Hannah years earlier so she could have avoided all the hassle and the emotional pain? The answer to that is obvious. So why does God let His children go through these long waiting periods?

We don't have all the answers to that, of course, but I think we have some answers in Hannah's case. And in the process of answering the questions, we learn something else about prayer.

Eli's two sons were worthless men. God was going to get rid of them, and Samuel was going to replace them. So God waited until Samuel was needed in His service. Then He allowed Hannah to conceive. And she was so desperate for a child that she promised to give him back to the Lord to serve Him.

What this tells me about prayer is that prayer is a lot more than making requests. The challenge of prayer is plugging into God's agenda. I'm convinced that the reason God doesn't give us some of the things we ask for is that He knows if He gives them to us now, He will never see them again. We will take the answers and run, and He will get no credit for them.

So what God often does is wait to answer our prayers until He knows He will be a full participant in the answer. Are you praying for something right now that may fall into this category? It's something to think about this weekend.

*"[Jesus] Himself would often slip away to the
wilderness and pray." Luke 5:16*

TOO BUSY TO PRAY
Read It: Matthew 26:36-41; Mark 1:35-39

An old gospel song says, "If you're too busy to pray, brother, you're too busy." Most Christians would say amen to that, I think, because we know how important prayer is. Unfortunately, a lot of our prayers never get spoken at all, or we pray in such a way as to try and manipulate God rather than seek and obey His will and His agenda for us. Therefore, we don't see prayer's power or results in our lives.

But if our understanding of Scripture is correct, prayer is foundational both to the individual Christian life and to the life and ministry of the church. You know what a foundation does. It anchors the whole building, gives it something solid to sit on. All else builds on the foundation.

It's no wonder, then, that Satan works overtime to keep us off our knees, keeping us busy, distracted, so we lose our regular in-depth communication with the Father. But there was one Person whom Satan could not get anywhere with when it came to trying to disrupt His prayer life. You already know from today's reading that this Person was Jesus Christ.

The Savior is our perfect model for a life of prayer. He began and ended His public ministry in prayer. We see Him on one of the busiest days of His life in Mark 1, getting up way before daylight to pray. Luke said He did this often. It was Jesus' habit to pray. In the Garden of Gethsemane, of course, He prayed with an agony of prayer we will never know.

No wonder the disciples looked at Jesus' prayer life and asked Him to teach them to pray. Ask Peter what He thought of Jesus' prayer life, and he will tell you it kept him from wiping out completely when he denied Jesus (see Luke 22:31-32).

And lest you say, "Well, that's Peter for you," let me remind you that the only reason we don't crash and burn is because Jesus is praying for us today (John 17:20; Hebrews 7:25).

The application is pretty obvious. If Jesus needed to pray, what does that say about you and me?

———— Think About It ————
If you're waiting for the Spirit to move you to pray, you're
missing something, because He already has moved you to pray—
through the instruction and example of the Word.

"At all times [we] ought to pray." Luke 18:1

FIRST THINGS FIRST
Read It: 1 Timothy 2:1-2

If prayer was top priority in the life of Jesus Christ, guess what ought to be top priority in the Church He purchased with His blood?

You could answer that just by reading today's verse or our text for the day. Paul was writing to Timothy, his son in the faith, who happened to be the pastor of the church in the great city of Ephesus. Paul wanted Timothy to understand how the church works, so he began with the important stuff: prayer.

Paul wanted to make sure that as pastor of the church at Ephesus, Timothy understood that prayer gets things going. Paul was saying, "Timothy, before you do anything else, pray. Before you teach anything else, teach your people how to pray."

Why? Because if God is not on your side, you are in trouble before you ever leave the starting blocks. Most of us understand this intellectually because we will say a quick, little prayer as we are running out the door in the morning. We say grace before a meal. We open our church services with prayer. They even open sessions of Congress with prayer.

But too few of us grasp the full importance of prayer, either for us as individuals or for the life of the church. Paul didn't want Timothy to be misled or misinformed about the place of prayer in the church.

As a pastor I really feel the weight of what Paul is saying. We in the church dare not fool ourselves into thinking that we can make things happen without prayer. It doesn't really matter how much the pastor preaches if the church is not a praying church.

It doesn't matter how well the choir sings or how nice the church looks. It had better be a praying church. That's why the services at our church start with the call to worship, when we urge God's people to pray and prepare to meet Him.

See, that's what you're doing when you come to church. You aren't coming to hear a sermon or a good song. You are coming to meet God. The pastor and the choir are vehicles through which God can speak to you, but they are not substitutes for prayer.

——————— **Think About It** ———————
Before anyone else talks to you about God, He wants
to talk to you Himself in prayer.

"I want the men in every place to pray." 1 Timothy 2:8

PRAYING MEN
Read It: 1 Timothy 2:3-8

Go outside today and look up and down your street. If someone threatened to attack the families on your street, do you think the men in those homes would come out into the street to defend their community?

I'd like to think they would. Well, our communities *are* under attack, but the invading army is invisible. We're engaged in spiritual warfare, and Paul lays the lion's share of the responsibility for repelling the enemy's attack at the feet of Christian men. The primary weapon we have to fight with is prayer.

We see the men's responsibility most clearly in verse 8 where the word *men* is not the generic word for the human race, but the specific term "males." But before we get to verse 8, we need to back up and see what this prayer should include.

Before I go any further, let me tell you what I'm not saying. I'm not saying only men are supposed to pray. The context here is the public worship of the church, and it's clear that in this setting men are to take the lead in prayer. But every Christian is to pray.

I'm also not saying that prayer is the only thing you do. It's just the first thing you do. You have to start with a divine frame of reference. You have to bring God into the equation, or your equation won't add up.

So Paul exhorts us to pray for everyone in authority in the public sector so that our communities will be at peace. But this is not just peace and quiet for the sake of peace and quiet. The object of this tranquillity is to free us from distractions so we can focus on living godly lives. It also promotes the spread of the Gospel so people come to the knowledge of the truth.

Someone may say, "Wait a minute. I thought the church grew best under persecution." That may be true, but we aren't told to pray for persecution. We are told to pray specifically for peace.

Christian men, we have quite a prayer agenda. Could it be that one reason our communities and our nation are deteriorating is because God's men are not praying?

——— **Think About It** ———

We're under attack, but the answer is not to take to the streets. The answer is to take to our knees.

"[I ask] that they may all be one." John 17:20-21

FUSSING, OR PRAYING?
Read It: James 4:1-3; 1 Peter 3:1-7

You've heard the old line about people who can't walk and chew gum at the same time. I don't know about that, but I do know there are some things that are so incompatible you can't do them at the same time. Like fussing and trying to pray, for example. Or to be more precise, it's impossible to be in disunity and yet see our prayers answered.

That's clear in a number of places throughout the Bible. Take a look at 1 Timothy 2:8 once more, and you'll see that the environment for prayer is the absence of "wrath and dissension." When the church prays, it must be done in a spirit of unity rather than division and strife.

Now we know that unity in the body of Christ is God's will, because Jesus prayed for it Himself. No group of people can accomplish much until they are agreed on what they're trying to accomplish. But prayer is not just a matter of getting people together. There's a divine element involved. God only operates in a context of oneness.

That's why Satan works so hard to keep believers from getting along. When we're at odds with one another, we aren't likely to even pray together, much less expect those prayers to get God excited.

The same principle operates at home. Peter stated it so plainly you can't miss it. If a husband and wife are divided, their prayers are hindered. And when a couple's prayers are hindered, the Devil has the key to that family's front door. So he'll work overtime to keep strife brewing in a home. And you thought the only reason you and your spouse are fussing is because you are not compatible!

In his no-nonsense style, the Apostle James gives us another angle on this thing of strife and prayer. Not only do we fight about stuff, but after we fight, we still don't get what we want.

Why? Well, in some cases it's because we should have prayed for it instead of fighting for it. But in other cases (v. 3), we don't get it because God isn't about to give it to us so we can blow it on ourselves. You can't fight and pray at the same time, so you need to decide which it's going to be.

——— **Think About It** ———
If you're at odds with another believer today,
better fix it before your prayer life breaks!

"The effective prayer of a righteous man can accomplish much."
James 5:16

EFFECTIVE PRAYING
Read It: James 5:16b-18

Yesterday we talked about how impossible it is for believers to be fighting with each other and praying effectively at the same time.

Let me make another observation on that today; then we'll see a great contrast in Elijah. You may be fussing with God right now about something you think you need. Since I'm not God, and since He doesn't share inside information with me, I can't tell you whether your request is legitimate for you or not.

I can say this, however. If God has decided not to grant your request, it won't matter how much you fuss or how hard you fight. Unless you can punch God out, you lose.

But if you're the right kind of person and your prayer request lines up with God's will, look out! You've got some power on your hands. That's what happened with Elijah, a guy just like you and me.

You say, "What do you mean, the right kind of person? I'm a Christian. Isn't that enough?" Well, yes and no. All believers are clothed in the righteousness of Christ, so all believers stand righteous before God.

But you know as well as I do that Christians can live like non-Christians and sometimes worse. So there's a righteousness we need to be practicing daily as we allow the Holy Spirit to cleanse and fill us. Just like you don't want to drink out of a dirty cup, God doesn't want to hear the prayers of a Christian whose life is all fouled up with junk.

James says Elijah did some very serious praying. You can't pray very long in an unrighteous condition without God taking you to the real issue, your heart. If you aren't living a clean life when you start praying, you soon will be as the Spirit points out your sin—or else you will stop praying.

Now don't miss the point. Elijah was just like us. In fact, I know he was like other men, because he was scared of an angry woman, Jezebel. Elijah wasn't perfect, but the whole orientation of his life was to please God—and his prayers moved heaven. Is that a goal you can achieve? Believe it!

——— **Think About It** ———
God didn't answer Elijah because he was a supersaint,
but because his prayer was made from a pure heart,
and it lined up with God's purposes.

REFLECTION

Whenever we preachers start talking about effective prayer and refer to biblical examples like Elijah, someone usually responds, "Yeah, but that was Old Testament stuff. Things were different back then. Miracle things like that don't happen anymore."

Well, let's look at this a little closer. First of all, I don't want to argue with James because he was inspired, and I'm not. He wouldn't have used Elijah if he didn't think we had any hope of imitating his example. Second, James doesn't say to pray for a miracle in the weather like Elijah got. The point is the kind of person the prophet was. Elijah was human, and he was righteous. You and I can make that list.

James has so much to say about prayer throughout his epistle that I want to leave you this week with another list, a prayer checklist you can use to evaluate your prayer life and the attitude of your heart. The prayer God hears and answers is:

1. Offered out of a clean heart.

2. Offered with a seriousness and intensity that show you are not just throwing out a few wishes to see which ones God might pick up on.

3. In line with God's purposes. The entire context of Elijah's prayer (1 Kings 17–18) shows that it was not for him, but to show Israel the power of the true God.

4. Offered with an undivided heart (see James 1:6-8). A double-minded person doesn't get God excited at all!

"O LORD, revive Thy work in the midst of the years." Habakkuk 3:2

TRICKLE, OR SHOWER?
Read It: Nehemiah 8:1-18

Remember how exciting it was to buy that first home and get all moved in? Well, chances are you've lived in that home long enough now to know that a new structure does not necessarily solve all your problems.

Many people who have bought houses are still trying to turn them into homes. The reality is that unless you fix the folk who are occupying these houses, you have not resolved your problem.

That's something of the situation Nehemiah and the people of Israel were in by the time we come to chapter 8. They had accomplished a great feat by rebuilding the walls of Jerusalem, making it a safe place to live, and restoring the honor of God's name.

They had fixed the city. Now it was time to fix the people who would be living in Jerusalem by calling them to confess their sins and rededicate themselves to the covenant and the Law of God. These people had been exiles, so they were starting over in their homeland. They needed to hear God's Word again and get their lives in line with it.

Nehemiah, with Ezra the scribe, was intent on preparing the people spiritually, getting them ready for revival. That's exactly what broke out in Nehemiah 8–10 as a spirit of revival moved among the people.

The revival started when the Word of God was opened and read to the people, and they responded by donning rough sackcloth and putting dirt on their heads as signs of repentance (9:1). Then prayer kicked in as a period of confession and worship broke out and the Israelites humbled themselves before God.

It's in this setting that the great prayer of 9:5-38 was offered, probably led by Ezra. We're going to study this prayer during the week because it has so much to teach us about the subject.

We're hearing a lot of talk about revival today. Thankfully, a lot of people are also praying hard for revival. That's often the way it starts. And the more people pray, the more seriously they take God. How's your "serious quotient" when it comes to Him today?

——— **Think About It** ———
If God responded to your prayers based on their
seriousness and the intensity with which you prayed, would
the resulting answer be a trickle or a shower?

*"The descendants of Israel . . . confessed their sins and the
iniquities of their fathers." Nehemiah 9:2*

ON OUR FACES
Read It: Nehemiah 9:1-4

I don't know what your definition of a revival is. The Bible's definition is when people commit to God's agenda and live in light of His holiness.

That's why there can be no revival without a serious understanding of our sinfulness. People say, "There's so much Christian activity going on; America must be getting ready to have a revival." I think not. Prayer is the lifeblood of revival. In order to have a national revival, God's people have to go on their faces before Him. I don't see many believers doing that.

Serious, expectant prayer is also key to revival in the church. You can't have a church revival unless the church is willing to go on its face before a holy God. You can't have a societal revival unless society is willing to go on its face before a holy God.

And, of course, you and I can't have personal and family revival unless we are willing to go on our faces before a holy God. If you want to see an example of personal and national revival, read Jonah 3 where the people of Nineveh repented from the king on down. They even put sackcloth on the animals.

God saw their repentance and spared the Ninevites. It can happen here if "My people who are called by My name humble themselves and pray, and seek My face and turn from their wicked ways" (2 Chronicles 7:14).

This is what we see unfolding here in Nehemiah 9. Notice the elements of this revival as the people of Jerusalem come before God in confession and repentance. Sackcloth was a rough, uncomfortable cloth that would definitely keep you alert. Putting dirt or dust on the head was another sign of sorrow for sin.

Fasting is giving up a craving of the body because of a greater need of the spirit. It is closely tied with prayer because you pray during what would normally be mealtime.

Now I don't know about you, but for most people giving up eating to pray is taking prayer seriously. I often tell my people that until you fast and pray about a need, you haven't done everything you can do.

——— Think About It ———
You may look better than others around you, but they're not the standard. God is the standard, and He demands holiness.

"May Thy glorious name be blessed and exalted above
all blessing and praise." Nehemiah 9:5

GOD IS SOMEBODY
Read It: Nehemiah 9:5-15

You know what happens when you get serious about prayer and getting your life clean before God? You start realizing who He really is, what He has done, and what He can do. Just ask the Israelites of Nehemiah's day.

When the people of Jerusalem, under the leadership of Nehemiah and Ezra, had prepared themselves spiritually, the leaders stood up and led the congregation in prayer—the longest prayer recorded in the Bible.

This is one awesome prayer, so full of good stuff we could spend several weeks right here studying and meditating. One lesson we can learn from this prayer is right here in the first section, which is all about God. Note the repetition of the phrase "Thou didst," and you'll get the picture.

In other words, the main purpose of prayer is to get us focusing on God, not to get His attention so He can focus on us. The Levites led the people in acknowledging that God is bigger, greater, and more glorious than they could have ever imagined.

Why is this so important? Because we forget whom we are dealing with. If we're not careful, we can become like Pharaoh (v. 10), who said, "I am Pharaoh. Moses, you come down here talking about God this and God that. I am Pharaoh. I'm God around here!"

But God said, "Say what?" Then He gave Pharaoh a lesson in power. That's why the Bible says that of all the sins God hates, pride is at the top of the list. God hates a prideful look. He hates people expanding their chests, puffing themselves up, and saying, "I am somebody!" Says who? Somebody has been lying to those people. Pharaoh got all puffed up; then God blew on him and puffed him away!

So we have men and women today who shake fists in the face of God, who basically say with their mouths or lives, "God, I don't need You." But you can't pray very long and very seriously and hold that attitude.

When you start praying and humbling yourself before God, He starts revealing Himself to you and reminding you of what He has done.

——— **Think About It** ———
So many of our prayers begin with a nod to God, but then
we start talking about us and never get back to Him.

"Bless the LORD, O my soul, and forget none of His benefits."
Psalm 103:2

FORGETTING TO SAY THANKS
Read It: Nehemiah 9:16-25

After three and a half weeks of studying prayer, I hope you'll agree with me that prayer does some wonderful things in our lives.

One of the things prayer is designed to do is make us grateful for all that God has done for us. Now if you know your Old Testament, you realize how much Israel had to thank God for. In this prayer in Nehemiah 9, the Levites have just recounted some highlights of God's goodness to Israel (vv. 5-15). And the people were so grateful they fell on their faces in appreciation, right? Not according to verses 16-17.

You know, they have appreciation banquets for people who have done great things. Well, you should hold an appreciation banquet for God every time you wake up, because no one can do what God does.

But today's verses remind us that instead of bowing down in grateful prayer, the Israelites tried to turn back in ungrateful unbelief. They were supposed to be on their way to Canaan, but they wanted to backtrack to Egypt.

When you get stubborn on God, you start going backwards. When you tell God, "I am going to have my own way," God says, "Fine. You are on your way back to Egypt." As a pastor, I have seen this in the lives of people who are delivered from habits and then go back to those habits.

In other cases, God is trying to make a marriage work, but the people want to go back to being single again. Before, they were on their knees praying, "O Lord, I have to get married. Please, Lord, give me a mate." He answered that prayer, but now one or both of the spouses have started being stubborn and independent of God, and they want to go back to being single.

So the Israelites got stuck in the wilderness because they disobeyed. But this section of the prayer is filled with the good things God continued to do for them. The good news is that God's grace is greater than your sin. If you get right with Him, He will take care of you even in the wilderness.

God can show you a lot of stuff when you start praying!

--- **Think About It** ---

What do you need to thank God for today? What do you
need to be reminded of? Find out on your knees.

"Thou art a gracious and compassionate God." Nehemiah 9:31

CHECK THOSE STABILIZERS
Read It: Nehemiah 9:26-38

The 1985 earthquake in Mexico City toppled a number of buildings, including a thirteen-story building called Nuevo Leon. The whole building just toppled over.

This building was not supposed to collapse, because it was equipped with hydraulic stabilizers. These are mechanisms that allow a structure to move when there is an earthquake, stabilizing it and allowing it to ride out the quake without collapsing.

Well, they found out later that the hydraulic stabilizers were not working on the Nuevo Leon building at the time of the quake, so the structure crashed down even though it had everything it needed to stand tall.

I think you can see how this story illustrates the lives of those who name the name of Christ. Many of us are going through earthquakes in our lives, and we're toppling over because the spiritual stabilizers God has built into us are not being used. They are out of service, rusted and frozen up from disuse.

I think prayer is one of those often unused stabilizers. It was for Israel at various times, and it is for us. Our text this week has given us a great picture of what happens when an entire people get plugged back into God in prayer.

By the end of this prayer (v. 38), the people are ready to make a new covenant with God, put it in writing, and sign it. They want God to hold them liable. They're getting serious about this business of being God's people. They're saying, "We never want to come this way again."

There's another stabilizer in this passage: the grace of God. It can enable you to stand tall in any situation, but the way you tap into God's grace and power is by going before Him on your knees and on your face if necessary.

Do you know why you don't want to spend a long time without being serious with God? Because there is too much disaster in between. It is hard to try and fix things up that have been messed up. It's better to keep your stabilizers in good working order so they won't get broken.

――――― **Think About It** ―――――
The time to find out whether your prayer life works is not when
the ground under you starts rocking and rolling.

REFLECTION

Let's see, if you started this book at the beginning of the year, it ought to be a little warm and springlike where you are this weekend.

I say that because this would be a great weekend to take your Bible and go out under a tree or beside your favorite body of water and spend some time meditating on Nehemiah 9.

I said earlier this week you could spend a lot of time on this prayer. So why not do that this weekend? Open your Bible and work your way through each section of the prayer.

When you come to the verses praising God for His creative and sustaining power, His love, and His grace, offer those words back to Him in your own prayer of praise.

When you come to a petition that relates directly to you, make it your own by asking God to do a work in your life.

When you read the verses that relate how God was faithful to Israel throughout its history, plug in your own history and recount God's mercy to you.

Finally, when you read those verses that recount the stubbornness and unbelief of the Israelites, plead with God not to let that kind of hardness creep into your heart. By the time you're done, the book of Nehemiah—and your prayer life—will never look the same to you again.

SEVEN

◇

TRANSFORMING SOCIETY

Our Role in a Lost World

If you want to start an argument in an empty room, bring up the subject of the Christian's proper response to secular society and culture. There are several alternatives, each defended passionately in various Christian circles. Should we denounce society, withdraw from it, or engage it in battle? I say, how about transforming it? God has a strategy for transforming society. Our job is to execute it. Read on.

"Humble yourselves . . . under the mighty hand of God, that He may exalt you at the proper time." 1 Peter 5:6

RULING THE JUNGLE
Read It: 1 Peter 5:8-9

Our nation is faced with a crisis of social deterioration the likes of which we would have thought unimaginable a generation ago. We seem to be a culture gone berserk.

To say that our society is in need of radical transformation is to state the obvious. Over the next four weeks we'll be talking about how we got into this mess and what God's Word has to say about getting out of it. We're in a "culture war" today, but before we go off waving our swords, we need to know who the real enemy is.

The real enemy isn't school administrators or the media or liberals. The one behind the scenes pulling the strings is the evil one, Satan himself. He's the enemy.

One reason there is so much satanic influence in schools, media, and government is that Christians have abandoned the culture and handed it over to the world. If you hand culture over, Satan will take it over.

The Bible calls him a "roaring lion" because, like real lions, Satan rules by intimidation. Lions roar to scare and intimidate their enemies. They roar after the kill so the jackals and hyenas will be too afraid to run up and snatch it away, even though they can if they work together. Satan rules our society with a lot of noise, because he knows he cannot stop the people of God from taking society back if we ever decide to *be* the people of God in society. But we're intimidated by the roar. The reason our culture is deteriorating is that Christians are nowhere to be found except in church. There is no morality being handed down anymore.

When we were growing up, even if your mama and daddy didn't give you a moral frame of reference, your schoolteacher did. Or the people next door did. Why? Because Christian morality permeated the culture. Not everyone was a Christian, but most people had a moral frame of reference by which they made decisions. That is no longer the case, because the influence of God is no longer being felt in the culture. We've got to raise a whole new generation of people who know and follow God.

--------- **Think About It** ---------
If we Christians will humble ourselves under God,
He will give us the power to take our culture back.

"As the Father has sent Me, I also send you." John 20:21

TRANSFORM, DON'T CONFORM
Read It: 2 Chronicles 15:3-6; Jeremiah 29:1-4

When Jesus Christ comes back, we won't have to worry about transforming culture, because He will set up His kingdom rule. But in the meantime, we've got a world to reach for Him and for our children and grandchildren who are coming along behind us. We've got to hand them some kind of a world.

So what is the role of the Christian in society? Well, I believe the Bible has a lot to say about that. Jeremiah 29:4-11 illustrates this foundational principle: Society is transformed when God's people execute His strategy in history. The only way to make the world a better place is for Christians to get busy being people of the world. Now I don't mean worldly, but involved in history in a Bible-centered, Christ-centered way.

The Prophet Jeremiah was writing to the Jews in exile in Babylon. The question was how they were supposed to function in such an environment. Well, the first thing they needed to do was regain their spiritual clarity.

Babylon was a pagan city. It had no fear of God—a lot like American culture today. But just as the pagans around us are not the real problem, so the Babylonians were not Israel's real problem. In verse 4 God says, "The reason you are in this mess is because I sent you there. And the reason I sent you there is that you forgot Me."

See, God delivered Israel to the Babylonians in 597 B.C. because His people had become pagan. So God said, "Since you want to be pagan, I'll send you to live with the pagans." It was the failure of God's people to be His distinct, unique people that caused Him to judge them. This was an old problem, as 2 Chronicles 15 reveals.

As I've said before, if God is your problem, then God is your only solution. It doesn't matter whom you elect or what programs you start if we as God's people lose our spiritual perspective. We have to see that God has put us here for a reason. Earth is not just a place to wait for a ride to heaven.

――――― **Think About It** ―――――
When the church fails to be the unique people of God, it leaves
a hole in the spiritual "ozone layer," and the culture gets
burned by the effects of sin.

"Let him labor, performing with his own hands what is good."
Ephesians 4:28

DON'T COUNT ON PHARAOH
Read It: Jeremiah 29:5, 27-28

This passage gives a second principle of God's strategy to transform society: It's transformed when His people develop economic stability.

See, the Prophet Hananiah was telling the Jews not to make themselves at home, because God was going to rapture them out of Babylon soon (Jeremiah 28:11). But Hananiah was a false prophet, because he was giving the people a false hope.

There's nothing false in our hope that Jesus is coming back. But in the meantime, He didn't rapture you to heaven the moment you were saved because He has work for you. At the heart of this work is evangelism, but we're also responsible to make this world the best possible place to live.

So Jeremiah told the people to start building and planting because they were going to be there for a while. In other words, "Develop economic independence. Don't depend on the Babylonians to fund your Jewish work. Don't depend on the pagans to provide you the wherewithal to live."

It's still a good strategy today. Pagans spend their time and money trying to make you like them. They're not going to fund you to make an impact for Christ upon them. Like it or not, we can't discuss ministry without discussing economics because ministry costs. God says, "If you are going to pull off My program, you must have economic independence."

Let me show you something. In Deuteronomy 28:12, God told Israel that if they would obey Him, they would be a lender to other nations but never a borrower. Reverse that and you see what happened when God's people were disobedient. They became debtors. They were plunged into poverty. They had to depend on pagans for their livelihood.

So Jeremiah told the people to cultivate economic stability. That's why at our church in Dallas we have economic development programs, why we teach people skills so that they become employable and not have to depend on the government. I'm not talking about getting rich or building your own economic empire. I'm talking about the ability of God's people to do His business His way because they are using His resources.

——— **Think About It** ———
As long as you are working for and dependent
upon Pharaoh, he will never let you go.

"Go into all the world and preach the gospel to all creation."
Mark 16:15

WINNING THEM IS JOB ONE
Read It: Colossians 1:28-29

We haven't gone far in our study of the transformation of culture, but I need to clarify something. When you talk about Christians' responsibility to the culture, some people start getting nervous. They're afraid you're going to obscure the Gospel in favor of social concerns. Most of America's churches tried that in the late nineteenth and early twentieth centuries when the social gospel was the rage, and it failed.

To forestall such thought, let me say that when it comes to the lost, *evangelism must be first.* I'm not talking social gospel. We must win people to Christ. Without Him it doesn't matter how much money they have or how good the job is. If they die without Him, they die without hope.

I'm not saying that we downplay evangelism to favor economic development or other programs to transform culture. But I'm saying that we still have to live in this world. Since we have to live and raise children and grandchildren here, we are responsible to recapture our society for Jesus Christ, point people to Him, and promote His righteousness in society.

Jeremiah told the exiles in Babylon to forget the false hope that they would be back home in two years, for if they believed that, they would sit around doing nothing, making no difference, waiting for their liberation. Does that scenario sound familiar? Some Christians' attitude toward the culture today is, "Hey, the world is falling apart anyway, and Christ is coming back soon, so let's just sit here and wait for the rapture."

Some people ask me, "Evans, don't you believe this world's getting worse and worse? Don't you believe things are falling apart?"

I say, "Yes, I do."

They say, "Then why polish the brass on a sinking ship?"

My answer is, "For the same reason you eat and bathe and jog even though you know you are going to die." Just because you are going to die someday doesn't mean you sit by and hasten the process by neglecting your body. Actually, I have a much stronger reason than that. Jesus commanded us to be salt and light. That says it for me!

——— **Think About It** ———
Are you making anyone around you thirsty for Christ?
Are you shining your light into their darkness?

"Be strong, and let us show ourselves courageous for the sake of our people." 2 Samuel 10:12

FAMILY SANCTITY
Read It: Nehemiah 4:14; Jeremiah 29:6

Today we come to a third principle from God's Word for changing a pagan society. Society is transformed when we recapture family sanctity. God told the Israelite exiles through Jeremiah, "Do not decrease." Wait a minute. Do you mean God wanted His people to bring children into the world in that wicked society? Yes, and the more the merrier.

We saw earlier that the purpose of children is to stamp the image of God on future generations. Why worry about that? Because we just might be here for a while. But people today say, "Kids are an inconvenience." No, kids are the greatest investment we can make, because with children we secure the future.

You see, in biblical times there was no Social Security or other "net" to catch people and hold them up when they got old. The responsibility for caring for aging parents fell to the children. So one benefit of raising a family was that it ensured the care of the parents. They would always have a place to live as long as they had children to take them in.

Another benefit of raising children was to see them grow up to love and serve the God their parents loved and served. This is the idea of children being a crown to their parents. There was nothing more satisfying for an Israelite parent than to see his children walk in the Lord's ways. Being in exile didn't change these realities, so God told the Jews to be fruitful and multiply. And in some cases, it would be their children who would return to Israel someday and rebuild it.

But today we've messed up the concept of family sanctity, and it's messing up our culture. Kids need families so bad they will join a substitute family known as a gang. Why? Because Dad doesn't have guts enough to stay home, and Mother doesn't have dedication enough to place the kids above her career. So the children go out into the streets.

Satan knows that God's long-term goal is to bless a society through its families. But we live for the now, today. We become slaves to our desires, we lose our families, and we deteriorate. How goes it in your family today?

--------- **Think About It** ---------
Satan wants our families because he wants the future.

REFLECTION

I remember what it was like growing up in the inner city of Baltimore, Maryland, not that many decades ago.

If I did something bad ten blocks from my house, more than likely a neighbor who saw me do it might grab me by the shirt collar and say, "Boy, you know your mama doesn't want you out here acting a fool like this."

Then this woman, whom I might not even know, would drag me home to my mama, introduce herself, and tell my mama what she saw me doing. My mama would then invite her in for coffee and cookies, and they would go about discussing my errant activity.

Then my mama would say goodbye to her new friend and spank me because I had embarrassed the family in the neighborhood.

Try to correct a kid like that in your neighborhood today, and you might find yourself staring down the barrel of an Uzi! We have lost something very valuable, that sense of family and community that grew from shared values and concern for one another.

You can't pass enough laws to make people care like that. It has to come from the inside, which is why the only hope for our society is the people of God taking the Word of God home and then into the world, and giving it out in our words and actions. It starts at home. This weekend ask God to help you hold on to—or recapture—your family. If we don't get this one right, we may not have much of a future.

"We [did not] eat anyone's bread without paying for it."
2 Thessalonians 3:8

WHOSE WELFARE?
Read It: Jeremiah 29:7; 2 Thessalonians 3:6-12

Our fourth principle in this section will give the week an interesting start. Society is transformed as Christians exercise social responsibility.

Jeremiah doesn't say to *take* welfare from the government. Only those unable to work or temporarily in a position where they can't work should be on welfare. But there is to be no long-term dependence on government.

That's not why government was established. It's the church's job to empower people to live responsible lives. The church is not to take the place of your individual or family responsibility. But the church's task is to equip you to be responsible and then make sure you are responsible. That's why Paul issued his famous order to the church at Thessalonica. You don't give charity to people who refuse to work. When their stomachs start growling, they start working.

The idea is to help people develop responsibility, which means helping them develop skills so they become employable. This is urban ministry. Jeremiah is talking about pagan Babylon. Why seek its welfare? Because God's people were the only ones left.

That is, unless we Christians seek society's welfare, it will fall apart. And guess what? You will fall apart with it, because even if you don't live in the inner city, its overflow will catch up with you in the "burbs." There is nowhere to run anymore. We have run out of running room.

So let's seek the welfare of the city. Let's get people of righteousness back into the political and economic scene. Let's get teachers who will teach right and wrong back into the classroom. Let's deal with the racial problem, which isn't downtown but at eleven o'clock on Sunday morning—still the most segregated hour in America. We have a standard of truth that transcends all of our categories.

If we would obey the truth, we would understand that there is no such thing as a black Christian or white Christian or Hispanic Christian or Asian Christian. There are only Christians, and if we would come together, we could shake society for Christ and see it change!

——— **Think About It** ———
Black is only beautiful if it's biblical,
and white is only right if it agrees with holy Writ.

"The plans that I have for you . . . [are] plans for welfare and not for calamity." Jeremiah 29:11

DOING IT HIS WAY
Read It: Jeremiah 29:8-11

Today we're looking at our final "Jeremiah principle" for transforming society. Society is transformed when God's people decide to start doing things His way. This is what God was saying to the Jewish exiles in Babylon. "Let's do things My way for a change. Stop letting the false prophets or anyone else tell you how it's supposed to be done."

What we need today are Christians with the guts to say, "I don't want to live this way anymore. I don't want my family to be raised this way anymore. I'm going to use the time and skill God has given me to be one of His change-agents."

That's why I like Paul. You couldn't intimidate him. They came to Paul and said, "We are going to kill you."

He said, "That's cool. 'To die is gain.'"

They said, "Okay, we won't kill you."

"That's cool too. 'To live is Christ.'"

If we had that kind of perspective, we'd come together as believers and make a real difference for our children and for future generations. We can't solve all the problems. I'm not saying that there won't be more crime or further social deterioration. But society's transformation starts with us.

At the theaters and on television they have previews of coming attractions. They always show you the hot clips of the upcoming movie or TV show because they want you to buy a ticket or tune in next week.

Well, one day there is a big show coming to town. God is the Producer, the Holy Spirit is the Director, Jesus Christ is the Star, and it will be a world-wide production called the "Kingdom of God." But until then God has left behind some previews of coming attractions. That's you and me, and we are supposed to be the hot clips so that when people see us functioning the way God intended, they say, "That's hot." And when they ask, "How can I buy a ticket to the show?" we can tell them they don't have to buy one; the price has already been paid! We can give them the good news of Jesus Christ.

――――― **Think About It** ―――――
When all else fails, "Thus says the LORD" is not a bad alternative!

> *"Do not be overcome by evil, but overcome evil with good."*
> Romans 12:21

OUT OF THE SALT SHAKER
Read It: Matthew 5:13

AIDS is a devastating disease because it destroys the body's immune system, leaving viruses free to attack the body. For an AIDS sufferer, a virus that would ordinarily cause only a cold produces pneumonia.

Just as God has given the human body an immune system, He has given one to society as well. It's called the church. We are God's "disease fighters" to keep the viruses of sin from penetrating the culture, to keep cultural colds from becoming cultural pneumonia. It is our task as God's representatives on earth to reflect His interests in such a way that evil can't do its full damage because of the presence of righteousness in the culture. When you see a culture deteriorate, you are probably also seeing an anemic people of God.

We as the people of God have been so withdrawn from culture that we have turned our society over to the unrighteous to rule. When Christians pulled out of public education, politics, and the media, then righteous decisions left with them.

We have been called to penetrate society. Of course our first calling is to win people to Christ. I dealt with that last Thursday. Having given a man Christ for his eternity, we must also give him Christ for his culture. We must give people hope in history. The absence of righteousness in our culture has everything to do with the absence of God's people in our culture.

That's why one of my favorite words is *alternative*. It embodies what the people of God ought to be—divine options in history. We are to represent the interests of God's kingdom in the marketplace, not only in the excellency of our work but also in the testimony of our character.

But far too many of us are like the Susan B. Anthony dollar, which looked like a quarter. People got confused, so Sue's coin fell into disuse. It was worth a dollar, but it looked like "chump change." Sadly, that describes a lot of Christians when it comes to making a difference for Christ. We don't spend well in the marketplace where people need to hear, see, and feel the reality of Christ. Jesus called it being "salty." Have you made anyone thirsty for Him lately?

———— Think About It ————
The whole point of salt is to leave the shaker and hit the meat, right?

"You are the light of the world." Matthew 5:14

WE'RE IT!
Read It: Matthew 5:14-15; John 8:12

The last time I checked, the purpose of a light was to shine. That's all it is supposed to do. But that shine means a lot when you're in the dark.

People say, "This world is dark." That's because the world is not the light. What else can a sinful place be but dark? The world is lost and without any direction because the world is not the light. Jesus is the Light, and we are to reflect Him.

In the original text, the meaning of what Jesus said in verse 14 really jumps out at you. The idea is, "You disciples and nobody else are the light. You are it." Remember, Jesus is talking to His followers here. That's you and me. He's saying that if this world is ever going to see His light and come to the knowledge of the truth, it will be because we let His light shine through us.

If we were to go into a building on a pitch-dark night, turn out all the lights, and even cover up all the windows, it would be so dark we would have a hard time moving around. There would be chaos as we ran into chairs, walls, and each other trying to get out of that building.

But if in the middle of all that confusion, I stood on a platform, pulled out a huge flashlight, and turned it on, guess what? I now run the show. Whoever has the light calls the shots when it's dark.

That dark building describes this dark world pretty well. People are crashing into everything, trying to find a way out of the darkness. We Christians are the light. We know Christ is the answer, to borrow a popular phrase from a few years ago. The tragedy is that we are not using the flashlight God has given us to give the world some light.

Turn your flashlight on, Christian, so people in darkness can see. And after you turn it on, hold it high so everyone can see it. Christianity is not a covert operation. We don't go slinking around in the dark to get our work done. There is no room for "secret-agent" Christians. We are not the spiritual CIA. We're people of the light.

---------- **Think About It** ----------

What we need is a group of people who are unapologetically Christian.
Are you ready to join up?

"All Scripture is inspired by God and profitable . . .
for every good work." 2 Timothy 3:16-17

GOOD THINGS vs. GOOD WORKS
Read It: Matthew 5:16; Ephesians 2:10

The way you verify your words is by your works. Biblically speaking, good works are not the same as good things. Sinners can do good things. Lost people can build hospitals and orphanages and feed the poor. But sinners cannot do good works. So what's the difference?

Good works are God-created, God-inspired works. Good works can help transform society because they have the power of God behind them. So somebody had better be asking where we can find God-created, God-inspired works. The answer is in His Word. That's what Paul told Timothy. That's what separates us from the world.

We not only have biblical goals, but we also use biblical means to achieve them. And as Jesus said, the aim of all good works is to glorify God. There are plenty of good things sinners do without even giving the slightest thought to what God thinks about it.

Now when Paul wrote this, the New Testament wasn't even completed yet. Today we have the full revelation of God, the Old and New Testaments. We have God's mind on every issue, which explains my philosophy of ministry. I believe there is a biblical answer for everything. Now some people don't like that; some people don't want to hear that, but there is a biblical answer for everything we face in life.

See, if you came to me and asked how you could glorify God by doing good works that please Him, I would open my Bible to give you an answer. If the elders and deacons at my church came to me and asked, "What work should this church be about?" I would open my Bible and show them what God has called the church to do. By the way, I would do the same thing if the president said to me, "We've got a messed-up country. What should we do?" I would go to the same standard. If you want works that are going to truly transform society, you go to the Word.

The word *glorify* means to show off. We're supposed to show God off. Don't apologize for being a Christian. No one else is apologizing. Homosexuals aren't. Racists aren't. If they can go public, so can we.

——— **Think About It** ———
How are your neighborhood, your town, and your kids' school
different because you are around?

REFLECTION

My favorite TV program while I was growing up was *Superman*. Clark Kent was a bumbling idiot. Lois Lane couldn't stand him; Jimmy Olson didn't respect him; he was always messing up. But, Lord, have mercy—don't let him find a telephone booth! The criminals of Metropolis would be wreaking havoc on the city, and someone would ask, "Where's Superman?"

I would be sitting on the floor with my brother. Clark Kent would take off his glasses and unhook his tie. I would look at my brother and say, "There he goes!" My man would go inside a telephone booth or closet or something and come back out with a red and blue jumpsuit on.

Then my man would go streaking across the sky, arrive on the scene, and change everything. He would catch bullets with his bare hand, bend gun barrels, and toss crooks around, all because who he really was came out, and he stopped hiding it under his suit.

It's time for Christians to take a trip to God's telephone booth. We need to take off our old suits—our timid "Clark Kent" way of thinking, living, and talking—and put on our spiritual jumpsuits so we step back out into the world in which we live and become "faster than speeding sin, more powerful than public unrighteousness, able to leap evil in a single bound."

May God help you to be His man or woman and stand up for Him. Ask Him right now to prepare you to represent Him next week at the office, in the classroom, or at the shop.

"Righteousness exalts a nation, but sin is a disgrace to any people."
Proverbs 14:34

A LOT OF PRAYING TO DO
Read It: Nehemiah 1:1-11

The book of Nehemiah tells about a remarkable man who knew God, knew what society needed, and brought them together. Few people are nation-builders. Even fewer are nation *re*builders. Nehemiah was one. We need to spend time with him. We'll take the last two weeks in our study on transforming culture to consider Nehemiah—the book and the man.

The tip-off to the kind of man Nehemiah was is here in chapter 1. He was "cupbearer to the king" of Persia (v. 11), an Israelite living as part of the community in exile. When he learned about the degradation and the deterioration in his homeland, the first thing Nehemiah did was pray. The prayer recorded in this chapter shows that Nehemiah definitely knew how to pray. He prayed on behalf of himself and his nation, asking God to forgive their sins and to give him another opportunity to turn things around.

Nehemiah also knew that God could work through the Persian government, because he asked God to give him favor before King Artaxerxes, to whom Nehemiah was a trusted adviser. Nehemiah was willing to use his strategic role to help rebuild the community of God back in Jerusalem.

Nehemiah 1 teaches us an important principle about cultural transformation. He understood that the deterioration of culture is first and foremost a spiritual issue. Until the spiritual dynamics have been addressed, you cannot properly address the social, economic, or political realms.

We keep trying though. People have meetings and draw up strategies. Because God's people have failed to a large degree to inform the culture of the spiritual dynamics involved in rebuilding a community, nothing that is put in place will do the job right. For example, our society has touted abortion as the answer to unwanted children and teenage pregnancy, and now it's legalized. But abortion is the shedding of innocent blood.

At the same time, people are decrying the horrible increase in violence. Well, the Bible makes it clear that when people shed innocent blood, God will require it at their hands. What we are seeing is not coincidence, but God's judgment. We had better get busy praying!

——— **Think About It** ———
This is a spiritual issue, and things won't happen until people like you and me bring righteousness into the public square.

"Rest in the LORD and wait patiently for Him." Psalm 37:7

THE RIGHT TIME
Read It: Nehemiah 2:1-3

It took four months for Nehemiah to begin to see an answer to his prayer about the desperate condition of Jerusalem. God doesn't work on our timetable. So Nehemiah learned to wait, just as we must learn to wait.

Now you would think that anyone who dealt with politicians every day—Nehemiah being a top-level adviser to the king—would be used to bureaucratic delays and government red tape. But waiting on God to move is a whole lot different than waiting on someone downtown or in Washington to push papers. We saw yesterday that the transformation of society is a spiritual issue, which means nothing will really happen until God shows up.

God is worth the wait because when He shows up, He shakes things up. Being sad in the king's presence could have cost Nehemiah his life, because it was against Persian law. Nehemiah's job was to cheer the king up, period.

But God gave him favor with the king and just the right words to say. Let me show you what I mean. Notice that in verse 3 Nehemiah did not mention Jerusalem by name, even though Jerusalem was the place that needed rebuilding. He just talked about the home of his ancestors.

A little bit of Bible history will tell you what's going on here. Back in Ezra 4:21, Artaxerxes had ordered a halt to the rebuilding of Jerusalem. He had allowed it, but he got word that if Jerusalem were rebuilt, it would pose a threat to the stability of the Persian Empire because the people would stop paying taxes. So Artaxerxes became concerned and ordered the rebuilding stopped, which was accomplished by the use of force. Nehemiah knew his history, and he understood the politics involved. So he just talked about the plight of his people.

But Artaxerxes was no dummy. He knew what city his cupbearer was talking about. But God knew the right time for Nehemiah to bring up the subject. Four months earlier, and the king might have had him killed. Are you waiting for the next election to change things? Waiting on God will be a whole lot more fruitful.

——— **Think About It** ———
Let God do things in His timing, and His plan will unveil itself. In the meantime, rest and wait—and keep praying.

*"There is no authority except from God, and those which exist
are established by God." Romans 13:1*

KINGS AND *THE* KING
Read It: Nehemiah 2:4-5

If there ever was anyone in a strategic position to make a dynamic impact for God, it was Nehemiah at the moment described in today's text. And what a job my man did.

I like this account for a couple of reasons. God arranged the timing so perfectly that when Nehemiah let the king know what was on his heart, Artaxerxes was open to the suggestion—even though he had a little political problem with Jerusalem, as we learned yesterday. The second thing I like here is Nehemiah's prayer (v. 4). Now whom was he talking to? The King of Persia. And whom was he praying to? "The God of heaven." Nehemiah was dealing with two kings at the same time.

One of the kings was in control of the Persian Empire, but the other King was and still is controlling heaven. Nehemiah was getting ready to make a request that the earthly king do something about Jerusalem. But first he asked the heavenly King to do something about the earthly king.

Nehemiah was asking God to intervene in the government He had established and that He controlled. Nehemiah understood that there is no dichotomy between politics and religion, despite our modern-day nonsense that they don't mix. Nehemiah realized there was a king, Artaxerxes, and then there was *the* King, the God of heaven. He was not going to deal with a king without dealing with the King.

I've said this before, but it bears repeating. The purpose of government is to be a minister of God to judge evil and to reward good. The Bible says governmental authorities are God's servants, though they may be unsaved.

But God did not place on government the responsibility for transforming culture so that it reflects His righteous standards. That's our job as God's people. Unless we are influencing government so that it has a divine standard by which to operate, government won't know which way to go. That is why you need Christian politicians, Christian lawyers, and Christian city council members. The reason most governments don't carry out God's agenda is because God's people are not influencing them.

———— Think About It ————
Are you trying to get something done through earthly "kings" without consulting the King? You need to think again, because it won't work.

"The king's heart is like channels of water in the hand of the LORD;
He turns it wherever He wishes." Proverbs 21:1

READY TO MOVE
Read It: Nehemiah 2:6-9; Psalm 24:1

Will you be ready when God gets ready to move? If you're going to make an impact on your community, if your church is going to take part in the transformation of this society, you need to have a plan.

That's what Nehemiah had. During those months he was waiting on God to answer his prayer, Nehemiah wasn't just daydreaming. He had a definite idea of what it would take to rebuild Jerusalem, and he had a definite time in mind. So when God turned the heart of King Artaxerxes around like a channel of water, Nehemiah was all set. It was divine sovereignty and human planning and responsibility working in perfect harmony. Sovereignty and planning go together. They are not in conflict.

Some people go to one extreme and say if God is going to do it, then why should we do anything? When He wants to make it happen, it will happen. The other extreme says we don't need God. We'll do it ourselves.

Both extremes are wrong. God definitely arranged for Nehemiah to go, and go with "clout," because it was God's divine timetable. God's sovereignty is necessary, because He has to balance what He is doing in your life with what He's doing in someone else's life so that "all things work together for good."

We can't do anything without God because Psalm 24:1 reminds us that He owns it all. Nehemiah couldn't have gotten those letters to the king's forest by his own scheming. But when the King of heaven decided Nehemiah needed some of *His* royal timber, He simply moved Artaxerxes to draw up the letters. That wood belonged to God, not to the king of Persia. But Nehemiah still had to ask. He needed a government grant to accomplish his plan, so he asked for it when he realized God was answering prayer and giving him favor before the king.

When you realize that Nehemiah didn't know he was going to have that conversation that day, you can see how thoroughly he had thought everything out. He knew his responsibility was to be ready when God in His sovereign wisdom said it was time to move.

─────── **Think About It** ───────

God's sovereignty means He decides what happens. Your planning
means you are ready whenever it happens.

"Resist the devil and he will flee from you." James 4:7

IN YOUR FACE
Read It: Nehemiah 2:10

Can you imagine Michael Jordan coming back to the bench talking about, "I could score a whole lot easier if I didn't have that other guy putting his hands up in my face all the time"?

Michael's coach would tell him, "Michael, if there were no opponent, it would be easy to score. We're paying you millions to score with that guy in your face."

As Christians, we have an opponent in our face too. Whenever you decide to do something significant for God, Satan will show up, usually in the person of people like Sanballat and Tobiah. Not everyone wants their culture transformed by the influence of godly people. It displeased these men that Nehemiah had come to seek the welfare of Israel. They took it upon themselves to stop him. See, Satan's job is to keep God's people from carrying out God's will.

By the way, this isn't just true for the big projects such as rebuilding a community. Satan's job is to destroy you and your family because he knows Christian families populated by committed Christians are the foundation to transforming society. So he spends day and night plotting your demise. Just like we have angels assigned to us, Satan has demons with our names and addresses on their "to do" lists.

That is why the Bible says, "Our struggle is not against flesh and blood" (Ephesians 6:12). Do we need to fear Satan and his demons? No, not at all. We need to resist and overcome them in the power of Christ.

Nehemiah wasn't afraid of his adversaries, but neither did he take them lightly. For the rest of his rebuilding project and well beyond it, he kept a close eye on those characters.

But too many of us are like puppets on a string to Satan. All he has to do is yank our string a little, and we go where he tells us to go and get mad when he tells us to get mad. Once you understand what Satan is up to, you will get down on your knees and say, "Not today, Satan. Not me, not my marriage, not my family, not my community—because we are submitting ourselves to God."

————— **Think About It** —————

Stand firm for God and against Satan, and the Sanballats
and Tobiahs of this world will melt like snowmen in summer.

REFLECTION

I love the story about the day Hall-of-Fame baseball player and home-run king Hank Aaron came to bat in the All-Star game. Yogi Berra, the great Yankee catcher, was catching. Yogi loved to talk to hitters to distract them. I used to do that myself when I was a catcher. You get behind that hitter and say stuff like, "Big man, little stick." You ask him, "How's your mama?" You play with his mind and talk to him.

Yogi Berra was great at that, so when Hank Aaron came to bat, Yogi started in. "Hank, you're holding your bat the wrong way. You should be able to read the label."

Aaron just kept his focus on the pitcher and didn't say anything. Berra was chattering away, trying to get Hank to worry about where the label on his bat was instead of concentrating on the pitch.

Finally Aaron had heard enough. "Yogi," he said, "I didn't come up here to read. I came up here to hit."

That's keeping your focus and concentration where they need to be. Nehemiah had that kind of focus. He didn't let anything distract him. He was about God's agenda, and he knew what he had been called to do.

How about you? If something is distracting you from what God wants you to do, put it behind you this weekend.

"You shall not oppress your neighbor, nor rob him." Leviticus 19:13

THE HIGH COST OF LEAVING GOD
Read It: Nehemiah 5:1-5

If anyone doubts the relevance of God's Word to today, all that person needs to do is read Nehemiah 5. Even as Jerusalem was being rebuilt and the Israelites were reestablishing themselves in their land, serious conflicts arose that were tearing the community apart.

As we'll learn this week, the problems revolved primarily around money. The people were giving their time to building the walls, which meant they didn't have the normal opportunities to earn a living. Some families did not have enough food to eat. So the first problem was poverty. The Bible is clear that the poor are to be taken care of, but these people were being exploited.

The second problem is in verse 3. Other Jews had property, but they had to mortgage it to survive. They had to buy the right to exist by taking things that they had worked hard for and using them as collateral to buy food. So the community was also facing the problem of growing debt.

The third problem was the taxes imposed by the Persian government (vv. 4-5), which the people had to borrow money to pay. You know you're in trouble when you have to borrow to pay your taxes. Why were the Israelites returning with Nehemiah from exile in this mess? Why were they being choked to death economically by poverty, debt, famine, and high taxes? Because they had left God in the first place.

You can't always see the roots of a community's problem just by looking at the immediate circumstances. Israel's problems went way back. If the people had not forsaken and disobeyed God, they would not have been in Persia, and they would not be dealing with the king's taxes.

If the Israelites had not left God, they would not have been a debtor community but a loaner community. If they had not left God, the poor of Jerusalem would have been taken care of.

You've got to go back and straighten out spiritual things first. When you see an economically depreciating community, you know something is wrong spiritually because God promises to meet the needs of His people.

——————— **Think About It** ———————
This same dynamic works in individual families too. If you're struggling, don't overlook the possibility that something may need to be dealt with spiritually.

"'If I am a father, where is My honor? And if I am a master, where is My respect?' says the LORD of hosts." Malachi 1:6

GOD'S BUY-BACK PROGRAM
Read It: Nehemiah 5:6-8

Do you ever get mad when you see people being exploited? Nehemiah got mad when he heard about the problems the people of Jerusalem were having. Did he get mad that some people were making money in their businesses? There is no commandment in the Bible that says, "Thou shalt not make a legitimate profit." It's okay to make a profit, but you cannot do it by exploitation or greed.

Verse 7 says Nehemiah was so angry that he had to get off in a corner to cool down and to think about how he was going to handle this mess. He wasn't ready to talk to anyone yet. Once he had a talk with himself and I'm sure some prayer time too, Nehemiah was ready to contend with the nobles and the rulers. He called the whole congregation together to get the problem straightened out.

You say, "How can you call a congregational meeting about the way a man does his business?" Because when you name the name of Jesus Christ, you don't just do business. You are supposed to do business to the glory of God, so if you are exploiting people, it's a sin.

If you are a Christian, you are called to excellence in everything you do. God expects it. He never wants leftovers. That was the problem in Malachi's day. God looked at the flawed sacrifices the people were bringing and said, "Would you offer that to your ruler? He doesn't want it, and neither do I."

So Nehemiah called a congregational meeting and instituted a buy-back program to get back Jews who had been sold into slavery because of the hard economic conditions. See, whenever you lose something you ought to have, you have to have a redemption program.

We need a buy-back program today. We have a generation of children who need to be bought back from the worldly influences we have sold them to. Some wives and husbands need buy-back programs in their homes. What have you lost that needs to be bought back, redeemed?

——— **Think About It** ———

God instituted a buy-back program for you. He lost you in the Garden of Eden, and He bought you back at Calvary. That's why He calls you to act like a redeemed person.

"Whatever you want others to do for you, do so for them."
Matthew 7:12

DON'T MAKE HIM LOOK BAD
Read It: Nehemiah 5:9-13

One of the best things you can do to impact your community for Christ and transform your culture is to maintain a spotless public testimony. Why? Because you are a representative of the eternal God. When you do poor business, you make God look bad. When you cannot pay your bills, you make God look bad. When you refuse to be responsible for your actions, you make God look bad. When you fail to care for your family, you make God look bad.

Nehemiah told the rulers and nobles of his day to give the people back their property and the interest money these nobles got by overcharging the people. There's a way to start a revival. Suppose every Christian businessperson went back to everyone he or she had done sloppy work for and said, "I didn't do a good job. Since I'm a Christian, I represent Jesus Christ. So let me make it right with you."

The principle here is restitution. You messed it up; you take responsibility to get it fixed. You don't just say, "I'm sorry; it will never happen again." You fix that mess. This is what Nehemiah demanded.

This principle is New Testament also. You remember Zaccheus (Luke 19)? He came down out of that tree when the Lord saved him and said, "I am going to pay back everyone I cheated four times more than I stole." So the businessmen of Jerusalem agreed with Nehemiah and promised to do right. But that wasn't good enough for Nehemiah. He called the priests and made them swear an oath. This was a "self-maledictory" oath, meaning you call down doom on yourself if you don't fulfill your promise.

Actually, we make commitments like that today. If you are married, you made an oath. You promised to love, honor, and cherish your partner in sickness and in health, for richer or poorer, as long as you both shall live. Then you said, "So help me, God."

That was a "self-maledictory" oath, like Nehemiah shaking out his robe as a sign that if you don't fulfill the oath, then the punishment will come upon you. Got any promises you are behind in keeping? Better catch up!

——————— **Think About It** ———————

If we're going to have renewed communities and a transformed culture,
God's people will have to start keeping their promises.

"In speech, conduct, love, faith, and purity, show yourself an example of those who believe." 1 Timothy 4:12

SHOWING THE WAY
Read It: Nehemiah 5:14-16

There never seem to be enough good leaders to go around. Leaders can't take a community any higher morally or ethically than they've been themselves, just as a pastor can't take a church higher spiritually than he's gone himself.

That's why studying the life and accomplishments of Nehemiah is like a breath of fresh air. Today and tomorrow we'll be wrapping up our study in how to transform culture, and we're stopping at just the right spot—with the portrait of a godly leader. Fix this picture in your mind, because we need to find a lot more Nehemiahs today.

After Nehemiah made the nobles and rulers shape up in the way they treated their fellow Jews who were in need, someone could have asked, "Hey, what about you, Nehemiah? Do you practice what you preach?"

According to these concluding verses in chapter 5, the answer was yes. Nehemiah set a great example for his people. He looked over his twelve-year governorship and concluded that he had honored his God. Notice what he did and did not do.

First, unlike his predecessors, Nehemiah did not allow power or wealth to corrupt him, because he feared the Lord. That tells me you can be a Christian politician. You can serve in the government and still fear the Lord. You can be in business, law, medicine, and fear the Lord. You can be anything and honor God.

Nehemiah knew that power and wealth can corrupt. So rather than lounging in the governor's mansion and enjoying all the "perks" of office, he set himself to work on the wall of Jerusalem. He did not tell other folk to do what he was not willing to do. He led by example. We need leaders today who set the example. I don't mean being perfect, but making the effort to do it right and being open to correction when they fail.

People at my church will tell you the senior pastor isn't perfect. I fail and make mistakes. The issue isn't whether I sin, but whether I'm setting the example I ought to set and being accountable for my actions.

——— **Think About It** ———

You're a leader whether you know it or not. Someone is watching you. What kind of example are you setting?

"Remember me, O my God, for good, according to all that I have done for this people." Nehemiah 5:19

REMEMBER ME?
Read It: Nehemiah 5:17-19

We all want to be remembered. And we all will be—just for different things. Nehemiah wanted to be remembered too. But he wasn't worried about having a civic luncheon and getting the "Citizen of the Year" award. His concern was what God thought of him.

Now Nehemiah was a wealthy man. Anytime you are feeding 150 people on a regular basis, you have some money to buy food. Since he did not take the governor's allowance (v. 14), Nehemiah was feeding all these people out of his own pocket.

There's nothing wrong with being rich as long as you got there the right way. Nehemiah not only got there the right way, he used his wealth to benefit his people. He didn't take from the government, then sit back, and say, "I got mine. You get yours somewhere else."

Don't forget, this is a politician making this prayer in verse 19. If there is any prayer that politicians—and you and I—need to be able to make today, it is this prayer of Nehemiah's. Why? Because one day your world is going to collapse. I guarantee it. One day things are going to go all wrong, whether it's a financial, health, or family problem. When these things hit, you want to be able to pray, "Lord, remember me."

Now my question to you is, if you prayed that prayer today, what would God remember about you? Would He look down and say, "Yes, I remember you. You were faithful. You used what you had for My glory. You made Me a priority. You served people. You were not selfish. You honored Me, and when you blew it, you confessed it. I remember you."

No one wants God to say, "Yes, I remember you. I remember that you never had time for Me. I remember that I was last on your priority list. I remember that you gave Me the leftovers of your time and energy and resources. I remember that you cut corners in your work. I remember that you gave your family little of your time. Yes, I remember you."

When you call on God, how is He going to remember you?

——— **Think About It** ———
Whether your thing is business or politics or whatever, the ultimate issue is what God remembers you for.

REFLECTION

A young violinist was giving a concert one day in front of a large crowd. He ended his concert with a flourish, and all the people stood up and applauded, shouting, "Bravo! Bravo! What a performance!" But the young man put his head down. As the people continued to clap, his eyes began to fill with tears. There was no smile on his face.

All of a sudden as the applause began to die, an old man sitting up in the balcony stood up and began to clap. As soon as the violinist saw that, a smile came across his face. He wiped the tears from his eyes. He smiled and held up his violin and walked off the stage.

A man in the wings said, "How come you were sad when the people stood up, but when that old man stood up, you became glad again?"

"Because the old man was my violin teacher," the young musician explained, "and unless he stood up, my concert would have been a failure, because he is the only one who knows all the nuances of the music I played. He knows exactly how each piece is supposed to be played. It does not matter whether the people stand and applaud. I want to know if my teacher is going to stand and applaud."

My friend, unless God is standing and applauding, we really haven't done anything. Don't be fooled by people's applause. Make sure that Jesus Christ says, "Well done, good and faithful servant."

EIGHT

FOLLOWING JESUS

What It Means to Be a Disciple

The day that Jesus first said, "Follow Me," to a group of Galilean fishermen, He launched His people into the fascinating and challenging process of becoming His disciples. We tend to think of disciples as those New Testament men and women who hung around Jesus, listened to Him, and tried to do what He told them to do. Although we can't walk alongside Jesus today, that's a pretty good description of what we're supposed to be doing today, because we're disciples too. Let's find out what it means to be a disciple—and what it takes.

"Take My yoke upon you, and learn from Me." Matthew 11:29

LEARNING AND GROWING
Read It: 2 Peter 3:18

What does it mean to be a disciple? What does a disciple look like in real life? What do we have to do today to be disciples? Those are good questions. We're going to try and answer them over the next four weeks as we look at the subject of discipleship and some of the fascinating people Jesus called to be His disciples.

Let's start with a definition. The Greek word for disciple means learner. A disciple is a student. That means he has some data, some information he needs to receive from his teacher or discipler. A disciple needs to hear and to know what the teacher wants known.

But gathering information is not enough. So the disciple must also practice what he is learning and develop the skills his discipler wants him to perform. The process of discipleship is not concerned alone with how much data you can absorb. It is also concerned with how much you can do. So if a disciple does not move from data to execution, the process has failed. The Apostle Peter said we are to grow in grace, not just knowledge.

A surgeon goes to medical school and learns all the parts of the body and all the equipment used for surgery. But they don't turn him loose until he has done an internship. The professors know there is a major difference between learning in a classroom how to cut somebody open and cutting somebody open. What difference does it make whether the process of discipleship works or not? Just ask someone lying on an operating table!

Now let me give you a definition of New Testament discipleship. It is that process of spiritual development that occurs in the framework of accountable relationships in the local church, whereby Christians are progressively brought from spiritual infancy to spiritual maturity. Then they are able to repeat the process with others.

That's a mouthful, so we'll break it down this week and next as we answer the questions above. Note especially the last part of that definition. Discipleship is meant to be reproduced. As you become a more mature disciple, you teach others what you have learned—not to make them like you, but to make them like Jesus.

─────── **Think About It** ───────

You can come to church every Sunday, year in and year out, and actually be worse off if you aren't *doing* what you're learning.

*"The things you have learned and received and heard and seen
in me, practice these things." Philippians 4:9*

HOW FAR HAVE YOU GONE?
Read It: Matthew 10:24-25a; Luke 6:40

The goal of your life and mine is to move in the direction of spiritual maturity and likeness to Jesus Christ. That's discipleship. As I said yesterday, discipleship is a process of spiritual development. The best place to go to understand what that means is to the Teacher Himself, the Lord Jesus. He is the One who has called us to be disciples, so He gets to set the parameters of discipleship.

Today's text is a summary statement. Jesus is looking at the back end of the process when a disciple has been through it and has reached the level of maturity desired by the teacher. Luke's version brings out this aspect, talking about a student who "has been fully trained."

Look at what Jesus said here. He gives the two basic components of discipleship: the disciple and his master, or teacher. The goal of the teacher is to move the disciple in the direction the teacher desires. We saw yesterday that this includes both the imparting of knowledge and the development of skills. A teacher shows a student how to do something and then gives him opportunities to practice his skills. All this requires time. Jesus spent over three years with His disciples, and they still had a lot to learn.

You do not get saved today and become everything God has called you to be tomorrow. Discipleship is a process. Now that ought to be encouraging to you as you seek to grow in grace. But don't let it become an excuse for dragging your feet. Discipleship is guaranteed if you stay with it, but it is not automatic.

Here's a little formula I think will help you see the process. When it comes to being a disciple of Jesus Christ, *rate* multiplied by *time* equals *distance*. Some people have been saved for years, but they are almost as immature today as they were the day they got saved. They've had plenty of time, but their rate of speed is negligible. Therefore, they've moved very little distance toward maturity.

What would the results show if this formula were applied to your Christian life?

--------- **Think About It** ---------

You don't become a mature disciple of Jesus overnight. You do not wake up mature. But you should be moving in the direction of maturity.

"We have the mind of Christ." 1 Corinthians 2:16

TORTOISES AND HARES
Read It: 1 Corinthians 2:12-16

Why is it that some people who have been saved for a relatively short period of time seem to mature faster, grow stronger, and move farther down the road of discipleship than other people who have been saved for many years?

At least part of the answer is in the discipleship formula I gave you yesterday. Disciples who break from the starting blocks with a burst of speed and never look back are going to cover a lot of ground in a hurry.

You see, if I'm running, and you're walking, you may start out before I do, but I will arrive at the finish line before you do. Now I know the old story of the tortoise and the hare as well as you do. But remember, the hare lost the race because he kept fooling around and looking back, wasting his God-given ability. He would have made a lousy disciple.

Make no mistake about it. Jesus doesn't play favorites among His disciples. It's true that we differ in gifts and abilities, but the Bible says we all have the mind of Christ. We all have His Spirit. We can all reach the level of spiritual maturity described in today's reading.

So when you see Christians who can't get their marriages or moral lives together, who can't control habits or their tongues, who can't seem to get a handle on their thought processes, who can't ever seem to get past the nagging problems and upsets that keep them in the dumps—when you see Christians like this, it's not because God is playing favorites.

The problem is that their discipleship mathematics are out of whack. They have forgotten that rate multiplied by time equals distance. The Corinthians were a good example of this problem. Today, tomorrow, and Friday we are going to examine this classic passage in chapters 2 and 3, which talks about where these believers were and where they should have been in their Christian growth. As we proceed, ask God to show you where you are on the spectrum we'll be talking about—and what you may need to do in light of where you are.

——— **Think About It** ———
Whether God has called you to be a tortoise or a hare,
just run your race well, and God will reward you accordingly.
Stop worrying about the other guy.

"We are no longer to be children, tossed here and there."
Ephesians 4:14

GROW UP!
Read It: 1 Corinthians 3:1-3

How do you know if you're growing as a disciple of Jesus Christ? How do you know if you're moving along at the proper rate of speed given the time you've known Christ? According to the Apostle Paul, you need to take a close look at your diet and your discipline. The first three verses of 1 Corinthians 3 tell us that what you are able to digest and the way you behave say a lot about your spiritual maturity or lack thereof.

Just as it's possible for our physical development to be arrested and stunted, Paul says it's possible for Christians to have arrested spiritual development. It's even possible for Christ's disciples to start looking and acting like "mere men," that is, non-Christians.

Now some professing Christians look like non-Christians because they actually are. One of my great concerns as a pastor is people who only think they are saved and use the excuse that they are carnal to justify their sins. Joining a church or signing a card does not a Christian make.

But there are genuine disciples who have been born again and aren't living like it. If you came to the nursery at our church in Dallas and saw baby bottles and baby food jars, saw kids fighting over toys or whatever, you wouldn't think twice on it. Babies need milk and baby food and toys.

But if you walked into a class of college-age young people or a class of married couples and saw people drinking milk out of baby bottles and fussing and fighting, you'd first double-check the class name on the door, and then you'd probably check out!

Well, that's what the Corinthian church looked like spiritually. And sad to say, that's what a lot of churches today look like. Jealousy, strife, and immaturity are as alive and well in the church of the twentieth century as they were in the church of the first century.

Do these verses describe you? I sincerely hope not. Check your spiritual diet and discipline today—and if need be, get rid of any baby bottles you see setting around.

--------- **Think About It** ---------
You can't become a disciple of Jesus Christ without responding
to His call to forsake your old life, take up your cross,
and follow Him (Mark 8:34).

"Long for the pure milk of the word, that by it you may grow in respect to salvation." 1 Peter 2:2

MILK vs. MEAT
Read It: Ephesians 4:14-16

At first reading, today's verse and today's text may seem to be in conflict. Paul tells us not to be children anymore, yet Peter tells us to desire the milk of the Word. The two texts aren't contradictory, of course. They're written to people of different spiritual ages. Peter makes it clear he's writing to new Christians, baby disciples. Paul is writing to people in Ephesus who have had time to grow and needed to move on from milk to meat.

You see this same thing in the church at Corinth. From the time Paul had established the church to the writing of 1 Corinthians was a span of about five years. Now in five years, a baby is supposed to do some growing. He may not be mature, but a five-year-old can understand a lot of things a newborn can't.

A five-year-old who's still on Pablum is a sad thing. So is a five-year-old Christian who's still playing in the crib. A new Christian is going to have newborn struggles. But if you are five or ten years old in Christ, and you still can't walk, we have a problem. If you are a teenage Christian and all you can get down is milk, there's a problem.

Remember our discipleship formula—rate multiplied by time gives us the distance traveled. Want to know one way you can test whether you're traveling at a good rate? Here's the test. Which ministers most to you, the "show and tell" kind of service or the teaching of God's Word?

See, many people will say, "We had church today. I know because I shouted. I got happy." That's baby food. There's nothing wrong with it, but spiritual growth occurs not just when you shout, but when you learn more about Jesus and what He wants from you, and you go out committed to obeying Him.

Paul calls it "speaking the truth in love" (v. 15) and says it's essential to spiritual growth. When you can hear and receive the truth of Christ, even when it confronts and convicts you, and adjust your life to it, you know you're covering some ground.

--------- **Think About It** ---------
A disciple should be growing in knowledge of the Lord
and developing skills in Christian living.

REFLECTION

Remember those exhilarating early days of your Christian life when you couldn't get enough of God's Word, you couldn't wait to be with God's people, and you couldn't find enough time to do all the praying and seeking God's face that you wanted to do?

That's the problem with too many of us, isn't it? We have to think awhile to recall times like these, because they're in the past tense. Now our days are full of work and bills and kids and chores around the house and a few TV shows, sports events, and rented movies.

Well, what I described at the top of this page may sound like super-saint to you, but I believe that's to be the normal experience of a growing and developing disciple of Jesus Christ.

Does that mean you're always on a high, always soaring from one mountaintop to another? Of course not. There are still jobs and bills and kids to take care of. But if you allow your walk with Christ to be pushed to the end of the line like a beggar looking for a few scraps among the leftovers, your growth will be stunted, and you'll wind up a spiritual midget.

It's easy to diagnose the problem. But what's the answer? Well, I think the answer is to fall in love with Jesus Christ all over again. If you do that, you'll find time for Him. So instead of asking the Lord to give you more hours in your day, pray that He will give you more love in your heart for Him. I guarantee that's a prayer He'll answer!

"Upon this rock I will build My church." Matthew 16:18

IT HAPPENS IN CHURCH
Read It: Ephesians 5:23-27

Reading today's text, you might think I got mixed up and slipped in something from the marriage and family series. Actually, when you read Ephesians 5, you realize that these verses are among the strongest statements of Jesus' love for the Church in all of the New Testament.

Why is that so important for the subject of discipleship? Being a Christian disciple means following and imitating Jesus, right? That includes loving what He loves and hating what He hates. Now if you're a disciple and your teacher says to you, "This is so important that I'm going to die for it," you'd sit up straight and pay close attention.

That's how much Jesus values the Church. And that's why today discipleship occurs in the context of the local church. That's the second part of the definition of discipleship I gave you at the beginning of last week.

The first principle is that discipleship is a process of spiritual development. We looked at that pretty thoroughly last week. Later this week we'll consider the other two elements of that definition before spending our final two weeks looking at some very interesting New Testament disciples.

Let me add two words that explain what I mean by the context of the Church: *accountable relationships*. You can be born by yourself, but you can't grow by yourself. You cannot become a fully mature disciple by yourself. So when you hear people talking about, "Well, you don't have to go to church. You can worship God in your heart," what those people are trying to do is give you a theological-sounding excuse for their spiritual laziness.

But you cannot grow apart from dynamic involvement in the body of Christ. If He can die for the Church, it won't kill you and me to show up at the church!

Did you know the word *disciple* only appears in the Gospels and Acts? After that it isn't used. Why? Because once Jesus went back to heaven and established His Church, He turned over to the Church what had been His personal ministry of making disciples. So if you're not dynamically involved in the church, you're missing the action!

——— **Think About It** ———

We're to hold each other accountable for our growth as disciples. You won't find anybody who will do that for you except at church.

"God has so composed the body . . . that the members should have the same care for one another." 1 Corinthians 12:24-25

GOD'S ANTIBODIES
Read It: 1 Corinthians 12:14-27

I was talking to a doctor friend of mine not too long ago. I love talking to doctors because they almost always give me dynamite sermon illustrations! This brother did not disappoint. He explained that most people have cancerous cell growth a number of times, but they don't know about it because of wonderful little organisms called antibodies that God has already built into our bodies.

My physician friend said renegade cells will decide to take off and do their own thing, becoming cancerous and gathering other cells around them. (Just the way some church members do!) These renegade cells call to their buddies, "Hey, blood, come on over here and grow wild with us."

So the issue in your body is, which cells are going to win, the healthy ones or the renegades? Well, the reason you don't know there may be a cancerlike growth in you until it really gets to be significant is that your body sends out these antibodies.

These guys get together and say, "Hey, there's a brother going off the wrong way. Let's get him!" So these antibodies go after the renegade cell and take care of it, and you don't even know it happened. All you have to do is be healthy, and your body will produce the needed antibodies.

Now the illustration doesn't fit at every point, of course, but basically this is what disciples are called to do for each other in the context of the church. When there is a need, when there is pain, when there is joy, when there is suffering, the church automatically sends out members of the body to take care of the need.

But you have to be in a body of fellow disciples to pull this off consistently. The test of our discipleship is not the programs we draw up. It's when we move to help others develop in their spiritual life. According to the Bible, you can't say to the other members of the body, "I don't need you." You may find out real soon how wrong you are.

———— Think About It ————
If you needed the ministry of the body, would anybody at your church know you well enough to pick up on your need and do something about it?

"For by one Spirit we were all baptized into one body."
1 Corinthians 12:13

LOVE AND TRUTH
Read It: John 13:34-35; 1 Timothy 3:14-15

Let me give you two more reasons why the church is so critical in the process of growing mature disciples who imitate Jesus Christ.

The first reason is relational. Jesus Himself issued the identifying mark for His disciples: our love for one another. God's people are so vitally connected that we're like members of the same physical body. The parts of your body are in dynamic relationship. Just smash your thumb or stub your toe, and you'll have a good biblical reminder of the interrelationship of your bodily members. Once you disconnect a body part, you cut off its ability to function because it is separated from the source of its life.

As Christ's disciples and members of His body, we're all in this thing together. That's why Paul calls the Church the "household of God." Your home is supposed to be the place where you give and receive love unconditionally. It takes more than a paid professional staff in a church to produce this kind of love. It has to come from each disciple in dynamic relationship with every other disciple. One person can't do it all either, because no one person has everything another person needs.

Another reason the church is so critical in the disciple-making process is that the church is where truth is found. Paul calls the church the "pillar and support of the truth." What do pillars and supports do? They hold up buildings. The church holds up the truth of God, preserving and passing it on so each generation of new disciples can operate from the basis of truth.

The church is the one place you ought to be able to go and get the truth. I hope you know there's not a lot of truth in the world now. There's a lot of shucking and jiving and game-playing out there, but there is a critical shortage of truth.

Well, in a biblically sound church you should always hear the truth, the whole truth, and nothing but the truth, so help you, God! So your first concern when you go to church ought to be, "Tell me the truth," not, "Make me feel good." Even if it makes me feel bad, tell me the truth.

––––––– **Think About It** –––––––
The church is not a gathering of strangers, like fans at a ball game
who just happen to be sitting next to one another.

"The goal of our instruction is love from a pure heart and a good conscience and a sincere faith." 1 Timothy 1:5

WHERE ARE YOU GOING?
Read It: 2 Corinthians 3:18

Today and tomorrow I want to go back to our definition of discipleship (see Monday of last week) and discuss the third and fourth components of the process.

The third aspect of discipleship is that it is a progressive movement toward spiritual maturity. Your experience of following Jesus should be taking you somewhere. The goal of discipleship is your spiritual maturity, which Paul describes in today's verse as being transformed into the image of God's glory.

The question we have to ask is, what do spiritually mature disciples—or at least disciples who are moving toward maturity—look like? Well, some of them look like people who once did not know how to control their passions. But they came under the teaching of God's Word, and now they understand how to maintain self-control with regard to their desires.

Other growing and mature disciples look like people who at one time or another have struggled and lost against just about every sin you can imagine, but now in the strength of Christ and the power of the Holy Spirit, they are living lives that are well-pleasing to God.

Now please don't misread me. I'm not talking about sinless perfection. Anybody who tells you that you can go through life and never sin has just sinned because that's a lie. But what I am talking about is maturity, where the normal thing for you to do is bring every area of your life under the control of Jesus Christ.

So what is maturity? Very simply, it is coming to the place where you think, judge, and react biblically to every situation. When it is the rule and not the exception for you to apply the Bible to your life; when you place every area of your life under the lordship of Jesus Christ; when you can say in everything, "Here I am, Lord. What do You want me to do?"—then you are a mature disciple of Jesus Christ.

The Bible calls it Christlikeness, because Jesus is intent on making you like Him. Who else is worthy for you to pattern your life after?

——— **Think About It** ———
Are you a growing disciple? Can you look back and see
definite signs of progress? Keep at it!

"Be imitators of me, just as I also am of Christ." 1 Corinthians 11:1

PASS IT ALONG
Read It: 2 Timothy 2:2; Hebrews 5:12-14

The final aspect of discipleship I want to consider is this. The process of disciple-making should be transferable to somebody else. You move from simply being a disciple to being a disciple-maker when you can take others through the process.

Paul put it in personal terms. Now I'm not sure many of us would want to sign our names under a bold statement like the one above, but there is nothing wrong with following people if those people are following Christ. A major part of Paul's ministry was transferring what he had been entrusted with to others.

The danger is, we can get so much truth that we get comfortable sitting on it. But if what you are learning is not changing how you live, if it does not help somebody else, and if it does not change the society, then what you are learning is a waste of time.

See, if you continue to take in the Word of God but don't do your spiritual exercises by applying it and passing it along, you get spiritually overweight. Then what was designed for your health becomes a detriment to you. You have to be exercising, sharing this stuff with other disciples. That's what Paul did.

Look at what the writer of Hebrews told his readers in Hebrews 5. They were called to be teachers, disciplers. You say, "But I thought that's what we hired a pastor to do."

Sorry, this job description is for every disciple. If you can't point to another person you're bringing along in the faith, you don't really understand what it means to be a disciple.

Hebrews 5 doesn't say it would be nice if each believer did this. We "ought" to be teaching and discipling others. It's imperative, not optional.

Any athlete will tell you it's easy to win games from an easy chair. It's something else to win them on the field. Too many churches are filled with "armchair quarterbacks" who see clearly what everyone else should be doing. But God has not called you to watch from the sidelines. He's called you to get into the game and help a "rookie" or two learn how it's done.

——————— **Think About It** ———————
Even if you haven't gone that far in your Christian life,
you can help somebody coming along behind you.

REFLECTION

I have been discipled by a lot of people, but preeminently by my father. It is mainly because of his influence that I am in the ministry today.

Whenever I begin thinking about my love for preaching and my burden to declare God's truth, I reflect on the fact that at the age of thirteen or fourteen, I would go with my dad and five or six other men from the church down to the street corners and watch my dad preach wholeheartedly as people passed by.

So when I was in college, I would take some students out on the streets of Atlanta, at the bus stops, and I'd preach.

My father would also take me to the local prison, and I would hand out things while he preached to the prisoners. And when I was in college, it wasn't unusual for me to go to the prisons and preach. My father had instilled in me his mind-set for ministry.

And now I want to take my eldest son, Anthony, Jr., with me whenever possible. As I was working on this series of studies on discipleship, it occurred to me that what I am asking my son to do is become a disciple, just as my father made me a disciple.

I was with Anthony not too long ago, and somebody said, "That boy looks just like you!" Guess what God the Father wants to say about you? He wants to look at Jesus, look at you, then look at Jesus again, and say to Him, "That disciple looks just like You!"

That's what discipleship is, a process of bringing you to the place where you look just like Jesus. How close is the resemblance right now?

"Behold, the Lamb of God who takes away the sin of the world!"
John 1:29

COME AND SEE
Read It: John 1:29-39

One thing that should mark every disciple of Jesus Christ is a burning desire to tell others His story. Show me a Christian who isn't witnessing, and I'll show you a Christian who doesn't understand what it means to be a disciple of Jesus.

That's why I love the latter part of John 1. There are disciples all over the place, and they are doing what learners and followers are supposed to be doing. They are learning who Jesus is, they are following Him, and they are bringing others to Him.

John the Baptist got things rolling with his unique witness. John was such a dynamic figure that he had his own disciples (v. 35), but that was just temporary. He was a disciple of Jesus himself. So when he saw Jesus, John did just what a disciple should do. He gave witness to Jesus as the Lamb of God, the long-awaited sacrifice that would not just cover sin, but take it away.

A preacher only does his job when people follow Jesus. So the next day the same thing happened again. This time two of John's disciples were there and took off after Jesus (vv. 35-37). John understood. He didn't say, "Behold me. I'm John the Baptist." He pointed to Jesus. John was a good disciple-maker because his disciples followed Jesus.

We know that one of these two disciples was Andrew, who, as we'll see this week, became the link to Peter and several other disciples who became apostles. Notice that Andrew made the right move for a disciple too. He started following Jesus. Jesus turned around and saw that Andrew and his companion had taken the first step. They were following Him. So Jesus asked, "What do you seek?" (v. 38).

In other words, "What can I do for you? How can I help you?" That's the greatest question anyone could ever be asked. Imagine Jesus asking you what you need. Here the two disciples wanted to know where He was going so they could follow Him. Underline in your Bible Jesus' response: "Come and you will see." We're going to hear that repeated a lot this week.

--- **Think About It** ---

The duty of a disciple isn't real complicated. We just
tell people where they can find Jesus; then we lead them to Him.

"We have found the Messiah (which translated means Christ)."
John 1:41

A NEW NAME
Read It: John 1:40-42

What would you do if you had just spent the day with Jesus? You'd probably run out and tell someone, wouldn't you?

Well, that's what Andrew did. He and the other disciple mentioned in verse 35, most likely the Apostle John himself, spent part of a day with Jesus. Then Andrew said, "I've got to tell somebody!" See, when you meet Jesus, you have to tell. Andrew had only been with Jesus for a few hours, and he felt that he just had to be a witness. He hadn't been to seminary. He hadn't been around Christians for years. But he had met Jesus, and that gave him something worth talking about.

The tragedy for a lot of Christians is that they did more talking about Jesus when they first got saved than they do now that they're "old hands" around the divine corral. But Andrew didn't have that problem. This was all new to him. Jesus was a Person, not a program.

The first place Andrew went was home, to his brother Simon. You know, the hardest place to talk about Jesus is to relatives. Most of us would rather talk to strangers, because relatives know us. With strangers we can say, "Do you know about Jesus?" But they can't scrutinize how we've been living. They can't see whether our walk and our talk are married. They don't know us. But when we go home, we can't be shucking and jiving.

So I like what Andrew did here. He went straight home and told his brother Simon about Jesus. Then he brought Simon to Jesus. Now Simon perked up when Andrew told him he had found the Messiah, the Anointed One, the promised Redeemer of Israel. When Jesus met Simon, He changed his name to Peter. Jesus was saying, "If you are going to be My disciple, we need to stop calling you what you were and start calling you what you are going to be."

Whenever you meet Jesus, you get a new name (Revelation 2:17). Have you come to Jesus and received your new name along with new life? Have you brought anyone else to Jesus lately?

--- **Think About It** ---

As a disciple you have a new name, a new destination,
a new heart, and a new job description. Your job is to
live like the new person you are.

"Jesus said to him, 'Follow Me.'" John 1:43

ANOTHER FOLLOWER
Read It: John 1:43-44

Philip was right in the middle of this wonderful chain reaction of discipleship we're studying this week. He played a key role here in the first chapter of John, and then he faded from the scene except for a couple of incidents we'll talk about today.

But I think Philip deserves some ink of his own. To begin with, he's the only one of this group of disciples who was sought out directly by Jesus. You can miss that important detail if you skim over verse 43 too quickly. All the others were either brought to Jesus by someone else or pointed to Jesus, as in the case of John the Baptist's two disciples.

Jesus went looking for Philip, which means Philip came to understand who Jesus was by direct revelation. In other words, Jesus wanted this man on His team. John gives us several clues in his book to the kind of character qualities Philip possessed that made him good disciple material.

Two of those clues are right here in this chapter. First, like the others, Philip obeyed when Jesus said, "Follow Me." And of course, Philip sought out Nathanael and brought him to Jesus too. If you don't have a brother to bring to Jesus like Andrew did, grab a friend. Philip was a follower and a "bringer."

John tells us that Philip was from the same city as Andrew and Peter, so they must have known each other. Maybe that's why we see Philip and Andrew hanging around together later in the book of John. They are linked in the text of John 6 at the miracle of the feeding of the five thousand. They're together again in chapter 12 when some Greeks want to see Jesus, and Philip and Andrew wind up escorting them to the Lord.

And on the night of Jesus' betrayal, it was Philip who said, "Lord, show us the Father, and it is enough for us" (John 14:8). Jesus answered him by name, a brief glimpse into what may have been a closer relationship between Master and disciple than we normally think.

Maybe it was because Jesus went looking for Philip and called him personally. Whatever the case, here is another classic profile of a good disciple.

--- **Think About It** ---

We can't all be like Peter, leading the way, but we can all be like Philip. He just kept bringing people to Jesus.

"It is [the Scriptures] that bear witness of me." John 5:39

THE BIBLE MAN
Read It: John 1:45-46

When it comes to Nathanael, we're dealing with a different breed of cat. Nathanael was the Bible man. Nathanael knew his Old Testament. So when Philip went to tell Nathanael about Jesus, Philip approached his buddy on the basis of what he knew from the Scriptures.

Notice how Philip stated his case in verse 45. He told Nathanael that everything he had read about and believed in the Scriptures concerning the coming Messiah was fulfilled in Jesus. What Philip was saying was, "Nate, you know the One you've been reading about and waiting for? Peter and Andrew and John and I have found Him.

"Remember when you read in Genesis 3:15 about the One who would crush the serpent's head? We found Him. It's Jesus of Nazareth. Remember the balm of Gilead and the Rose of Sharon? We found Him.

"Remember reading in Isaiah about the root of Jesse and the suffering servant? We found Him. Remember how much you love to read about the King who will sit on the throne of David? We found Him. His name is Jesus, and He's from Nazareth."

You ask, "Did Philip really say all of that?" Maybe not word for word, but that's the idea. He was inviting Nathanael to lay his Old Testament scroll aside for a minute and come and see the One he was reading about.

How do I know Nathanael was reading his Bible? Because rabbinic literature refers to the fig tree (look ahead to verse 50) as the place for meditation, sort of like going to the park today and sitting under a tree to read a book. The Jews would go and sit under a fig tree to read and meditate on the Scriptures.

Now Nathanael must have been from Missouri, because he said in verse 46, "Show me." His reference to Nazareth is less than flattering, but that was the reputation the town had in those days.

Then true to form, good old Philip just said the secret words of John 1: "Come and see." And the reason you know Nathanael was also good disciple material was that despite his deep skepticism, he was willing to be taught. He was willing to be corrected. How about you?

――――― **Think About It** ―――――
You don't have to argue with people about the Gospel.
Just bring them to Jesus, and He will take care of the rest.

"You are the Son of God; You are the King of Israel." John 1:49

CHECKING IT OUT
Read It: John 1:47-51

As I indicated yesterday, Nathanael had the heart attitude of a true disciple. When Philip went to tell Nathanael about Jesus, Nathanael said, "I don't buy it." But he was willing to give his friend the benefit of the doubt. He decided to see for himself. You can teach someone like that.

Jesus saw him coming and announced that here was an Israelite with a pure and honest heart. Nathanael was taken aback. How could someone from a nowhere place like Nazareth know him that well? Jesus flashed a little omniscience and told Nathanael that He had seen him under the fig tree.

That was enough for my man Nate. Jesus knew him, and that was all he needed to know. By the way, disciple, Jesus knows you too. And if He knows you, it really doesn't matter who else knows you. He knows you in private under the fig tree, and He knows you in public. He knows you.

So Nathanael confessed his faith in Christ, calling up a couple of those biblical names for Jesus that he would have known so well from his Bible study. He was laying these exalted titles on Jesus, and Jesus was accepting them because they were true. Nathanael exhibited the best traits of a disciple here: an open, honest, searching heart, a willingness to believe the evidence, a readiness to learn.

At verse 50 it started getting good. Jesus told Nathanael that if he thought that brief flash of divine omniscience was something, he had better stick around, because he hadn't seen anything yet.

Notice that Jesus referred to Genesis 28, the account of Jacob's ladder, to explain to Nathanael what was in store for him. That ladder connected heaven and earth, bringing God's angels down to earth to reveal God's plan to bless Jacob. And I believe on the way back up, those angels took Jacob's needs back to heaven to lay them before the throne of God.

Think about that one for a minute, and you might start shouting, because this is for you too. If you will take God at His Word the way Nathanael did, He will show you things that will blow you away.

──────── **Think About It** ────────
You don't have to know all the answers to be Jesus' disciple.
You don't even have to know all the questions!
All you need is an open and honest heart before Him.

REFLECTION

Do you get the idea after reading John 1 that this thing of being Jesus' disciple is really pretty straightforward? It really is.

Basically, being Jesus' disciple involves following Him—which implies obeying Him and learning from Him—and bringing others to Him. Sure, there are a lot of other instructions and commands given to us as New Testament disciples, but following and bringing pretty well capture the basics.

With that in mind, let me give you about four ideas to work on this weekend that I think will help you in your discipleship. The first one is *praise*. As soon as you finish reading this page, stop and praise God for the faithful disciple of His who led you to Jesus. If that person is still alive, a note or call of appreciation is in order.

The second thing I want you to do is *practice*. Grab a Christian friend and practice presenting the Gospel to him or her. Nail down the biblical path you would take to show someone his sin, his need of a Savior, and what he must do to be saved.

A third idea you can work on this weekend is to *prepare* a list of unsaved friends and family members who need to be brought to Jesus.

Fourth and finally, *pray* specifically for these people, asking God to give you opportunities to share the Gospel with them. He'll do it in ways you never thought possible—and that's when this disciple business gets to be fun!

*"If I have forgiven anything, I did it for your sakes
in the presence of Christ." 2 Corinthians 2:10*

PEOPLE, PEOPLE EVERYWHERE
Read It: Philemon 1-3

For our final week of studies on discipleship, let's look at an interesting, insightful relationship between a disciple-maker and his disciple: the Apostle Paul and Philemon, whose book carries the same name.

Philemon is one of those books you will miss if you thumb through your Bible too fast. Yet it has a powerful message not only for "the church in [Philemon's] house" (v. 1), but also for the church today. Philemon shows us what it means to follow Christ when it comes to forgiveness and reconciliation among people.

Somebody once said that he could be really happy if it weren't for people. People have a way of messing our lives up. The problem is, you and I are people too, and there are so many people running around that we keep running into them wherever we go.

In fact, the slave Onesimus found out that even when you run away from some people, you run into other people. You know what I'm talking about. You change jobs to get away from troublesome people, and you run smack into other bad-news people on your new job. Same thing often happens when people change churches.

Since we humans are here to stay, we had better learn how to relate to each other. Fortunately, we have God's Word to guide us. Relationships are one of the most important topics in the Bible, particularly in Paul's letters to various churches where people of all sorts were rubbing shoulders.

Philemon was evidently a prominent person in the church at Colossae (Archippus [Philemon 2] is also mentioned in Colossians 4:17). Apphia was probably Philemon's wife. Onesimus was his servant, actually his slave. From what we can tell, Onesimus stole money from Philemon and ran away. The punishment for a runaway slave in the Roman Empire was death, so Paul had a definite relationship problem on his hands.

Paul was a Roman prisoner when he wrote this book, so a lot of folk were being "done wrong" here. This week we'll see how it all fits together.

─────── **Think About It** ───────

The old blues song says, "Somebody done done you wrong."
Is that true for you today? Then get to know Philemon this week,
and you'll learn how to handle that hurt.

"[God] has committed to us the word of reconciliation."
2 Corinthians 5:19

LOVE *THAT* PERSON?
Read It: Philemon 4-7

It's obvious that Paul loved Philemon like a brother (v. 7). And he considered Onesimus to be his spiritual child (v. 10). One reason Paul felt this way was that he had brought them both into the kingdom. Paul is setting Philemon up gently for the request he's going to make of him.

These are amazing verses. Think how it must have made Philemon feel to know that his spiritual father and discipler saw this much love and faith and knowledge in him. If you're on the learning end of a discipling relationship today, you couldn't do any better than to pray that God would make you this kind of disciple.

And if you're working with younger believers either individually or in a group, notice Paul's delight in seeing Philemon's spiritual maturity. There is no joy in the world quite like that of seeing your spiritual children grow.

Now I haven't forgotten that we're talking about what being a disciple means in terms of our relationships with others. Paul commends Philemon on his love for Christ and for his fellow believers, which is going to be important when he tells Philemon he's got a new brother he needs to love and accept, Onesimus.

See, Philemon couldn't say, "I love God, but I hate Onesimus because he stole from me and ran off." John says the way you show your love for God is by loving your brother. Conversely, if you do not love your brother, something is seriously wrong with your love for God (1 John 4:20).

You say, "Yeah, but you don't know what he did to me." God's response is: "You don't know what you did to Me. But I demonstrated My love toward you while you were still a sinner. My Son died for you when you were at your ugliest" (Romans 5:8).

Paul knows there is one name Philemon does not want to hear, so he's easing him into it. All of us have that one person whose name we don't want to hear, especially if the subject is forgiveness and reconciliation. It is a good thing God didn't feel that way about you and me when our names came up for salvation!

———— **Think About It** ————

If you have that one person you can't bring yourself to love, you need to get that mess fixed. Take the first step yourself if that's what it takes.

"Go your way; first be reconciled to your brother, and then come and present your offering." Matthew 5:24

USEFUL AGAIN
Read It: Philemon 8-14

Did you know the Greek word *Onesimus* means useful? Now there's some real irony. What's more useless than a runaway slave—and thief to boot? But Paul says that's all past. Onesimus will live up to his name now (v. 11). What happened? When Onesimus ran away from Philemon, he ran smack into Paul in Rome. Because of Paul the useless young man was turned around.

You know by now that it was dangerous to run into Paul, even in prison. One time he had guards chained to him in eight-hour shifts. Poor guards. They didn't have a chance. Paul said at one point that the whole "praetorian guard," the guys guarding him, had heard about Christ (Philippians 1:13).

The slave has become a saint. Relationships have changed. Once you come into the family of God, your status changes. You start all over again.

Paul brought out the meaning of Onesimus's name to make a point. Onesimus was now useful to Philemon. So Paul was sending him back, although Onesimus was also useful to Paul and Paul wanted him to stay.

See the discipler/disciple relationship between Paul and Philemon in verse 8. Paul could have ordered Philemon to do the right thing. Yet as his spiritual father, Paul appealed to him based on their bond. He cared about his relationship with Philemon and didn't want to presume on it.

Notice that this wasn't one-sided. Restoring broken relationships requires not only forgiveness but restoration. Onesimus needed to go back to pay back what he'd stolen from Philemon in terms of money and missed work. So Paul asked Philemon's permission to send Onesimus back (v. 14).

Now this is where we often miss it. We say forgive and forget. No, sin must be atoned for. God did not forgive and forget our sins until Jesus did the atoning. See, things can't be right vertically with God until they're also right horizontally with each other. Jesus said we need to fix our human relationships before we can talk about bringing God the kind of worship He wants. Anybody you need to talk to today?

——— **Think About It** ———
As forgiven people, we have no right to withhold
forgiveness from anyone else.

"Forgive us our debts, as we also have forgiven our debtors."
Matthew 6:12

EQUAL IN CHRIST
Read It: Philemon 15-20

Sometimes it's really hard being a disciple of Jesus Christ. You know why? If you try to follow and obey Jesus long enough, sooner or later He's going to ask you to love and accept somebody you don't even *like*.

As we saw yesterday, Paul wanted to keep Onesimus with him. But Paul wasn't so selfish as to ignore Philemon's feelings and the fact that he'd been wronged. So Paul said Onesimus had to go back to square things.

But I want you to notice a great principle here. Even though Onesimus had some restitution to make, the only right way Philemon could take him back was as his "beloved brother," no longer as his slave.

You almost hear Philemon saying, "The man who stole from me?" Yes. "The guy who messed me over?" You got it. "Now I'm supposed to receive him as my beloved brother?" Right again. What Paul was saying was that Onesimus was now much more than what he had been when he ran away.

Now don't misunderstand. Paul did not mean that Onesimus's job description had changed. He may still owe Philemon money and work, but he wasn't to be treated as his slave.

Here's the answer to those who wonder why the Bible doesn't come right out and denounce slavery. Paul knew that if slaves and masters got saved and started treating each other as beloved brothers, slavery as an institution would collapse of its own weight. Slavery is so morally reprehensible that you can't have two disciples of Jesus Christ fulfilling His command to love one another while one disciple is the property of the other.

Now that's not to say this would be an easy assignment for Philemon. We're still talking about two human beings whose relationship has been badly damaged. And they were from two different social classes. But once a man has been to Calvary, he is your equal.

So Paul put it on the personal level (vv. 17-18). The way Philemon treated Onesimus would be a reflection of how Philemon felt about Paul. But Jesus said the same thing in Matthew 25:40. How you treat the "least" of His followers is how you treat Him.

--------- **Think About It** ---------
If Jesus took your treatment of other believers as reflecting
your love for Him, would you be glad or embarrassed?

"Be kind to one another . . . forgiving each other, just as God in Christ has forgiven you." Ephesians 4:32

A SECOND CHANCE
Read It: Philemon 21-25

How do you know when to give somebody another chance? Now I'm not talking about forgiving a person for doing you wrong. A disciple has only one option there: to forgive. But forgiving somebody is different from giving that person another chance to maybe mess you over again. We've been talking about relationships and reconciliation from the standpoint of what it means to be Christ's disciple. But does being a disciple mean being an easy mark? When do you take the risk?

There's a very clear answer to that question in the book of Philemon. Paul knew Philemon was asking himself the same question. How did he know Onesimus wouldn't really clean him out again and take off?

The answer is that before Paul wrote, he had put Onesimus to the test. Paul had been with Onesimus and worked with him. He was able to tell Philemon, "I've got good news. Mr. Useless is now Mr. Useful again. I've checked him out. He's for real. Fact is, I'd like to hang onto him myself."

Now we don't have a record of what happened when Onesimus got back, but we can assume everything went well. One church father even said Onesimus later became the bishop of Ephesus, although we can't know for sure. But he was worth the risk Philemon had to take.

There's another fascinating example of a man who made good on a second chance: Mark (v. 24), or John Mark, as he was called in Acts 15:37. He went out with Paul and Barnabas on their first missionary journey, but he got scared and went home to Mama (13:13).

Paul said no more chances for him, but Barnabas was ready to take a risk with Mark, even if it meant splitting with Paul (15:37-40). And Mark proved himself. Later he became a valuable helper to Paul (2 Timothy 4:11). Mark was with him in Rome as he wrote this letter to Philemon.

There are two extremes in dealing with broken relationships. One is to skip what happened, try to ignore it. The other is to hold a grudge and ruin your spiritual life. A faithful disciple chooses forgiveness and reconciliation—the way of the Cross.

——————— **Think About It** ———————
If you're afraid to give somebody a second chance,
ask God for His wisdom in the situation (James 1:5).

REFLECTION

Philemon has a lot to teach us about relationships, especially about the changes that occur in relationships when the people involved are disciples of Jesus Christ.

For instance, Philemon is a great book for dealing with issues like slavery and social class differences. And as we learned this week, Philemon is great for dealing with conflicts and making things right with folk who have done us wrong.

Verse 1 really sets the stage for the message Paul wanted to get across to Philemon—and the message the Holy Spirit wants to get across to us today. Paul identified himself as a "prisoner of Christ Jesus" and called Philemon his "brother."

See, Paul defined himself and Philemon based on Calvary. The reason Paul was a prisoner and Philemon was a brother was because they had been to the Cross. They had received Christ as their Savior and were His followers, His disciples.

Onesimus had received Christ too, and now Philemon needed to define Onesimus based on Calvary, not based on his social standing. Even though Philemon was a wealthy man, because of the Cross, he and Onesimus were equals. Period.

Do you see how being true disciples of Jesus Christ is the only hope for the pervasive and persistent problems of racial and class discrimination that plague our society? Once you start defining people by what happened at Calvary, you won't be talking about who's better. In Christ we're all equal. Period.

NINE

◇

TRIALS & TRIBULATIONS

Getting Out from Under
Your Circumstances

Are you doing okay under the circumstances?
Well, what in the world are you doing under there?
God wants you to get on top of your circumstances,
because He never designed life to put you under. He does
have some very important lessons He wants you to learn,
such as His sufficiency for your need, His strength in your
trials, and His power over your archenemy, the Devil.
That's our outline for the next four weeks,
as a matter of fact. I hope you'll find some new joy
and encouragement for the journey.

"Do not work for the food which perishes, but for the food
which endures to eternal life." John 6:27

GOING FOR THE BREAD
Read It: Matthew 14:13; John 6:1-4

You may not think we're going to talk about trials and tribulations when you see that we are beginning with one of Jesus' greatest miracles, the only one recorded in all four Gospels: the feeding of the five thousand. But I want to study this incident both for what it teaches us about God's provision and because it served as the prelude to a great trial of the disciples' faith.

The reason this miracle is recorded more than any other is that at this point excitement about Jesus Christ had reached a fever pitch. It came two years into His ministry, and His popularity was going through the roof.

John 6 records that it happened during the Passover, the celebration of Israel's deliverance from Egypt. The death angel passed over every house covered by the blood (Exodus 11:1–12:36). Now the reason this is important is that John wanted his readers to make the link between Israel under Egypt and Israel under Rome in his day. Israel in the Old Testament wanted deliverance from Egypt. The Jews of Jesus' day wanted deliverance from Rome.

The Old Testament prophesied that when Messiah came, He would deliver His people and bring in a new kingdom. They would be under the hand of God. So by now it has become apparent to the Jews that Jesus was a great candidate for this position. He has been healing people and performing many other miracles. The problem, though, was that the people wanted the goodies Jesus was handing out, but they didn't want the message He was preaching. They were saying, "This Brother's bad. The blind see, and the lame walk, and demons are cast out. He's our Man to feed us and lead us out of Roman bondage."

In fact, they were so intent on getting the good stuff that Mark 6:33 says they outran Jesus to this location. This is serious popularity. This is superstar treatment. The crowd was big because the people wanted to see what Jesus would do next (John 6:2). As we will learn, however, they wanted Jesus to be their King on their terms, not His.

─────── **Think About It** ───────

Are you trying to have Jesus on your terms instead of His?
It won't work. He is either Lord of all or not Lord at all.

*"Since then the children share in flesh and blood, He Himself
likewise also partook of the same." Hebrews 2:14*

OUR CARING SHEPHERD
Read It: Matthew 14:14; Mark 6:34; Hebrews 4:14-16

I want you to see something wonderful about Jesus Christ today. If you
read the verses above, you've probably picked up on the theme: Jesus
knows where you are and what you're going through, and He cares.

When this huge crowd gathered, Jesus looked out and saw broken people with broken lives. They had brought their sick and their lame, people with all manner of problems. And Jesus felt compassion for them.

That tells us a lot about Jesus Christ, because it says that He is more
than just a Person of power. He is One who cares. I'm here to tell you today
that Jesus knows what you are going through. Jesus feels your pain. See,
the beauty of the Incarnation is that when God became man, He could
feel what we feel.

We need a Person like that because we're like sheep. Mark says Jesus
had compassion on the people because "they were like sheep without a
shepherd." There are three things you need to know about sheep: they
are dumb, defenseless, and directionless. It's not flattering, but it's true.

These people were groping for direction. They were defenseless, ripe
for plucking. How many times have we been deceived into going to the
wrong places, doing the wrong things, thinking the wrong thoughts, hanging out with the wrong people? We are defenseless and directionless.

So Jesus was moved with their suffering. And when you bring your
needs to Jesus today, you're coming to someone who knows what you are
talking about, not only because He is God, and therefore He knows everything, but also because He is man, and He can feel what you feel. That's
why Jesus is the only One who can be the mediator between God and us.

But please take note. Jesus can do much more than just sympathize
with you. His power can overrule your circumstances. His compassion can
deal with your situation. He healed the sick that day (Matthew 14:14),
and He fed them too. I don't know what impossible situation you may be
facing today, but when you bring Jesus Christ into the equation, you have
someone who can surmount the insurmountable.

——— **Think About It** ———
Before you encounter your next trial, you need to know
that Jesus cares and can do something about it.

"When He has tried me, I shall come forth as gold." Job 23:10

THIS IS A TEST
Read It: Matthew 14:15-16; John 6:5-7

It's interesting to read about this miracle in the various Gospels because you pick up important little details. Mark 6:31 says Jesus and the disciples were tired when this happened. They wanted Him to dismiss the crowd, to give the benediction so they could go home.

But Jesus told them to take care of the crowd's hunger. He asked Philip, whom we met a few weeks ago, how he was going to feed so many people. Now we know from John 6:6 that Jesus was testing Philip. He knew what He was planning to do. When Jesus asks a question, it's not to learn new information. When Jesus inquires of you, it is to test you.

Philip had been with Jesus for about two years. He had seen Him change water into wine. He had seen Him heal people. Jesus was now ready to put Philip to the test. But Philip thought Jesus should have been answering the question, not asking it.

You may be facing an insurmountable situation right now, and rather than Jesus answering you, it seems that He's asking you, "What are you going to do?" In other words, "You mean you haven't come up with anything yet?"

You say, "But, Jesus, I'm coming to *You* for answers."

Jesus responds, "This is a test. Were you in church last Sunday? Were you listening? This is a test."

Philip pulled out his calculator and figured out that they were way short. So he enlightened Jesus. "Now, Jesus, pay attention. Come back to the real world. Two hundred denarii won't even begin to dent this deal."

Are there any Philips in the house? We've all been there. We look at an insurmountable circumstance and see only that it can't be done. So we come to Jesus and say, "Lord, this is all I've got. It's not near enough, so I guess we'll have to forget it."

The problem with that is that the issue is not what you have. The issue is what Jesus has, what He can do. And He already knows what He wants to do in your circumstance. He's just waiting for you to figure out what He already knows—that you can't do it by yourself!

--------- **Think About It** ---------
When you're talking to Jesus, put away your calculator.
Don't try to limit what He can do for you.

"All things are possible with God." Mark 10:27

HERE, LORD
Read It: Matthew 14:17-18; John 6:8-9

Yesterday we saw that Philip didn't have much hope of anything being done about the circumstance they were facing, because all he could see was how little they had.

But there was another disciple on the scene, Peter's brother Andrew. Philip said, "Forget it." Andrew said, "I've been scouring around, and I found a boy with his lunch." Barley loaves were little pancakes, the poor people's food. It would be like us having sardines and crackers for dinner. While Philip saw no way the people could be fed, at least Andrew saw some hope. Not much, to be sure. He still had limited vision.

But as I said yesterday, what can or can't be done is never the question when Jesus is on the scene. The issue is the will of God, not the size of the problem. Regardless of what you're facing, the question is always, what is the will of God? He can always afford whatever He chooses to do. There is never a lack of resources with God.

Now there was a third person present that day. That little boy was the star of the show. He hadn't gone to seminary, hadn't been trained in theology, didn't have all of that knowledge. All he knew was, "Jesus would like your lunch."

This boy was poor, but the little that he did have he made available to Jesus. I don't know what the boy thought or what he was going through. All I know is that at some point he said, "Here, Lord."

Now he could have started talking about, "It's my lunch. My mama made this lunch for me, and neither Jesus nor anyone else is getting it." He could have been like a lot of us who want to go through the spiritual motions but don't want to give Jesus what we have. We want to keep it to ourselves. This little boy gave Jesus what he had.

Is there anything God wants from you that you are holding back from Him? Whether it's your skills, your financial resources, or whatever, if you hold out on God, you lose. And others whom God would have blessed through you lose too. Jesus can make more of what you have than you ever could anyway!

--- **Think About It** ---
Never be afraid to give something to Jesus.
He knows what to do with it.

*"In everything give thanks; for this is God's will for you
in Christ Jesus." 1 Thessalonians 5:18*

SAY THANKS
Read It: Matthew 14:19-21

What a wonderful contrast there is between the way Jesus responded to this situation and the way His disciples responded. He gave thanks. We would have been complaining. I'll bet when Jesus said, "Let us give thanks," Philip and Andrew were looking at each other thinking, *Give thanks for this?*

But Jesus was thankful for what He had. Most of us would have started our prayer with, "How come I only have crackers and sardines? Lord, You promised to meet all my needs, and I need more than this." Most of us would have been fussing and complaining, "How come I don't have more?" One of the tragedies today is that we don't have enough Christians who know how to give thanks for what they already have.

Jesus gave thanks for two reasons: He had something, and He was anticipating more. Did Jesus need more than five loaves and two fish to feed five thousand men, plus women and children? Of course He did. But He knew what Paul later told us. Don't come to God with anxiety, but come with thanksgiving to let your need be known (Philippians 4:6). Don't come to God without saying thanks first.

So Jesus broke the loaves and fish, and there was so much food that everyone on the premises ate until he was stuffed. The writer lets us know that this was not some little thing where everyone got a nibble or a crumb. So that there would be no doubt or confusion, he said that the people ate until they couldn't hold another bite.

See, when we're talking about our circumstances, we have to get away from worrying about the sardines and crackers we have. Otherwise, all you'll see is what's at the bottom of your little lunch box.

So Jesus did the job with just five loaves and two fish, because He knew what to do with them, and He knew where to go. He went to the Father, but He didn't go griping. He went with thanksgiving.

You may not have much, but if you have a compassionate Christ who can get to an all-powerful Father, you've got everything you need.

———— Think About It ————
Until we learn to give thanks for what God gives, we won't see Him supernaturally take what's given and multiply it to make more out of it.

REFLECTION

I hope that if you forget everything else you read this week, you'll take this truth with you: When you kneel before our all-powerful God, the equation changes. There is a new agenda you have just brought to the table.

If we as God's people really get hold of this, we will stop robbing God of our time; we will stop holding onto our five barley loaves and two fish, afraid we won't have anything left. We will be more like the lad in our story this week, saying to the Lord, "Here is what I have. Take it, because I know that if I give it to You, something real will be done with it."

Our subject for the next few weeks is trials and tribulations, but the truth is that for many of us, our circumstances are working out pretty well right now. We're doing better than we've ever done financially. The family is healthy and intact. Things are relatively quiet.

My concern is that if this describes your life today, don't forget God, or you'll actually be poorer than when you had less. See, if you don't bring God into the equation, it doesn't matter what you have. It will never be enough, because the Prophet Haggai said if you forget God, you're putting your wealth into a bag full of holes. It will dissipate.

But when you bring what you have to God, He can do amazing things with it. Do you believe that? If you're not absolutely sure, don't let this weekend pass without settling the issue with God.

"Why do you call Me, 'Lord, Lord,' and do not do what I say?"
Luke 6:46

NOT YOUR SUGAR DADDY
Read It: John 6:14-15

If you want to know why more people don't see God at work in their circumstances, all you have to do is read today's text. After Jesus had fed the multitude, the people said, "This has got to be Messiah. He's the One. Get Him! He's going to be our King whether He likes it or not. Anyone who can take sardines and crackers and turn them into Moby Dick sandwiches ought to be King!" We are talking welfare like you've never seen it before.

But Jesus withdrew. He was not interested in being their "Sugar Daddy." He was not interested in being their new welfare system. He's not interested in being yours either, by the way. Jesus is interested in building the kingdom of God. If all you want from Jesus is His goodies, He's going to do with you like He did with the crowd in His day. He will withdraw from you.

See, Jesus does not hang out with people who want His benefits but don't want a relationship. He's not going to walk with people who get up in the morning and say, "Lord, give me what I need today," but never get around to, "Lord, make me what you want me to be today."

He's also not excited about people who say, "Lord, give me recognition on my job even though I'm too ashamed to give You glory among my co-workers"; or, "Lord, give me more money in my pocket even though I can't make any available to Your kingdom"; or, "Lord, sharpen my skills even though I won't use them for Your kingdom."

If that's the way you pray, God may help you out a time or two like He did the people in Jesus' day. But over the long haul, if you only want a welfare relationship with God, He won't hang out with you, because He came to be your King of Kings and Lord of Lords, not your spiritual Sugar Daddy.

God wants a relationship with you. When you come to Him for Him alone, then you will see Him overcome the insurmountable circumstances in your life. If we are going to be the people of God, a people He can bless and use, we've got to do it His way.

─────── **Think About It** ───────
Do you want Jesus or just His goodies?

"We also exult in our tribulations, knowing that tribulation
brings about perseverance." Romans 5:3

A REASON TO REJOICE
Read It: James 1:2-4

If you're not in the middle of a trial right now, just hang around. None of us can dodge trials. So we need to find out the resources God has given us to deal with trials.

What is a trial, anyway? It's an adverse circumstance that God allows or even brings about in the lives of us His children to deepen our faith. We'll see this week that trials are not designed to sink our boat, but to help us improve our navigation skills. In the words of the Apostles Paul and James, we can actually rejoice when we undergo trials, because we know God is doing something special in our lives.

Now trials can come from a number of directions. Sometimes God sends you a trial to teach you a specific lesson. At other times, it comes simply because you live in a sin-cursed world, and the curse rubs off on you. So you become the victim of a crime or accident or illness that crashes into your life.

Sometimes trials are the result of your own sin. You yield to a temptation that leads to a set of circumstances that are tough to deal with. And don't forget that the enemy can attack you with trials for the purpose of bringing about your spiritual defeat.

So my concern is not so much the source of your trials, but what you do when they show up. How you respond to cataclysmic circumstances has a lot to do with what shape you're in when you come out on the other side. The good news is, you're not out there alone, because no matter what the source of your trial is, God has the situation well in hand. He can work out His purposes even in a trial you may bring on yourself.

One great way to learn how to deal with trials is to watch others in the middle of one. So starting tomorrow, we'll get into a boat with the disciples and row out to the middle of the Sea of Galilee. Stay with me, and you'll learn that even when your boat starts to rock, Jesus Christ has authority over your trials.

——— **Think About It** ———

You're either in the middle of a trial, just coming out of one, or just heading into one. Better be ready!

*"He will not allow your foot to slip; He who keeps you
will not slumber." Psalm 121:3*

HIS IDEA
Read It: Matthew 14:22-24

God's Word has some great lessons for us in this classic story of a trial-by-storm the disciples underwent. We'll deal with it the rest of this week and into next week, because I don't want to shortchange you on the good stuff God wants to teach us.

Notice first that Christ controls the very existence of a trial. Matthew says, "He *made* the disciples get into the boat" (my emphasis). This whole trip was Jesus' idea, not theirs. The disciples wanted to stay where they were, because Jesus had just miraculously fed five thousand men. The disciples liked this action.

See, they were just like the crowd who wanted to make Jesus their "welfare" King. As we saw last week, Jesus wanted no part of it. But from the disciples' standpoint, this king business sounded like a good idea. But what the disciples wanted and what they needed were two different things. They wanted royalty, but what they got was a rowboat in a storm, because that's what Jesus wanted them to have.

So there were the disciples being battered by the waves and wind. The harder they rowed in one direction, the harder the wind pushed in the other direction. Mark pictures them "straining at the oars" (Mark 6:48). These boys were sweating. And they didn't even want to be out there.

Are you in a storm today? Can you feel the wind pushing against you? You say, "Tony, I'm not only in a storm, but I'm being pushed backwards."

I hear you. I've been in those kinds of trials too. The first thing I want to tell you about trials is that for a Christian, there is no such thing as random, pointless trials. If Jesus sent you into the storm, His authority is reigning over it even though it may be raining on you.

If you are in a trial, God has a point to it. God can even hit the target with a crooked arrow. He can take a trial caused by our sin and failure and still make something out of it. The power and authority of Christ are not threatened by trials.

--- **Think About It** ---

Since that rowboat ride was Jesus' idea, He must have known what He was doing—just like He knows what He's doing in your life today.

"Take courage, it is I; do not be afraid." Matthew 14:27

HE CAN FIND YOU
Read It: Matthew 14:25-27

By the time Jesus came to the disciples in their trial, it was late—and dark. But He came right on time with the word they needed. That's what He wants to do for you too. Let me show you three ways Christ can encourage you in your trials.

First, because Jesus is God, He knows exactly where you are, and He can find you even in the dark. By now the disciples had been out in the boat about twelve hours without Jesus. So it wasn't when the storm hit that Jesus showed up, but He did show up. He may not have come when they wished He would, but He came on time.

Have you ever been in the middle of a trial and wondered where Jesus was? You've been out there on the stormy sea fighting for your life, and no Jesus. No problem—at least not for Him. He'll arrive on time.

Second, remember that what you see is not necessarily all there is. What the disciples thought was a "sho-nuff" serious problem, a ghost coming out to scare them, turned out to be their salvation in the Person of Jesus.

The very thing that could be looking like the worst possible problem for you may be the thing the Savior uses to deliver you. What you may see as a source of great fear may be God's way of saying, "Take courage." Trials have a way of clouding your vision so that you may not really be seeing what you think you're seeing. That's why you must always look for Christ.

A third source of encouragement in trials is Jesus' authoritative word, "Do not be afraid." See, He did not change the disciples' circumstance. He changed them. He did not deal with what they were facing on the outside. He first calmed them down on the inside.

Jesus will do the same for you in your trials. Your circumstances are no sweat for Him. He can walk right over the top of your storm, because He's bigger than your problem. He wants you to learn that you can face the enemy on the outside because Jesus is with you on the inside.

——— Think About It ———
Jesus has you on His radar screen, and He will come just when you need Him. And He has no problem getting to you.

"Lord, save me!" Matthew 14:30

JUMP INTO JESUS' ARMS
Read It: Matthew 14:28-31

Let me give you another important truth you need to know about your trials: Christ loves you even as He tests you.

When Peter stepped out on the water, he started out great, because he started out by faith. It took a lot of faith to step out of that boat. But he got in trouble when he took his eyes off Jesus and started looking at his circumstances. Now this was the same storm Peter had already been watching for about twelve hours. But it looked different out there on that dark water. He let what he saw around him control him. His faith faltered.

The moment Peter took his eyes off Christ, the trial started swallowing him up. If your trials are swallowing you up, it's because you are looking at the wrong thing. You are looking at your trials. I know you can't just close your eyes and ignore them, but they are not to be your focus.

Well, at least Peter had the good sense to cry out to Jesus for help as he was going under. He went to the right place, because Jesus loved Peter far too much to let him go under. Notice there was no delay in Jesus' response. He grabbed Peter "immediately" (v. 31). Even if you are going under, Jesus loves you enough not to let you sink.

In fact, I believe that one major purpose of trials is to teach us that we can't make it ourselves and that we can't figure it out, and all we can do is pray, "Lord, save me!" His love says yes to that admission of need and dependence upon Him.

Of all the temptations you need to resist in times of trial, the greatest is the temptation to think Jesus must not love you very much, or this wouldn't be happening to you.

Recently, my granddaughter Kariss got scared by our dog Casey. He ran toward her, and she screamed and came running to me yelling, "Poppy, Poppy! Casey is going to get me!" Then she jumped up into my arms—and from up there, everything looked different. She wasn't afraid anymore.

Has your trial got you scared? Jump up into Jesus' arms. From up there, your trial won't look so fierce anymore. It may still bark, but you're in Jesus' arms now!

———— **Think About It** ————
Jesus loves you far too much to let you sink under the waves.

REFLECTION

Some years ago when airlines first started transatlantic flights to Europe, they noticed that on some flights the plane would arrive an hour or so ahead of schedule without the wear and tear on the engine normally expected for that length of flight.

The airline people could not understand it, because they did not know as much about the weather as we do today. So as they began trying to figure out how this could happen, they discovered a weather phenomenon known today as the jet stream.

When an airplane gets into the jet stream, it is propelled forward by the wind so that even though it may be going the same air speed as a plane not in the jet stream, it is really going faster, because it is carried along by the force of the jet stream winds. So rather than fighting the air currents, a plane in the jet stream is actually being carried on the air.

Your trials may have you in turbulence right now. You may feel as if you're flying in the face of a strong wind, just as the disciples were rowing against a strong wind. What you need to do is catch the "Jesus stream." When you catch that Jesus stream, He will carry you along in the way you need to go.

If you catch the Jesus stream, He will take you where you are trying to go; He will get you there ahead of schedule, and you won't experience all the wear and tear you would if you tried to go it alone. How do you get in the Jesus stream? Just cry out to Him, "Lord, save me!" He will!

"We know that God causes all things to work together for good to those who love God." Romans 8:28

WHEN HE'S GOOD AND READY
Read It: Matthew 14:32; John 6:21

A final truth I want to share with you about trials is this: Christ will bring your trial to an end when He has accomplished what He wants through it.

When did the wind die down? When Jesus got into the boat with the disciples. And when did Jesus get into the boat? When He was ready. He had been up in the mountains praying earlier and could have gotten into the boat when the wind first started blowing. He didn't have to wait until the storm hit. But He got into the boat when He was ready.

That means no amount of fussing and crying and complaining is going to change what God wills to do. People say, "I'm mad at God." Big deal. It's okay to be honest with God, but you have to understand that He is working His will and His program, and He is not going to get into the boat until He wants to get into the boat.

Let me show you what happens when God is at work in your trials to bring about His will. John says that when the storm died down and the disciples looked around, "the boat was at the land to which they were going."

In other words, when the storm was over, they had arrived at their intended destination! They thought Jesus had sent them out to drown. But He planned for them to reach the other side (Matthew 14:22).

What I am saying is, don't get so upset about your trial that you forget it may be the very thing God is using to take you where He wants you to be. Let Him do His thing His way, because even when circumstances seem to be going against you, God can work it all out for good, because that's the business He's in.

Romans 8:28 is the *modus operandi* of the God we claim to love and serve. It's not the exception; it's the rule. It's only when you understand that God is working His plan through your trials that it makes any sense at all to count them as joy (James 1:2).

———— Think About It ————
The disciples thought they were going to drown, and all the time the storm was taking them where they wanted to go in the first place!

"Thou art the Christ, the Son of the living God." Matthew 16:16

SOMEBODY SPECIAL
Read It: Matthew 14:33

This is our last day on the subject of Jesus' presence in and authority over our trials. Tomorrow we begin looking at Christ's authority over the demons and the Devil himself.

But today we've got a great truth to finish up this part of our series with: The only right response we can make to Christ's authority over our trials is to worship Him. When Peter and Jesus stepped into the boat, everything was calm. The disciples knew Jesus was somebody special.

Did you know this was the first time the disciples acknowledged Jesus' deity, even though they had been with Him for about two years? They had seen all the miracles, but it just now dawned on them: "You really are who You say You are."

See, a lot of us have a problem. We still don't understand who Jesus is. If we did, we would be contacting Him a lot more regularly. If we really knew who He is, we would be focusing on Him more.

We would also be bringing our trials to Him, asking not for a quick fix to make us feel better, but for His will to be done. Worship is a priority response when you're in the middle of a trial.

You know, I like those three Hebrew boys Shadrach, Meshach, and Abednego. King Nebuchadnezzar said, "If you don't bow to me, I'm going to throw you into this fiery furnace."

My men were cool. They said, "Our God whom we serve is able to deliver us." They knew their Bible history. They figured any God who could open up the Red Sea and drown an army could certainly find a little bit of water to put out old Nebby's fire.

But I really love what they said next: "But even if He does not, let it be known to you, O King, that we are not going to serve your gods or worship the golden image that you have set up" (Daniel 3:18). These boys understood the priority of worshiping the true God, and not even a *fiery* trial could make them change their focus.

When Jesus sends you out into the middle of the sea in your boat, He isn't sending you out to drown you. His authority can see you through any trial!

————— **Think About It** —————
If you're not worshiping, your boat is going to keep on rocking.

"Our struggle is not against flesh and blood, but against . . . spiritual forces of wickedness." Ephesians 6:12

OUR ARCHENEMY
Read It: Matthew 25:41; Ephesians 6:10-12

If you're going to get out from under your circumstances and live in spiritual victory, you'll have to become proficient in spiritual warfare. Let's look at Christ's power over the forces of hell.

Spiritual warfare started when the Devil challenged the authority of God in heaven and led his coup d'etat. Satan's influence must have been enormous, because one-third of the angels followed him (Revelation 12:4). These fallen angels came to be known as demons or unclean spirits. They are the Devil's army, his foot soldiers. They are the denizens of hell, a place created with the express purpose of being the eternal prison for Satan and his angels.

What Satan has done is emulate heaven in creating an organizational structure—a demonic government, if you will—whose job it is to carry out hell's agenda in thwarting the program of God.

Our battle is against this government of demons. The words Paul uses to describe hell's hierarchy are governmental words lifted right out of the ruling Roman regime. "Rulers" refers to those demonic princes who guide the affairs of the satanic realm. "Powers" execute Satan's program. Under them are the "forces" of darkness, the workhorses, the lieutenants and sergeants who make sure those programs are properly implemented.

Finally there are the wicked spirits, the privates who go out and take the marching orders to the field of battle. When you became a Christian, you became a target. All of mankind is targeted, because the Bible says that "the whole world lies in the power of the evil one" (1 John 5:19). His government is all over the place.

But let's not give Satan more power than he possesses. Unlike God, Satan is not omnipotent or omniscient. He's more powerful than any human being or the whole race collectively, but not as powerful as God.

Because demons exist, they can only be addressed by the authority of Christ. That is, because our warfare is in a spiritual realm, it can only be won by wielding spiritual power.

——— Think About It ———
Actually, the only real power demons have over you and me
is the power we give them by yielding to temptation.

"When He ascended on high, He led captive a host of captives."
Ephesians 4:8

PRISONERS OF WAR
Read It: Mark 5:1-10

In Mark 5 we have a premier case of demon activity in the New Testament. We're introduced to a madman with an "unclean spirit" (v. 8). When these demonic unclean spirits do their thing, what do they do?

Well, we are told in verse 2 that this man lived in the realm of death. He came out of the tombs. So his worldview was one of death, morbidity. We learn from verse 3 that he possessed unusual strength. He was also suicidal and ran around without clothes (see v. 15). This is a stark picture of the degradation demons try to heap on human beings.

So the man is demon-possessed. Now the demons know who Jesus is. That's consistent throughout the Gospels. Demons are always forced to recognize Jesus because He is God. But there seems to be a dual recognition going on here. The demons have to bow to Jesus, but they'd never plead for His help. The man also bowed before Jesus. He needed help, and he knew Jesus was the only One who could help him. You can see the totality of his possession even in the structure of the text, because there is no clear distinction between the man speaking and the demons speaking. It's one of the saddest pictures of helpless humanity in the Bible.

The man was in torment because of the demons. The demons were in torment when Jesus showed up. Why? Because Jesus was giving His word. Jesus was speaking. The word of Christ was producing the potential of torment. If it's a spiritual issue, there will be spiritual crisis, because there is a war going on. I've never heard of a war where there wasn't conflict.

"My name is Legion," the demon answered Jesus through the man when Jesus asked for his name. A legion in the Roman army was six thousand soldiers. This man needed the authority of Christ to battle an army.

Now why didn't the demons want to be expelled from the man? Because demons only fulfill their reason for living when they are tormenting others. They exist to perpetuate and extend the agenda of hell. But when Jesus said go, they had to go!

———— Think About It ————
The power of Christ over demons is the power in which
you can stand against the forces of hell.

*"When He had disarmed the rulers and authorities, He made
a public display of them." Colossians 2:15*

THE REAL DEAL
Read It: Mark 5:11-20

Did you know that God also uses demons for His purposes? He's so sovereign that He not only uses the good angels to do His work, but He uses the bad angels too.

You really see that in today's conclusion of the story of the demon-possessed man. When Jesus ordered the demons out of the man, they wanted to enter the pigs. Now pigs were unclean animals in Scripture, so these unclean spirits wanted to inhabit unclean animals. They are messing with my pork chops here.

Jesus granted them permission—to teach an object lesson. This man was written off as insane. Jesus wanted to point out, "That's not true. Let me show you the real deal here." So He let the demons enter the pigs.

The pigs then immediately committed suicide. This was also an object lesson of what evil spirits can do. You can be grazing one minute, having a good time, and the next minute go downhill so fast that your life isn't worth a nickel. That's what demons can do. Only Jesus can do something about that. See, no matter what counsel you get for your problems, unless you are getting it together with Jesus Christ, you are going to plunge downhill and be drowned in the circumstances of life.

You say, "Tony, that's all well and good. I hear you. But what do I do? I am not Jesus. Jesus could speak, and the demons would leave. How do I have power over the demons today? That was back in the first century. What do I do in the twentieth century?"

Well, Jesus told His disciples in Luke 10:19-20, "Don't get excited because you have authority over demons. Get excited that your name is written in the Lamb's book of life in heaven."

What was Jesus saying? He was saying, "Get excited about what your salvation has done for you." You don't need to go around looking for an exorcist. You need to understand who you are in Christ. In Christ you have authority. In Christ you are equipped for spiritual warfare. In Christ you don't need to drown in your circumstances. That's the real deal.

──────── **Think About It** ────────

Jesus Christ has to be your authority, because the forces of hell are involved in spiritual warfare, and He defeated them on the Cross.

REFLECTION

Satan and his demons are real, make no mistake, but they're beaten enemies in the power of Christ. Let me give you three "R's" for dealing with demonic attacks.

1. *Recall* what Christ has done for you in relationship to the demonic realm. Read Colossians 2:14-15 and 1 Peter 3:22. We are not just talking about what Jesus did on earth, but what is happening right now while He is seated at the right hand of God. The demons are still subject to Him.

2. *Resist* the Devil (James 4:7). This is not just the power of positive thinking. Resisting Satan includes submitting to God. To submit to God means not compromising with the Devil's agenda. How do you resist Satan? By putting on the full armor of God (Ephesians 6).

3. *Rely* on God to do in and through you what you could never do for yourself. If God thought you could live the Christian life on your own, He would not have had to indwell you by the Holy Spirit. You're indwelt by the Spirit because you need a power bigger than you. You need somebody who has experience in this kind of warfare.

The Holy Spirit is an experienced general in God's army. He's been fighting demons for a long time. He knows how they move, when they move, where they move, and what they move with. When you are filled with the Spirit (Ephesians 5:18) and submitted to God, you are well-armed for spiritual warfare.

"The ruler of the world is coming, and he has nothing in Me."
John 14:30

NO CONTEST
Read It: Matthew 4:1-2

We've saved the best for last. In this final week of our current series, we want to study the triumph of Jesus Christ over the prince of darkness himself, "the great dragon . . . the serpent of old . . . the devil and Satan" (Revelation 12:9).

There are so many good things to enjoy in these verses that it's hard to know where to begin. The greatest benefit of Christ's victory in head-to-head spiritual warfare with Satan is that it confirmed the eternal victory of God's kingdom. When the Old Testament closed, it was still not clear who the winner was, because Israel was so inconsistent and unfaithful. But when the book of Matthew opened with God becoming a man in the Person of Jesus Christ, the battle between heaven and hell became personal. And it was no contest.

Along with the cosmic consequences of Jesus' triumph in the wilderness, His temptation holds very crucial lessons for us in our battle against the enemy of our souls. We want to focus on these lessons this week.

Please note what led up to this event. Matthew 4:1 begins with the word *then*, which points back to the end of chapter 3. There we find the account of Jesus' baptism, His public "coming out," a victorious moment. That often happens to us as well. Right on the heels of a victory comes a satanic attack. So we need to understand the context in which the battle was launched.

Notice that it was God's idea for Jesus to go into the wilderness. That is, Jesus is on the offensive, not on the defensive. God set out to demonstrate Christ's superiority. This event wasn't the Devil's call, but his opposition was still real.

You know, I'm awesome when I play basketball by myself. I can win when I play by myself, because there is no competition. Put someone in front of me waving his hand in my face, though, and it's a different ball game. The proof of how good you are is when you are opposed. Do you quit when the Devil starts waving his hand in your face?

——— **Think About It** ———
God allows you to be tempted so that you might prove that "greater is He who is in you than he who is in the world" (1 John 4:4).

"Man does not live by bread alone, but . . . by everything that proceeds out of the mouth of the LORD." Deuteronomy 8:3

OPERATION BREADBASKET
Read It: Matthew 4:3-4

Why was Jesus tested in the wilderness? Well, you remember what happened with the first Adam. He was tested in the Garden of Eden. Satan came onto God's territory, got Adam to sin, and Adam got kicked out of a garden into a wilderness.

The last Adam paid Satan a return visit on his territory. Jesus went into the wilderness to defeat Satan and get back for us what was lost by the failure of our forefather, Adam. By His victory, Jesus reclaimed us from the wilderness so He could bring us someday to the paradise of God, which is heaven.

Now the Bible says God does not tempt anyone (James 1:12). But He does test us. What's the difference? As we have seen, testing is designed to validate our victory in Christ. But tempting by the Devil is designed to defeat us spiritually.

So Jesus came under Satan's temptation. Jesus had fasted for forty days and nights in preparation for spiritual battle, so the first temptation was "Operation Breadbasket." Now what does that tell us about the Devil? He had been watching Jesus' fast. He knew Jesus was hungry. Remember that, because Satan knows what you're up to even when what you're up to is spiritual. Satan knows your intentions.

Satan was questioning God's provision. He was saying to Jesus, "God hasn't given you what you need." Have you ever felt that way? It's been forty days, and God hasn't supplied yet. You're hunting for a job, and He hasn't given it to you yet. You've been praying for a raise, and it hasn't come through. You've been waiting for a mate, but God hasn't given you one yet. Satan says, "God is really not that good, because if He was good, you would have what you need by now."

What did Jesus say? "It is written." There was more to this issue than food. Jesus answered temptation with the Word. How much more we need to use the Word against our enemy. We need to learn that we don't live by bread alone but by the Word of the One who provides it.

——— **Think About It** ———

God did not give you the Bible to decorate your coffee table or to carry under your arm but to wield like a sword.

"You shall not put the LORD your God to the test."
Deuteronomy 6:16

JUST JUMP!
Read It: Matthew 4:5-7

Did you know that the Devil knows the Bible? During the temptation in the wilderness, he even tried out Jesus' own words on Him: "It is written" (v. 6). Why did Satan do this? He was saying to Jesus, "I can't get You to act independently of God, so let me work through Your religion." So don't get all ruffled because people use the Bible to promote their agendas. Hell uses the Bible. Satan says, "Well, since you don't want to act independently of God, let's put it all on God."

He took Jesus to the pinnacle of the temple, about four hundred feet up, and quoted Scripture to Him about how God would catch Him if He jumped, thereby proving His Messiahship to Israel as He miraculously floated down to earth. So the second temptation was to question the plan of God. See, Satan offered to help Jesus fulfill God's plan for His life. After all, He was the Messiah, wasn't He? What's wrong with proving it?

Let me tell you something: God does not need Satan's help to get you where He wants you to go. Let me tell you what Satan was really saying. "You can skip the Cross, Jesus. I know every knee is going to bow to You and all that stuff, but if You do my plan, You can skip the Cross. You can be recognized as King of the Jews right here and now!"

What did Jesus say? "On the other hand" (v. 7). In other words, "If you're going to quote My Word, Satan, let's see the whole picture." You can never back God into a corner so that He has to perform a miracle for you. God has a plan, and when it's time for you to get that mate, that job, that promotion, you will get it. But don't go leaping off a temple. Don't go doing sinful things to accomplish spiritual goals. You don't have to compromise.

What you need is forty days of fasting and prayer in the presence of God. If you're going to defeat Satan, imitate Jesus. Know God's Word so well that no one can fool you into trying to achieve His will by taking shortcuts.

--- **Think About It** ---

If Satan knows the Bible and you don't, you are in big-time trouble, because you don't have anything to use against him.

"Seek first His kingdom and His righteousness; and all these things shall be added to you." Matthew 6:33

BOW!
Read It: Matthew 4:8-9

By the time we get to temptation number three in this great contest between Jesus and Satan, the enemy has cut right to the bottom line. By offering Jesus the kingdoms of the world in return for His worship, Satan has taken off his covering. He's now standing there with two horns, a pitchfork, and a red jumpsuit, saying, "Jesus, let me tell you what I'm getting at. Bow!"

That's what Satan wants from you too. He wants you to bow to him. Now he may not come out and say so at first. He didn't with Jesus. He may start with a food program. "Let's make some bread." But the goal is "Bow!" Or he may say, "Let's skip the inconvenience of the Cross and get there the easy way." But he's really saying, "Worship me."

This final temptation is the most blatant. No appeals to a real physical need. No quoting of Scripture. Just a straight-up offer of power and wealth beyond anyone's wildest dreams, all available if Jesus would acknowledge Satan as His master.

That's what Satan is after in your life and mine. He wants us to bow. He wants us to make him god. That is what he has always been after, to exalt his throne above the throne of God. And some of us have bowed. We have bowed at the altar of materialism. Our passion for stuff has driven us from God. When we were poor, we worshiped. When we were poor, we made time for God. Now that we have stuff, we don't have time.

The beauty of being in God's will is that what's yours is yours, and no one else can have it. You have to fulfill your responsibility, but you don't have to break your neck. You can enjoy Sabbath rest.

On the seventh day God rested. When you worship God, you can come to a day every week when you say, "I'm finished. God, whatever I've left undone, You are going to have to make up, because You told me to rest. I'm going to enjoy what I've done, because it is what I was supposed to do. If it wasn't enough, You pick up the slack."

--------- **Think About It** ---------
There's nothing like seeing God pick up the slack when you choose to worship Him instead of chasing stuff!

"You shall fear only the LORD your God; and you shall worship Him." Deuteronomy 6:13

WORSHIP *AND* SERVE
Read It: Matthew 4:10-11

Did you know you have no obligation at all to the Devil? When Jesus got tired of that mess, He told Satan, "Get out of here!" We owe the Devil nothing—not our worship or our service. But too many of us worship God on Sunday and then serve Satan all week long. But Sunday is supposed to be the precursor to what you do Monday through Saturday. After Satan laid out his best offer, Jesus laid out His bottom line. Worship *and* serve God only, period.

Based on Jesus' temptation, I believe that if you resist the Devil three times about any one temptation, he must leave you at that time when you use the Word. You say, "Well, he's not fleeing from me. He's all over me!"

Why? The problem may be you are not using the Word. That's the lesson I want you to take away from this week. The Devil is not impressed by what you know or think. He only leaves when the Word of God comes into play. Jesus hit Satan three times with God's Word, and he left.

Then the angels showed up. You know, sometimes God leaves you out there naked with just His Word. No angelic help, nothing except His Word. He wants to know, "Are you going to do anything with this?"

Now what do you think those angels did? Well, I can tell you what they did. Number one, they brought Jesus food because He was hungry. They also encouraged Him because that's what He needed. And they worshiped Him because that's what He deserved.

But they didn't do any of that until the spiritual battle was over. God's Word teaches that if you are His child, there is an angel assigned to minister to you. Angels are God's delivery boys. Their job is to deliver God's blessings, but only according to His timetable.

That means we need to adjust our focus to the authority of Christ. He's the One who has authority over the Devil. You can't beat the Devil. You can't overcome or resist him on your own. But you can in Christ's authority.

——— **Think About It** ———

One purpose of Sunday is to remind you that when you
go out into the world on Monday, you are supposed to take the God
you worship with you and serve Him alone.

REFLECTION

Suppose you are at home one night when a gigantic intruder breaks into your house and takes over. He makes you cook for him. He holds you hostage in your house, and you don't know what to do. He's just too big. Talk about a trial! Talk about being underneath your circumstances! You're in bad shape.

But then it dawns on you: "If I can just knock the phone off the hook and punch 911, I don't even have to talk, because they will have my phone number and can find my address."

So you knock the phone off and dial 911. All of a sudden a police car pulls up in front of your house. An officer emerges wearing a belt with firepower to get rid of your problem. He barges into the house and tells the intruder, "You must leave."

But the intruder won't be intimidated. So the officer calls for reinforcements. More police cars arrive at your house with all the firepower needed to get rid of your intruder.

Satan is an intruder in your house. He has come in to destroy and take over your life and hold you hostage to sin. But God has an emergency telephone number. You say, "What's that number?"

"It is written." When you dial it, the firepower from heaven comes down to remove the intruder from your house.

So the next time Satan barges in on your life, pick up God's Word and dial, "It is written." When you dial that number, heaven will give you everything you need to get this intruder out of your house!

TEN

◇

"HE WILL BE IN YOU"

The Ministry of the Holy Spirit

The Holy Spirit is the third Person of the Trinity. Quite simply, He is God. He is the invisible presence and power of the invisible God who indwells every believer at the point of salvation. The Holy Spirit performs a number of ministries within us, to us, and for us, and in this section we want to look at four of His operations on our behalf: His empowerment, His filling, the fruit He wants to produce in our lives, and the freedom He brings. There's nothing mystical about the Holy Spirit's work, but it is supernatural from beginning to end.

"[The Father] will give you another Helper, that He may be with you forever." John 14:16

ANOTHER HELPER
Read It: John 14:15-18; Acts 1:1-5

You can't talk about power in the spiritual realm without talking about the Holy Spirit. I wanted to get to the bottom line real quick as we spend this week talking about the empowering ministry of the Holy Spirit. The first truth we want to look at is this: The Holy Spirit provides Christians with a very powerful, indwelling presence. In Acts 1:4 Jesus commanded the disciples not to leave Jerusalem until they had received the promise of the Holy Spirit.

Jesus was saying don't leave home without the Spirit, because the power He promised (v. 8) would only be realized when the presence of the Spirit was realized. Jesus had promised earlier to come to His disciples after His death and resurrection (John 14:18). The way Jesus was going to come to them—and the way He comes to us today—was through the indwelling Person of the Holy Spirit.

In other words, you do not have to go back in time in order to be with Jesus. There is no such thing as wishing that Jesus were here. He is. That is why the Holy Spirit is called so often in Scripture the Spirit of Christ. It is the Holy Spirit who brings you the reality of the power of the resurrected and ascended Christ. If you want to be close to Christ, you must be close to the Spirit, because He is the Spirit of Christ.

Don't spend too much time trying to figure out how He is Spirit and Christ at the same time, and how the two relate, or you will probably jump out of a window. The mystery of the Trinity is beyond our ability to comprehend. Someone has said that if you try to explain the Trinity, you will lose your mind. But deny it, and you will lose your soul.

I like to picture the Trinity as a pretzel, all interlocked and intertwined. As I tell the people at my church, don't try to figure the "Trinity pretzel" out. Just enjoy it while you chew on it! The point is, when you have the Holy Spirit, you have all the power you will ever need to live the Christian life.

––––––– **Think About It** –––––––
You have no less of Jesus than those first disciples did.
You just have Him in the Person of the Holy Spirit.

"[God] gives the Spirit without measure." John 3:34

NOT VIRTUAL REALITY
Read It: Romans 8:26-27; 2 Corinthians 3:5-6

I want to take a little more time today to talk about the truth we studied yesterday, because it is so important for you to understand. The coming of the Holy Spirit to permanently indwell God's people means that we have unlimited power and spiritual resources available to us. In the Person of the Spirit, Jesus Christ's presence is now with each of us fully, because He is now present among us without the limitation of the flesh.

See, when Jesus was on earth, if He went to Peter's house to be with Peter, He couldn't be at your house or mine to fellowship with us. But through the indwelling Spirit you have Christ's fullness with you at the same time I have Christ's fullness with me. The same is true for His power.

The Apostle John wrote his first letter to second-generation believers who had not seen Jesus. Yet even though they had not seen or touched Jesus in the flesh, these later believers could have full fellowship with those who had (1 John 1:1-3).

Paul gives us some indications of the Spirit's powerful presence in today's reading. The Holy Spirit is actively at work in our prayers, interpreting them to the Father. He also gives life, which is the ultimate act of power.

When we talk about Jesus and the Holy Spirit in the same breath, as Paul does in 2 Corinthians 3:17, we are talking about two different Persons with one purpose, because, as we noted yesterday, they are both members of the Godhead. So when you have the Holy Spirit, you have Christ. And you have all of the Spirit, as John tells us in the verse above. The powerful presence of the Spirit allows you to enter into a realm of spiritual power that in your natural state you could never enter.

Right now you can go to an electronics store and buy a glove that goes with one of those video games. Or you can put on a helmet and other equipment and enter into the realm of the game you are playing. They call it virtual reality.

The Holy Spirit is *total* reality. He has taken us into another realm, the "heavenly places in Christ" (Ephesians 1:3). Nothing can top that!

———— **Think About It** ————

You have as much spiritual power at your fingertips as the next believer. The question is what you're going to do with it.

"Thy kingdom come. Thy will be done, on earth as it is in heaven."
Matthew 6:10

KINGDOM BUILDER
Read It: Acts 1:6-7

Not only is the Holy Spirit a powerful presence, but He is also accomplishing a powerful program called the kingdom of God. We know the kingdom was on the disciples' minds when they met with Jesus before His ascension. But their minds weren't on the kingdom. That is, they were interested in the kingdom coming their way, not Jesus' way. So He had to inform them that this was not what the Holy Spirit was all about.

One of the great problems we are facing today is the abuses and excesses coming from various groups regarding the Holy Spirit. They make the Spirit an end in Himself. But the Spirit is *not* an end in Himself. He did not come just so you could know the Holy Spirit. He wants to empower you to accomplish a great program, God's kingdom.

So if you are one of those Christians who goes around Spirit-hunting, you need to know that He does not display His power just to show off. God has a specific program in mind that He uses the Spirit's power to accomplish.

The kingdom of God is not first and foremost a place, although that will be true someday. The earth belongs to God, although His Son is not yet sitting on His throne. It will happen. On that day it will be evident to Satan and all of God's enemies that it was foolish to resist His kingdom.

But the primary concept of the kingdom is God's rule. When you become part of God's kingdom, you come under His rule. That's what the Holy Spirit wants to do in your life, bring you under the kingdom rule of God. So if you want to see Holy Spirit power, make sure you are involved in the kingdom.

See, if you are asking the Holy Spirit to bless your kingdom, that is not what God is doing. If all you want is another miracle so you can feel better or have more money, that is not kingdom work. That's the problem with so-called prosperity theology. It is not about the kingdom. God is after His kingdom, not after making you and me rich. Whose kingdom are you building today?

─────── **Think About It** ───────
If what you are doing is not building God's kingdom,
the Holy Spirit is not interested in empowering you.

"For God has not given us a spirit of timidity, but of power."
2 Timothy 1:7

HOLY GHOST POWER
Read It: Acts 4:13; 5:27-32, 40-42

A third truth I want to show you about the Holy Spirit's power is that He is creating a powerful people. Before the Spirit's coming on the Day of Pentecost, Jesus' disciples were a weak group of people. They were like timid Timothy. Peter denied the Lord. Others ran away because they feared the Jewish leaders who were after Jesus. But when the Holy Spirit came to live within them permanently, something drastic happened to their personalities. They became powerful proclaimers of the Word.

Understand, this didn't happen because their environment improved. In fact, the disciples were in far more danger in Acts 4–5 than they ever were during Jesus' ministry. They also did not get this power by taking a Dale Carnegie course or learning the power of positive thinking. What they got was Holy Ghost power.

Listen to me. The power of the Holy Spirit has nothing to do with the degrees on your wall. You can have all the degrees and be a defeated Christian. But if you have been with Jesus, others are going to know it.

We spend all this time trying to fix ourselves. We go to our therapist to find out who we were, who we are, and who we want to be. But the Bible says that when the Spirit took over these people, there was a personality change. All of a sudden these spaghetti Christians stood tall. The Holy Spirit can change a person from scared to confident, from intimidated to dedicated. If we aren't experiencing the Holy Spirit's power, we are going to be spiritual wimps running around from conference to conference looking for the newest secret, hoping the next program will do for us what only the Holy Spirit can do.

Sometimes people come for counseling and say, "I don't know what's wrong with me!" I know what's wrong. The Holy Spirit is not in control of that life yet. Because if He ever takes over, people will do things they cannot normally do and say things they cannot normally say. The Spirit is bigger than your attempts to fix yourself. He brings about a real change. Anybody who can change your personality is powerful!

——— Think About It ———
If you have been with Jesus, it's going to become evident
that something powerful is at work in you.

"You shall receive power when the Holy Spirit has come upon you."
Acts 1:8

ARE YOU A WITNESS?
Read It: Acts 1:8; 2:1-4

Here's a final truth to think about in relation to the Holy Spirit's power: The Spirit leads us to a powerful proclamation.

Verse 8 actually begins with a very strong contrasting word. Why? Because as we saw on Wednesday, the disciples were looking for the kingdom to be established at that moment. They wanted the kingdom to come because Jesus had said that with the kingdom would come power (Matthew 6:13). Jesus told the disciples that He was not going to give them an earthly, political kingdom at that time, but He was going to give them kingdom power, because the power of the kingdom is the Holy Spirit.

Notice that Jesus did not simply say, "You are going to witness for Me." He said, "You shall *be* My witnesses" (my emphasis). The emphasis was upon becoming something, not just doing something. If you get the being right, the doing will follow. One of the ways you know the Holy Spirit is taking over is that you are being Christian when nobody is telling you to be Christian. You are representing Jesus when nobody is telling you to represent Jesus. You are taking a stand for Christ when nobody is telling you to, because you have become His witness.

If you can go day in and day out, week in and week out, month in and month out, and never bring up the name of Jesus Christ to anyone; if you can go year in and year out without Jesus Christ radiating out from your life, then your problem is not that the church needs to come up with an evangelistic program. Your problem is that the Holy Spirit doesn't have you yet, because when the Holy Spirit gets you, a transformation occurs.

Look at Peter. When the Holy Spirit got him on the Day of Pentecost, the people thought he and the others were drunk (2:13). Not so, Peter said. Then he explained that it was the outpouring of the Spirit (v. 17).

Has anyone ever accused you of being so full of the Holy Spirit that they couldn't explain your behavior in ordinary terms? That's a charge a lot more of us Christians need to get stuck with a lot more often.

--- **Think About It** ---

You don't need more power if you have the Holy Spirit.
You just need to turn the Spirit loose.

REFLECTION

I didn't see the first *Crocodile Dundee* movie, but I remember the clip they showed when they were advertising it. Crocodile Dundee was walking down the street in New York City with his girlfriend when this guy jumps out to rob them. The thief whips out a knife and says, "Give me your money!"

The girl screams, "Be careful—he has a knife!"

You know by now that I like brothers who are cool. This brother is cool. He just smirks and says in his great accent, "That's not a knife." Homeboy reaches inside his boot and pulls out the scariest knife you've ever seen. He smiles and says, "*This* is a knife." The thief's eyes get big, and he takes off.

Why wasn't Dundee afraid? Because what would normally bring fear, a knife in your face, does not bring fear when you have something bigger and better working on the inside.

You have something bigger and better working on the inside of you, the Holy Spirit. Therefore, God does not want you to be intimidated by the world. You have the Spirit's powerful indwelling presence making you a powerful person accomplishing God's powerful kingdom program through the powerful proclamation of the Gospel.

What you need to do to unleash all this power is to pray, "Holy Spirit, I am yours. Have Your way in me. I will do what You want done the way You want it done. I will seek to glorify Christ and build God's kingdom. Be real in me because I want all of You. I give You all of me."

*"Arise, shine; for your light has come, and the glory
of the LORD has risen upon you." Isaiah 60:1*

WAKE UP, SLEEPER!
Read It: Ephesians 5:14-15

We're going to tread some familiar biblical ground this week as we study together the filling of the Holy Spirit. But let me assure you, we won't even begin to wear the subject out. These are foundational, life-changing truths. I want to remind you of them and help you make them real in your daily Christian life.

So let's begin with a simple review. If you are a believer, you have been baptized by the Spirit into the body of Christ. You are also indwelt by the Spirit, who will never leave you. These are givens for the true child of God.

But neither of these realities guarantees you all the benefits of the Spirit. The Spirit can be in you, and you can know very little of His power and influence. You can be in the environment of the Spirit and the Spirit's family, the body of Christ, and still know very little of His power and influence.

To receive the benefits, you must be filled with the Spirit.

Why is the filling of the Spirit so important? Because it is possible to be a Christian and yet be asleep—to be a Christian and yet be unable to make wise decisions. Now as we have said before, the problem here is not that you don't have the Holy Spirit. The problem is that He does not have you. The concern is not that the Spirit is not present in your life, but that you are not awake and alive to His presence.

The more consistently filled you are with the Spirit, the faster you will grow in your faith. The less filled you are, the slower will be your growth in your faith. So the fastest way to get from where you are to where you are supposed to be is to learn to live a Spirit-filled life. The absence of that means spiritual defeat and ultimately disaster.

The reason God gave us the Holy Spirit is that He knows something we tend to forget: It is impossible to live the Christian life on our own. If we could do it, we would not need the Holy Spirit.

--------- **Think About It** ---------
The purpose of the Spirit's filling is that He might become
the dominating influence in your life, that you might be
spiritually awake and wise.

*"You are not in the flesh but in the Spirit, if indeed
the Spirit of God dwells in you." Romans 8:9*

SOMEBODY TO LEAN ON
Read It: Ephesians 5:16-17

When I broke my leg playing football in 1970, they put a steel plate in my leg and wrapped it in a sixty-pound cast that reached from the bottom of my foot to my hips. They also gave me crutches, because I could not walk without something to lean on. I was too burdened down with the cast and too broken in my leg to pull off what I wanted and needed to do. I wanted to walk, and I needed to walk, but I was too weighed down.

Some of us came into the Christian life wearing a sixty-pound spiritual cast. We came into the light wanting to walk and needing to walk, but unable to walk because we were weighed down by a heavy cast. Maybe for you it was child abuse or other damaging circumstances. Maybe you grew up with parents who drank and showed you very little love.

You say, "I need to walk. I need to love. I need to keep my temper. I promised myself I wouldn't do those things, but this cast is so heavy."

Well, when God saved you, He gave you a crutch, Somebody to lean on with the strength to hold you up. That is the job of the Holy Spirit, because God is well aware of the number sin has done on you.

See, when you get saved, you do not lose the flesh. You bring it with you into the Christian life. Your flesh comes along kicking and screaming all the way. It has no intention of letting you go. In fact, you may have many of the same sinful propensities today that you had before conversion.

That's why you need to understand the will of the Lord for you (v. 17), which is to be filled with the Spirit. Your flesh has been contaminated by sin. When you come to Christ, you need supernatural help to live the Christian life.

Paul said he could find "nothing good" in his flesh (Romans 7:18). You and I have to sign our names to that one too!

——— **Think About It** ———

There is nothing in you that can enable you to live the Christian life
on your own. If you've tried it, you know what I mean.

"Walk by the Spirit, and you will not carry out
the desire of the flesh." Galatians 5:16

POWER TO PLEASE GOD
Read It: Ephesians 5:18

The Holy Spirit gives us the power to overcome the sin that we carry around within us because we still live in bodies contaminated by sin. This is the purpose of the Spirit's filling. To help you understand and appropriate the reality of this, let me make five observations about the exciting, powerful, yet often misunderstood verse we're reading today.

First, Paul is definitely talking about yielding control of your will to another. The drunk yields to alcohol. We are to yield to the Spirit. That's a big difference, but the principle is the same in each case.

Second, notice that the positive statement is a command. Paul is not saying, "If you'd like to, it would be nice if you were filled with the Spirit." He is saying that if you are going to please God, then you must be filled with His Spirit.

Third, this is a plural command. It applies to every believer. The Spirit's fullness is not for the elite few. There are Christians you may look at and say, "If I could just be like them. They love Jesus so much, and they walk so closely with Him. Why can't I be like that?" You can. The difference is the filling of the Spirit, not the fact that they have something you don't.

Fourth, this plural command is also passive. You can't fill yourself. This is the sovereign activity of the Spirit. That means your attempts to fill yourself are going to be very unfulfilling.

Fifth, this plural, passive command is also present tense, meaning it is a continuous action. You don't get filled today and expect it to cover you tomorrow, just like you don't eat Sunday dinner and expect it to carry you to next Sunday. The Holy Spirit's filling is a dynamic, moment-by-moment experience.

Why is it that way? Because we live in a world that depletes our filling. Sin depletes the filling. When you go against your conscience, it is depleted. So the Spirit's fullness is constantly being depleted, not because He is deficient, but because we are imperfect Christians who still carry the principle of sin around with us.

——— **Think About It** ———
Have you asked the Holy Spirit to fill and control
you today? He will, if that's your prayer.

"Let the word of Christ richly dwell within you . . . singing with thankfulness in your hearts to God." Colossians 3:16

EVERYDAY WORSHIP
Read It: Ephesians 5:19-21

Did you know that there's a debate about the meaning of today's verses? Many theologians and Bible teachers say these things Paul lists are the results of being filled with the Holy Spirit. Others say these verses give us the "how to" for getting filled. Now let me assure you, you can enjoy these blessings to the full whatever your view if you are filled with the Spirit. But I do think it's important to understand as best we can what's going on here.

I would like to suggest that both the "how to" and the result are present here. That is, while things like singing, giving thanks, and being subject to one another are results of the Spirit's filling, they also suggest how you get filled. I think Paul is saying that the way you get filled with the Spirit is by making worship a lifestyle. Here's what I mean.

Have you ever left church on "cloud nine"? You were full of the Lord's presence. What filled you was being in the environment of the redeemed, the family of God. What filled you was the intake of His Word, the inspiration of the music, the prayers, and all those things that add up to a worship service.

We have come to expect that kind of spiritual experience to happen only during a two-hour block of time on Sunday morning. But the way you get filled is to learn to do Monday through Saturday what you did on Sunday. The way you get filled is to make your life a worship service. That's what Paul meant in Romans 12:1-2. Read those familiar verses today and you'll see that what Paul is calling for there is actually a private worship service.

What Paul is saying is, when worship becomes a way of life, when you make this orientation to God your normal way of living, when you begin to live in the environment of the Spirit as a way of life, when you are perpetually in a mode of worship, then you cannot help but be filled with the Holy Spirit. Try it!

——————— **Think About It** ———————

God never meant for His fullness to die out by Monday morning. He meant for you to live every day in the Spirit's fullness—and you can.

"Blessed are those who hunger and thirst for righteousness,
for they shall be satisfied." Matthew 5:6

ARE YOU REALLY THIRSTY?
Read It: John 7:37-39

Only thirsty people drink. You say, "That's obvious, Tony." Well, it may be obvious, but in the spiritual realm it's important to understand. See, really thirsty people drink. They don't just talk about drinking. Many of us say, "I need to spend time with God every day." Then the next year we say, "Well, I haven't gotten around to it yet, but I need to spend time with the Lord." If you're constantly saying that, your problem is that you are not thirsty.

Alcoholics don't talk about drinking. They do some serious drinking. Jesus offered the living water of the Spirit to all who were spiritually thirsty. All they had to do was come to Him and ask, like the woman at the well (John 4:15). The way you know you are serious about the Holy Spirit is that you come. If you get thirsty enough, you will come. There must be the desire and then the action predicated on that desire.

Some Christians say devotions are so boring. They're boring because they're not a worship service. But when you come to your devotions spiritually parched and ready for the Holy Spirit to quench your thirst, your time with God will come alive. In fact, let me suggest a way to start if you have a problem being spiritually thirsty every day. Every morning when you get up, start with this simple prayer: "Lord, for the next twenty-four hours, I'm yours. Do with me whatever You want. Have Your way with me, because the only thing that matters to me for the next twenty-four hours is Your will.

"Whatever You bring to me today, I give back to you. I only ask You to remind me to consult You all through the day so that I bring the Spirit to bear on my life. I ask You to fill me with Your Spirit right now."

Start your day that way, add in a song and a few verses of Scripture, and after awhile you are going to start being late for work because the worship is so good! That's what God does when you are thirsty for Him.

--------- **Think About It** ---------
The reason many of us don't have more of the Holy Spirit's
power is that we're not yet thirsty enough to drink
of Him. How thirsty are you today?

REFLECTION

It's no coincidence that Paul follows the teaching about being filled with the Spirit with about sixteen straight verses dealing with family relationships.

The first place to apply the Spirit's filling is to the family. The problem is not opposite personalities or "irreconcilable differences." The problem is that nobody in that family has gotten drunk with the Holy Spirit yet. You say, "How's that again, Tony?"

I mean no one is willing to come under the Holy Spirit's control. The reason I know the Spirit-filled life works is not just because the Bible says it. I saw it work with a couple in our church where the wife told me, "In two months I'm gone."

So I asked her for the next two months to allow herself to be filled with the Spirit. I didn't try to change her mind or convince her to stay. I just asked her to be filled with the Spirit.

She said, "I can do that. I can't live with this man, but I will allow the Spirit to fill me." That is what she did for two months. The next time my wife and I met with this couple, they told us they were looking forward to the next twenty-five years together because God had transformed them.

They went on to tell us that some of the same problems were still there. What happened? They changed. Can I guarantee you that the filling of the Spirit will change your problems? No. But I can guarantee you that it will change *you*.

"I find then the principle that evil is present in me, the one who
wishes to do good." Romans 7:21

THIS MEANS WAR
Read It: Galatians 5:16-17

We're going to talk about the fruit of the Spirit this week, but before we can get to that, we have to do some weed-killing and cultivating. The flesh needs a job done on it, so let's begin there.

Don't misread Paul's statement about "carry[ing] out the desire of the flesh." He does not say that if you are in tune with the Spirit, you will not have fleshly desires. That is a false view of Christianity. One man told me, "I am so miserable because my flesh keeps wanting to sin." Well, he's clear on that. What is even clearer is that the flesh is unfixable. It will never change. It cannot be reformed. You can't change its nature. God has put a condemned sign on the flesh called death.

But Paul says you will not necessarily lose the desires of your flesh when you become a Christian. You aren't held guilty for having desires. The problem comes when you carry them out in illegitimate ways. The Spirit does not eradicate your fleshly desires. But He does give you the ability not to give in to those cravings.

When the Bible uses the word *flesh* in this context, it means the body contaminated by sin. Your body is not evil in and of itself, but it is like a house that is infested with roaches. We have been infested with spiritual roaches that, given the right amount of darkness, will come out of hiding.

No wonder Paul says that if you are a Christian, you live in a war zone. In fact, you *are* the war zone, pitting your unredeemed humanity against the Spirit of God. When the Spirit of God comes in, He goes to war. So if you can commit the same sins the same way you used to do when you were a sinner, it is probably because you are the same sinner you were when you were committing those sins.

One of the things the Holy Spirit does is let you know when He is ticked off. If there's a war going on inside of you, you ought to smell some smoke once in a while!

--- **Think About It** ---
If you never get a sin message from the Spirit,
you may not be plugged into the Spirit.

*"Having begun by the Spirit, are you now being
perfected by the flesh?" Galatians 3:3*

WANT TO, NOT HAVE TO
Read It: Galatians 5:18

Today's text is one of those powerful statements of Scripture you need to meditate on and enjoy for a few minutes. So that's exactly what we're going to do today.

Think about it: In the Holy Spirit, you are free from the law. Now that does not mean that law is no good. Because of all the abuses of justice today, law has gotten a bad rap. But law is good and necessary, because people are rebellious and lawless by nature. The flesh has to be restrained.

See, law isn't made for the law-abiding. If you're going the speed limit, that police officer on the side of the road isn't going to pull you over, congratulate you, and write you a thank-you ticket. He doesn't have time for that. His concern is the guy behind you who's doing seventy-five in a fifty-five-mile-an-hour zone.

His radar does not reward. It condemns, because that's what law does. So if you are trying to live your Christian life and achieve spiritual victory by keeping a set of rules, you are going to feel condemned.

If you are trying to find spiritual power in a list of do's and don'ts, you are going to be sorely disappointed. The law has no power to help you obey. All it does is give you the boundaries and the penalties for overstepping those boundaries. You're on your own after that.

But if you ever let the Holy Spirit take over in your life, He will free you from the law. He will give you the power to produce spiritual fruit and please God because you want to, not because you're afraid God will point His radar at you and pull you over.

It saddens me to see how many believers treat the Christian life like a life sentence. What an unspiritual, unfruitful way to live. The Christian life is designed to be a joy, not a load.

Paul asked the Galatians, "Having been supernaturally introduced to the Christian family by the power of the Spirit, are you now trying to be victorious by the power of your condemned humanity?" That's foolish, he says. Are you trying that same mess today? It's still foolish.

───── **Think About It** ─────

You may have burdens, but your life is not to *be* a burden.
Do you see the difference?

*"We are under obligation, not to the flesh, to live
according to the flesh." Romans 8:12*

NO PLACE TO HIDE
Read It: Galatians 5:19-21

You can know whether you are a spiritual or a fleshly Christian at any given moment. You don't have to wonder, because Paul says that if you are fleshly, everyone will know. There's no place to hide.

Today's reading is a nasty list of the flesh's dirty work, but we can't skip it, because we won't crave the fruit of the Spirit like we should until we've bit into this rotten mess. You've heard of the "dirty dozen." Well, here is the "filthy fifteen." We can divide this list into three categories of sin.

The first category has to do with morality: immorality, impurity, and sensuality. Immorality is the word *porneia*, the root of the word *pornography*. Immorality seeks to satisfy sexual cravings either by direct sexual contact or by feeding on sexual material.

Impurity has to do with your thinking. It means creating a thought life that is putrid and contaminated. Sensuality is flagrant sexual activity. Immorality can be hidden, privatized. Nobody knows it but you. Sensuality means that you have gone public. You have come out of the closet. You don't care who knows.

Paul then lists religious sin. Idolatry is worshiping other gods. Many of us go after other gods. We may even ride in them or live in them. Sorcery is *pharmakeia*, which should look familiar. It's the root of the word *pharmacy*. It had to do with the use of drugs for religious purposes. Some Bible versions translate it "witchcraft."

The third category is relational sins. The list is long and painfully familiar. Take "outbursts of anger," for example. "I just lost my temper!" Really? How about "disputes, dissensions, [and] factions"? "We can't get along!" The reason is one or both of you are operating in the flesh. Your conflict is a spiritual issue. It's not just about personalities.

Then Paul says, "There's a lot more, but I'm out of ink." Me too, at least for today. Suffice it to say your flesh has more ways to sin than you'd ever believe. Are you making it easier for the flesh to do its stuff? As Dr. Howard Hendricks used to tell us in seminary, "Cut it out!"

———— Think About It ————
This list is just a small taste of the deeds of the flesh.
That's why you have to walk in the Spirit. Any questions?

"Every good tree bears good fruit."
Matthew 7:17

SWEET STUFF
Read It: Galatians 5:22-23

What a relief to put a lid on those bad-smelling works of the flesh and get to the sweet stuff: the fruit of the Holy Spirit. You've probably heard a hundred sermons on this topic, so today let me just mention three characteristics of fruit. The first is that fruit is visible, just like the works of the flesh. Watch out for the tree in your backyard that is giving you invisible fruit.

The second characteristic of fruit is that it always reflects the character of the tree on which it grows. If it's an apple tree, you're going to have apples. If it's an orange grove, you'll see oranges on the tree. The fruit that comes out of a life controlled by the Spirit will reflect the character of Jesus Christ.

Third, fruit is always borne for someone else's benefit. You never see fruit chewing on itself. Any fruit that jumps up and says, "I don't want to be picked. I don't even want to be touched. Just let me hang here," is going to rot after awhile. Good fruit makes somebody want to take a bite of it.

The Holy Spirit wants to produce His fruit in you so that your children and your spouse can take a bite out of your life. Fruit exists for the benefit of another.

In contrast, all deeds of the flesh are selfish. The flesh says, "You made me mad. I'm not happy. You have what I want. You are irritating me."

But the fruit of the Spirit is God-centered and other-directed. The word is singular even though Paul lists nine kinds of spiritual fruit, because they all grow from the same tree. This is a special kind of tree. It can produce everything you need for every area of your life.

In other words, you don't have to go to the Holy Spirit for your religion and then to someone else for joy. You don't have to go to the Spirit for peace and then to some other place for love. You don't have to go to the Holy Spirit for patience and to somebody else for self-control. It's all on the Spirit's tree.

How's your fruit growing today?

--- **Think About It** ---

You know you are in the flesh if you are at the center of the program.

"Our old self was crucified with [Christ] . . . that we should no longer be slaves to sin." Romans 6:6

INSIST ON IT
Read It: Galatians 5:24-25

When I was growing up in Baltimore, I would play in front of the fire hydrant. My father explained to me that underneath the ground, that hydrant was connected to a dam that had more water than I could ever use. So as long as there was that unseen connection, there would always be an outflow from the hydrant.

All you are is a hydrant. The Holy Ghost is the dam. As long as you keep the connection tight, the water will continue to flow. So if you are living by the flesh and not by the Spirit, there must be damage in the underground pipe. How do you get the flow going again?

Paul gives us two analogies. Verse 24 talks about crucifying the flesh. If you belong to Christ, you have been crucified with Him (Galatians 2:20). Since Christ is the victor over sin and the grave by His resurrection, and since you are raised with Him, you are already on the victor's side.

The second analogy is a familiar one by now, that of walking by the Spirit. Walking implies first that you are going somewhere. Our destination is the will of God. Walking also assumes continuous movement. If a baby trips, he gets back up. We don't condemn a baby for falling down. But something is wrong if he doesn't try to get up again. If you blow it, don't stay there. Get up and start moving again. Finally, walking involves dependence. To walk, you have to place your weight on your feet and depend on your legs and feet to hold you up.

You say, "How do I know when I'm depending on God?" Simple answer: prayer. That's why Paul said to pray without ceasing. Bring everything you face to the Lord. Prayer is like breathing. Stop doing it, and you die.

You say, "It's hard to pray." Well, I grew up with a bad case of asthma. It was hard to breathe. But I can assure you that I insisted on it even though my bronchial tubes were congested. I never thought about not trying to breathe.

When sin congests us, it's hard to pray. But you must insist on it. Stop praying, and the flow stops.

--------- **Think About It** ---------

Get those tubes cleared up and keep praying.
Keep that connection to the Spirit flowing freely.

REFLECTION

Consider Galatians 6:8-9 for a few minutes with me: "For the one who sows to his own flesh shall from the flesh reap corruption, but the one who sows to the Spirit shall from the Spirit reap eternal life. And let us not lose heart in doing good, for in due time we shall reap if we do not grow weary."

Paul says if you want to understand the spiritual life, look at farming. The principle of sowing and reaping is simple. What you sow is what you get. If you sow fleshly seeds, you will reap a harvest of fleshly deeds.

So if there is a lack of spiritual fruit in your life, it's because there has been a lack of sowing to the Spirit. But you can turn that around starting this weekend. You can begin sowing seeds that will produce the sweet fruit of the Spirit.

And the beautiful thing about sowing is that you always get back more than you put in. So the apostle encourages you not to grow weary of sowing righteousness, because when harvesttime comes, you are going to reap a voluptuous return on your investment.

It's true that you can't pull up what you have already sown. You may have blown it spiritually, but the Holy Spirit knows how to plow up that field. He knows how to prepare the ground and turn over the soil so you can sow new seeds in the same soil.

So I urge you, let the Holy Spirit do some plowing and soil preparation on your heart. At harvesttime, you'll be glad you did.

"You have not received a spirit of slavery
leading to fear again." Romans 8:15

YOU'RE FREE
Read It: Galatians 5:1

We've got a great subject to end our study of the Holy Spirit with: His freedom. Slavery is not a very exciting position to be in, whether it's social, political, economic, or personal slavery. The Holy Spirit has come to make people free. The good news of the presence of the Spirit of God is that He is the Emancipator. His job is to set you free from those things that hold you in bondage.

Today's text states a central truth about spiritual freedom. God did not set you free so you could become a slave again. He did not release you so that you could be bound by sin once more.

In the case of the Galatian believers, some who followed Paul were trying to enslave the people to the old Jewish religious standards such as circumcision. This was serious stuff, as we'll see tomorrow, because it threatened the Galatians' faith in Christ and their dependence on Him alone for salvation.

This wasn't a difference of opinion over the color of carpet in the sanctuary. It was a battle for the spiritual freedom Jesus Christ paid a heavy price to procure and Paul paid a heavy price to proclaim.

Paul is so emphatic on the necessity of spiritual freedom that the way he states the truth almost sounds like a redundancy: "It was for freedom that Christ set us free." In other words, when He set you free, He intended you to stay free.

So if you are a Christian and you are in slavery today, you have a fundamental misunderstanding of what happened at the Cross. Now I need to remind you that freedom never means being free to do what you want. Freedom means that God has liberated us to fulfill the purposes for which He saved us.

Suppose a fish said, "I want to be free. Get me out of this water. I want to roam with the lions." So we "liberate" the fish from the river. He may be free of the water, but he will also be dead. Freedom for God's creation means fulfilling His purposes—and that includes you and me.

——— Think About It ———
If Christ set you free, why are you still wearing those chains on your mind or attitudes or actions or whatever is binding you?

"For we through the Spirit, by faith, are waiting for the hope
of righteousness." Galatians 5:5

DON'T CUT THE SUPPLY LINE
Read It: 2 Corinthians 3:17; Galatians 5:2-5

Whenever the Holy Spirit shows up, He brings freedom with Him. So if you are indwelt by the Spirit, yet you are all bound up, the Spirit is not having free rein in your life for some reason.

See, when you do not have God's rules as the guidelines for life and you do not have God's Spirit as your source of power to live life, you will be somebody's slave. The psychological term for it may be co-dependency or something else, but at bottom it is some form of spiritual slavery.

For the Galatians, the issue of Spirit-given freedom was very real. They had people in town trying to put them back into spiritual slavery. Paul thought it was serious enough that he said if they yielded, Christ would no longer benefit them.

In fact, he went on to say that if they gave up their freedom, the supply line of grace that gave them the ability to be all that God wanted them to be would be cut. This is serious stuff. Paul is saying that the Spirit's power to be what God has created you to be is cut off if you allow something else to bring you into bondage.

As we said yesterday, freedom doesn't mean living without rules. It means living under the rules of the Holy Spirit, which are liberating rather than confining. You may not be living freely, but if you are a Christian, you are free.

Today's verse gives the bottom line of this matter. Freedom comes when the Holy Spirit is at work in your life. The Galatians needed to be reminded of that, and so do we. It's like having to remind yourself sometimes that you are married. You may not feel married, but the fact is that if you stood before a preacher and exchanged vows with your mate, you are married. Now the question is, how much are you going to enjoy your relationship?

If you are in bondage to anyone or anything today, it is because the Holy Spirit has not been allowed to set you free. Claim your freedom in Him and drop those chains.

─────── **Think About It** ───────

If somebody else is playing God in your life, you can bet your
bottom dollar that God is not being God in your life.

"Do not turn your freedom into an opportunity for the flesh, but through love serve one another." Galatians 5:13

FREE TO SERVE
Read It: Romans 6:17-18; Galatians 5:13

Jesus Christ looked down through history and saw you trapped in sin and death and paid the price to set you free—free to become His slave, the greatest freedom of all.

You've heard it said that we are saved to serve. Well, that also applies to the freedom we have in the Holy Spirit. I remember as I was growing up, our family could not go to movies. When my father got saved, one of the things he cut out was movies. We couldn't go no matter how harmless the movie.

Now that bothered me because they came out with a movie called *Zorro* that I wanted to see because my boy had that black hat on with the cape and stuff. He was cool. So I snuck out to see *Zorro*. But I did sit in the back of the theater so that if it caught on fire, I would be able to get out.

Today I feel the freedom to go to a legitimate movie. My father is still not free to go to movies. I can't impose my freedom on him. I can't say because I'm free in an area that something is wrong with you if you aren't.

See, if God has not set my father free to attend a movie, but he goes because I put pressure on him, Paul says I am misusing my freedom to cause another brother to sin. We cannot sit in judgment on other people's convictions.

Some of us look at the things other people do or say or the way they dress and assume they must think they are really something. But you and I are not God, so we don't know who thinks what. We usually get into trouble when we start sitting in judgment on matters of conviction or opinion. Now that does not mean we suspend all judgment. God's guidelines are clear, so we're not talking about being open and accepting of everything.

Some clothes are immodest. Some movies are unfit because they are designed to produce lust. We can speak to matters like these. But we are not to wield our freedom like a club to knock other people into line with our thinking. That's not using our freedom to serve each other.

———— **Think About It** ————
We are free to serve, not to flaunt our freedom
and stifle someone else's spiritual growth.

"If therefore the Son shall make you free,
you shall be free indeed." John 8:36

FREE FOR SURE
Read It: Romans 8:1-2

One of the things the Holy Spirit has set us free from is the bondage of the flesh. In Romans 7 Paul described the onslaught of the flesh that sought to bring him under its control.

But then in chapter 8 he makes this great declaration of freedom. The flesh no longer has a vise-lock on you. If you know Jesus Christ, a new person has been placed inside your old flesh. You are a new person, but you are a new person living in an old house—your flesh, your body that has become so contaminated by sin that God views it as worm food. We've already seen that the flesh is bound for the scrap heap, but it's going down kicking and screaming.

Praise God, then, that although we are still living in this old prison-house of our flesh, we don't have to be its prisoner. The Holy Spirit has set us free from the law of sin and death. I have been liberated from having to follow my passions. I am not perfect. I fail, just as you do, but we no longer have to be in slavery to the flesh.

But don't get the big head about your freedom, because Paul reminds us in 2 Corinthians 4:7, "We have this treasure in earthen vessels, that the surpassing greatness of the power may be of God and not from ourselves." This is God's work.

When we try to get free in our own power, there isn't much to draw on. So we stay in bondage. That's why, for example, Christian counseling has to be more than helping people understand the history and causes of their problem.

If you come to me as your pastor, and I don't help you understand how the Spirit works in freeing you from your problem, how you are to walk in the Spirit, what it means to depend on the Spirit, and how you appropriate the Spirit's power, then I am asking you to use your human resources to solve a problem you can't solve.

The "law of sin and of death" is so strong the only thing that can break it is the "law of the Spirit of life."

——— **Think About It** ———
You are free not because of you, but because
there is a greater Power at work in you.

"The kingdom of God is not eating and drinking, but righteousness and peace and joy in the Holy Spirit." Romans 14:17

DYING TO PLEASE
Read It: Romans 14:1-8

Let me give you one more thing the Holy Spirit sets us free from: the expectations of others. Paul says that in God's kingdom, freedom comes from what God tells you on the inside, not what people tell you on the outside. We spend so much time worrying about what people want that we never get around to what God wants. With apologies to Barbra Streisand, people who need people in this way are the unluckiest people in the world.

Don't get me wrong. God expects us to be people-lovers, but He does not want us to be people-pleasers. Your first responsibility is to please the Lord, not the crowd. But we work so hard to gain acceptance from men that we lose acceptance from God. If that happens, there is no power, because the Spirit of God is only here to glorify Christ.

In the early days of my ministry, people-pleasing was a major concern. I could pull it off because there were only about twenty-five people. But as the church grew, people-pleasing became tougher. There were a lot more people to try and please. I was wearing myself out trying to please everyone when the Lord hit me with this one: "I have already died for them, Evans. You don't need to kill yourself for them too."

See, as a servant of Christ, I stand or fall to Him (v. 4). So do you. As I said, this doesn't mean we aren't to love people or that we're free to trample on their feelings and sensitivities. On the contrary, we are to accept one another with all of our foibles.

But if I'm going to do the job God called me to do, I have to be free from unrealistic human expectations. Paul goes on in Romans 14 to say that each one of us will give an account of himself to God, not to each other (v. 12).

When God has spoken, we need to move. This is why we are not to sit in judgment on one another. Listen, if God is in something, He is able to make His people stand whether we think they are able or not.

——— **Think About It** ———
Psalm 130:3 reminds us that if God kept score
on our sins, none of us would be left standing.

REFLECTION

Would you like a new taste of the Spirit's freedom? Let me suggest three steps to take.

First of all, you have to believe God's promise of freedom in John 8:36. You have to believe you are free and come out of the cage.

In other words, there has to be a change in your mind. You need to begin to think like a free person so you can walk like a free person. If you are bound, begin now telling yourself what God told you to tell yourself, that you are free. That's not the power of positive thinking. That's the power of *biblical* thinking. You are only telling yourself what God says about you.

Second, commit yourself to discipleship. You can only be free when you are fully committed to Christ's calling for your life, which is to follow Him. If you compromise on this, you will never be free. God will not free you up to half-step on Him. He will only free you if all of you belongs to all of Him.

Third, forgive somebody you need to forgive so God can set you free by forgiving you. Write that person a letter or make a call. Tell that person what you have been holding against him or her, and explain that your unforgiveness has you in bondage. Then tell that person you are freeing him or her from the offense so God can free you.

By the time you put the letter in the mailbox or dial the number, your burden will lift, and you'll be free.

Christ has set you free. Stop being a slave!

ELEVEN

◇

MIND & FEET IN GEAR

The Importance of Your Thinking & Commitments

A popular piece of advice these days tells us, "Get a life." Well, that's not a bad idea. God wants us to get a life—the life of Christ lived out through our minds and our bodies. But if we're going to be like Christ, we have to learn to think like Him and make the right kind of commitments. So let's explore how to get a Christian mind and then talk about how to put that Christian mind to work in the commitments we make.

"Be renewed in the spirit of your mind." Ephesians 4:23

NEW SOFTWARE
Read It: Romans 8:5-7; 12:1-2

"God gave you a brain. Use it."

How many times have you heard that? Well, it's about half right. God is concerned that you use your mind. But He's even more concerned about *how* you use your mind. He wants you to think from a divine frame of reference: a Christ-centered, Bible-centered way of thinking about every facet of life.

God wants to make sure that when you log onto the computer of your mind, the software you use is drawn from His Word. Paul calls it having the mind of Christ. For this week and next, we want to talk about how to develop and use a thoroughly Christian—that is, Christlike—mind.

Now, theologically speaking, we have an immediate problem, because the human mind in its natural state is as far from this ideal as the east is from the west. We learned in our last segment that these earthly bodies, our flesh, are destined for worm food because they are so contaminated by sin that God is going to discard them and give us new ones.

Well, our minds are part of that old makeup. They are corrupted by sin, but since we have to use them between now and the grave, God has undertaken a reclamation project for our thinking processes.

As redeemed people, we are to renew our minds after the mind of Christ and not after the pattern of this world. The reason Christianity is in such weak condition today is that the minds of Christians have become obsessed with a way of thinking foreign to the kingdom of God.

Romans 12 makes it clear that we need renewed minds. But they only come by the presentation of our bodies as living sacrifices to God and by a determination not to conform to this world.

If we are going to think Christianly, we've got some work to do. A recent awarding-winning book goes by the title *The Scandal of the Evangelical Mind.* It laments the lack of critical thinking among God's people and the lack of the will to do the work of thinking. Are you thinking like Christ today? Are you using the mind He gave you?

--- **Think About It** ---

If you are thinking worldly thoughts, don't be surprised
that you begin living a worldly life.

"You shall love the Lord your God . . . with all your mind."
Matthew 22:37

DUPES OR DISCIPLES?
Read It: Colossians 2:8-10

The problem with the human mind is not just that in its natural or unconverted state, the mind is contrary to God. That's bad enough. But there's also a cosmic battle being waged for the control of your mind. This world, under the control of Satan, is filled with every kind of "philosophy and empty deception" imaginable—and people by the millions are buying into these false systems. But Satan isn't satisfied with that. He's also after the minds of believers.

Now he knows he can't mess with our salvation, because we are secure in Christ. But if the Devil can mess with our minds and get us thinking like pagans, he can render us useless in our impact for Christ.

Let me give an example of how hard Satan is working to capture people's minds. Someone has pointed out that although the New Age movement has no world headquarters, no full-time missionaries on the field, and no coherent organization, it is attracting disciples at a dizzying rate.

Now we know that the New Age philosophy is about as mindless and silly as any "ism" going. Pay a few hundred bucks and learn how to be your own God. So if it's so mindless, why are millions of people flocking to New Age teaching? Who's behind it? I'll give you one guess. No human is smart enough to pull this off.

That's a good example of what passes for thinking out there in the world. But look whom we have to pattern our minds after: Jesus Christ, "the fulness of Deity . . . the head over all rule and authority" (vv. 9-10). Because He is complete, we are complete in Him—including our minds. Everything you need to develop a Christlike mind, you will find in Him.

The problem with many of us is that we are listening to John and Joe and whomever instead of to Jesus. When we stand before Christ, some of us will have to say, "Well, John told me . . ." To which Jesus will answer, "John's not even up here. What were you doing listening to him?" So I ask you the question I ask myself: Are we going to be Satan's dupes or Jesus' disciples?

─────── **Think About It** ───────

If you've ever wondered why you need to develop a Christian mind,
Colossians 2:8 should answer your question.

"Even when we were dead in our transgressions,
[God] made us alive together with Christ." Ephesians 2:5

KEEP LOOKING UP
Read It: Colossians 2:12-13; 3:1

We've said it a hundred different ways this year, but it keeps coming up in every topic we study: We are new people, completely new creations, in Christ Jesus. This is such a radical concept that the Bible speaks of it as nothing less than a death, burial, and resurrection.

Okay, that's our Theology 101 lesson for today. The question God's Word wants us to pursue is, what are the implications of our new identity? How should new creations in Christ look, act, and think? To help answer that last point, we will turn to Colossians 3 today and tomorrow.

Notice the command here in verse 1: "Keep seeking the things above." Why? Because that's where our life is. Since we died and rose with Christ, we're now citizens of heaven. And even though we may not arrive there for a few more decades, we need to take our mental cues from above.

What this verse tells us is that to develop a Christian mind, we have to shift our focus from earth to heaven. Now I know some preachers have used verses like this to tell people not to worry about anything on earth and just to think about the glories of heaven all day long.

That's not what Paul is saying. He's not concerned about teaching you how to live in heaven. That will take care of itself when you get there. Paul is teaching you how to live on earth with a renewed mind.

What this verse is saying is: "Take a good look at heaven so you will know how to live and think heavenly on earth." So if you are going to live and think heavenly in a hellish world, you've got to have heavenly software teaching your earthly computer, your mind, how to think.

Why should you keep looking up? Because that's where Christ is, seated at the Father's right hand in the place of honor, dignity, and authority. That means when you seek to think like Jesus Christ, you are seeking that which God honors and which pleases Him, because God honors His well-pleasing Son above all.

——— Think About It ———

Do you take your cues on how to think from the "tube" or the temple in heaven? Are you listening to Jerry or Jesus, to Sally or the Son of God?

"We are taking every thought captive to the obedience of Christ."
2 Corinthians 10:5

NO LOOSE THOUGHTS
Read It: Colossians 3:2-4

Did you know that Jesus Christ doesn't even want you to think apart from Him and His will? Pardon the pun, but you may need to think about that statement for a minute. If I read the Apostle Paul correctly, that's exactly what the verse above means. Our thoughts are not to run loose like a bunch of animals suddenly let out of their cages at the zoo.

After all, when do most of us get into trouble spiritually? Well, I don't know about you, but for many of the people I've talked with and counseled over the years, the problem started in the mind when they let their thoughts get out of control, and their actions followed.

That's not thinking with a disciplined mind. When Paul advises you to "set your mind on the things above," he's calling you to focus your attention and place your affections on the things of heaven.

Now this does not mean going around in a kind of hazy emotional cloud. Remember, we're talking about developing a Christian mind. We're talking about solid thinking, not tiptoeing through the tulips. This calls for a decision of the will and a determination of the heart to seek the mind of Christ. He's why we are to set our minds on heavenly things. Heaven is where He is, so if we're going to think like Christ, we had better be sitting at His feet, figuratively speaking, listening to Him.

How do you make that practical? One of our church members once asked, "Suppose you are a new Christian, and you don't know what the Bible says about a subject on which you need the mind of Christ?"

My answer was simply this: You track down the mind of Christ either through your own Bible study or through the teaching and guidance of others who you know look at life from a divine perspective. What I am saying is that the mind of Christ is not some elusive, cosmic force. Do you have a Bible lying near you right now? Does the Holy Spirit indwell you as your Teacher and Illuminator? Then you can know the mind of Christ!

--------- **Think About It** ---------
There's nothing more dangerous than a loose thought rolling
around in your head like a loose cannon on the deck of a ship.
Bring every thought captive to Christ.

*"He who is spiritual appraises all things, yet he himself is
appraised by no man."* 1 Corinthians 2:15

HOW'S YOUR THINKING?
Read It: Genesis 13:1-18

If you read the suggested Scripture passage for today, you might think
we forgot the topic at hand. No, actually I wanted you to see the process
we've been talking about fleshed out in real life. The story of Abram and
Lot and the choices they made regarding the land is a great example of
the principle Paul enunciates in 1 Corinthians 2:15.

Abram (still his name at this stage in his life) is the classic example of
a spiritual man, and this account is a classic example of a spiritual man
appraising—sifting, processing, understanding—a major decision from
a spiritual mind-set. Abram exhibits the mind of Christ.

You may remember the story. Abram and Lot were both wealthy men
whose herds grew so large they couldn't occupy the same space. Their
servants started fighting, so Abram offered Lot the opportunity to take
first choice of the available land.

Now what's interesting here is that Abram was the older man and had
the larger herds. He could have insisted on first choice. But what did he
do? He used a thought process just like the one Jesus Christ used centuries later in His earthly life and death. That is, Abram did not simply
look out for his own interests, but for the interests of others (see
Philippians 2:4), in this case his relative Lot. Abram appraised the situation from a spiritual perspective—and I have no doubt that Lot didn't
understand Abram's thinking. The spiritual person understands all things,
Paul says, but nobody can figure him out because he doesn't act "normal."

So Lot made the choice that took him toward Sodom, and today you
won't find anything left of Lot's land but ashes. But Abraham's land is still
around. You can even visit it if you wish.

The point is, the problem was not money. The problem was perspective. Lot wanted to settle down in close proximity to the world, and the
world devoured him. In fact, I believe that even if Lot had made the opposite choice, Abram wouldn't have headed toward Sodom, because he knew
it was bad news. He saw with spiritual eyes and thought with a spiritual
mind. What about you?

——— **Think About It** ———
Is your thinking spiritual . . . or predictable?

REFLECTION

Is Jesus Christ your life these days?

What I'm asking is not just whether you have accepted Him as your Savior. I mean does He dominate and possess your thoughts?

How do you know when someone is your life? When you think about that person all the time. When you can't get him or her off your mind no matter what you're doing.

If Jesus Christ is truly your life, that means when you open your eyes in the morning, your first thought is what He wants from you that day. It means that as you encounter various situations during the day, you are thinking, *What is the mind of Christ for this situation?* And it means you end your day with thanksgiving to Him.

It's Jesus in the morning, Jesus at noon, Jesus in the evening. It's being possessed by the mind of Christ.

Now you may call that fanaticism if you like, but everyone is fanatical about something. Some people are fanatical about their business or their money. Others are fanatical about that special someone. And, of course, still others are sports "fan"atics.

So don't get overly worried that someone might call you a fanatic if you get your mind saturated with Jesus. You aren't doing anything the world wouldn't do when it comes to getting fanatical about something it believes in. You're just getting fanatical about the right thing!

"We have the mind of Christ." 1 Corinthians 2:16

GOD'S BUTTERFLY
Read It: Colossians 3:5-6

This week we want to look at some very practical ways that having the mind of Christ should impact our lives. Usually when you start talking about setting your mind on heavenly things, someone objects, "If you do that, you become so heavenly minded you're no earthly good."

No, the idea is to become heavenly informed so you can become some good on earth. Our problem today is not heavenly minded Christians who are no earthly good. Our problem is Christians who are so earthly minded they are no heavenly good—people so obsessed with this world's way of thinking that they do not bring heaven's perspective to bear on life.

Now we've explained that you have died to the old you. The butterfly has been set free. You must no longer hang out in "Caterpillarville." You are now set free to roam the heavens as God's butterfly. Your job is to "consider" this as so (v. 5), to realize that you are now dead. Dead to what? Dead to your old life, which includes the unsavory list that follows in verse 5.

What does Paul mean when he says these things amount to idolatry? Because whenever you serve immorality, impurity, passion, evil desires, or greed, you have made those things your god because you have placed yourself under their control. You do not need to worship a wooden carving to be an idolater. All you need to do is serve and give yourself to something other than the true God.

Instead, your mind needs to inform your body that it no longer has to serve these gods. Why? Because God is going to judge those who do these things. Why would you want to hang out where judgment is about to fall?

If you knew there was going to be a drug raid at a certain location at 3:00 A.M., you'd be a fool to be there at that hour. You need to be as far away from that place as you can get. The same thing is true if you want to be governed by the mind of Christ. "Consider" yourself dead and run as far away as possible from the deeds of the flesh.

——— **Think About It** ———
Whenever you say, "I can't help myself," you're saying
that this thing controls your being. And if it controls your
being, it has become your god.

"You were formerly darkness, but now you are light in the Lord;
walk as children of light." Ephesians 5:8

DITCH THOSE SMELLY CLOTHES
Read It: Colossians 3:7-11

Remember what it was like before you were a Christian? If you were like most nonbelievers, it was no big deal to think what you wanted to think and be as greedy or lustful or whatever as you wanted to be. You could say like a lot of people, "There are three important folks in my life: me, myself, and I."

But if you know Christ, you have been called to consider a new reality. You are not the same person, and therefore you don't have to do the same things you used to do. You have the mind of Christ.

Now in theology there is positional truth and practical truth. Positional truth refers to your state before God. Practical truth refers to your lifestyle in light of your state. The Bible calls us to act like the children of God we are. We have the mind of Christ, so let's use it.

When I used to jog, I would get up early, hit the road, and run for about five and a half miles. By the end I was drenched with sweat. You really wouldn't have wanted to keep close company with me at that moment. So I would go home and take a shower. I would wash off all the stench and come out smelling good. Now I would have been foolish to put my smelly jogging clothes back on. It would be illogical. What sense would it make to spend time getting clean, only to go back into the dirt from whence I was cleansed?

Let me tell you, if I had come out of the bathroom in my jogging clothes, Lois would have rejected me. Our fellowship would have been seriously interrupted. Why? Because the purpose of the shower was to wash me and introduce me to clean clothes. The Bible says that when you met Jesus, you were washed. You were made pure, and all of your unrighteousness was removed. How can you then go back and put on the dirty clothes of your old self again? It doesn't make sense. That's the point Paul wants you to get. Got it?

--------- **Think About It** ---------
When you and I got cleaned up by Christ, He also washed away
those old distinctions by which we used to judge each
other (v. 11). We all look the same in Him. Got it?

"With humility of mind let each of you regard one another as more important than himself." Philippians 2:3

SET APART FOR GOD
Read It: Colossians 3:12-14

If you are going to use the Christian mind you already possess, if you are going to reflect the mind of Christ, you must understand what it means to be holy. A lot of people are afraid of that word. It means to be set apart. For the Christian, being holy means being set apart by God for His purposes.

Our church used to meet in a school building. That building was holy on Sunday, set apart for God's use. When people walked through the doors on Sunday, they had to change their thinking about that building, because it was not the same place even though it was the same building.

Why? Because it was set apart. It was holy. In the Old Testament, they set everything apart to God. That's why when people ask me to dedicate their children, I have to explain what that means. It means they are committing to raise their children a certain way because the children have been set apart for divine purposes.

One way you know you are acting on your new identity in Christ and thinking with His mind is the way you treat others in His body ("one another," v. 13). If you are a hateful Christian, an unforgiving Christian, you don't know who you are.

That's why Paul says you need to "put on love" (v. 14) the way you would get dressed in the morning. If you had lived in Jesus' day, you would have put on a robe over your undergarments and then tied a girdle or a belt around it. Everything was held together by the belt.

That's the picture Paul had in mind when he said, "Make sure you are wearing love, because it holds everything else together." I see two extremes in many churches: truth without love, and love without truth.

If you have truth without love, you've got haughty, proud people who brag about how much they know. But if you have love without truth, some of the people who love will hate the people who don't love, but who defend the truth. You must have truth with love, because love binds everything together.

───── **Think About It** ─────

If you're a Christian, everything in your life is supposed
to be holy, set apart by God for His use.

"Let the peace of Christ rule in your hearts." Colossians 3:15

YOUR UMPIRE
Read It: Colossians 3:15-16

If you are walking in obedience to God, one of the benefits He gives you is peace. Now I don't mean circumstantial peace. You are never going to have 100 percent circumstantial peace. I'm talking about inner contentment and calm despite circumstances.

If you don't have that peace, something is wrong in your walk with the Lord. It's a red flag. See, the mind of Christ is one in which His peace rules. He says, "Peace should rule." The word for *rule* means umpire. What does an umpire do in a baseball game? He calls the game. He tells you whether you are safe or out. He calls the shots. Let the peace of God call the shots in your life. Let His peace be your umpire.

Sounds great, doesn't it? But how do you keep the peace of God ruling in your heart? The answer is in verse 16: "Let [an act of the will] the word of Christ [the Word of God, the Bible] richly [abundantly] dwell within you."

The key word is *dwell*. It means to be at home. See, some of us have this kind of relationship with the Word: "Word of God, you can visit me on Sunday at church. You can visit me on Monday evening in my family life. But in my work life, Word of God, the door is locked. And, Word of God, don't start telling me how to think. I keep my mind to myself. After all, as long as I only think it, I'm not hurting anyone."

But God is saying, "I want access to the whole house, including your mind. I want to make My Word at home in your heart. I want My Word to dwell in you abundantly. I want it to rule. Don't shut out My Word."

Notice how the daily operation of God's Word involves the mind: "With all wisdom teaching and admonishing one another." The Psalms contain those life situations we need to think about. "Hymns and spiritual songs" are directed toward God and toward one another in His name.

If you want God's peace to rule you, get His mind by letting His Word rule you.

--------- **Think About It** ---------

Do you have a private room in your heart where you say, "Word of God, I don't let anyone in that room"? If so, don't expect God's peace.

"Whether, then, you eat or drink or whatever you do, do all to the glory of God." 1 Corinthians 10:31

IN THE NAME OF
Read It: Colossians 3:17

Most of us end our prayers with these words: "In Jesus' name, amen." You need to understand what God's name means. It is not a magical phrase. God's name is special. Jesus taught us to pray, "Our Father who art in heaven, hallowed be Thy name" (Matthew 6:9).

In the Bible, a person's name wasn't just something to distinguish one person from another. A name was a reflection of the person's character. For example, *Elohim* is the Creator, the God who said, "Let there be," and there was. *Yahweh* is the covenant-keeping name of God. That's the God who makes a promise and does not back away from it. That's the God you can depend on. One day you might call God *El Shaddai,* the "Lord God Almighty." That's the God who does whatever He wants to do.

So when you talk about the name of God, you are talking about more than just a name. You are talking action. You are talking power. You are talking authority. But God only lends His name to those things that are in harmony with His character.

So when Paul tells us to do everything "in the name of the Lord Jesus," he means make sure Jesus okays it. The only way you can know what Jesus will approve of is by having His mind.

A lot of people are doing a lot of things they didn't get God's okay to do. Have you got God's approval for what you're doing? Not if you are living in sin, you haven't. If you are greedy, you didn't get the okay to put Jesus' name on that. If you are immoral, you didn't get approval for that from Jesus. If you are unloving to your wife, you didn't get that from Jesus.

See, the Bible can tell you to live a new life because there is a new you. When you said yes to Christ, you got a new mind. Now you can say yes to the new and no to the old. You have the ability to do whatever you do in the name of Christ.

——— **Think About It** ———

If you're using God's name the way He meant it to be used, you're only using it to help you do the things that please Him.

REFLECTION

One of the biggest lies we all tell is when people come over for a visit or a meal and we say, "Please make yourself at home."

Now I know we want to make our guests feel comfortable, and there are little social niceties we repeat. But when we say, "Make yourself at home," there's a lot we *don't* mean by that.

You don't mean, for example, that your guests are free to go into your bedroom and closet and see what's there. They can't open your desk and read your personal papers. That's not what you mean by making themselves at home.

You also don't mean that your guests can take off their shoes and socks and prop their feet up on the table. So when you tell people to make themselves at home, you don't mean, "Take over my house as though it were your own and do whatever you want to do."

But guess what? That's exactly what God wants to do when you invite His Word to make itself at home in your heart. The Word wants to visit your bedroom, look in your closet, read your letters, and check out your bank balance. Your response is to let the Word of God invade every crevice of your life.

I'm convinced that many Christians don't come to church more often because they don't want the Word of God to get too personal. They don't want it getting into their business.

What about you? Is the Word free to inspect every nook and cranny of your heart? Is it free to critique your mind? I pray that it is, because otherwise you'll never really know what it means to function with the mind of Christ.

*"Trust in the LORD with all your heart, and do not lean
on your own understanding." Proverbs 3:5*

YOUR GOLIATH
Read It: 1 Samuel 17:26-27

What is your Goliath today? Maybe it's that marriage you can't get together. Maybe the Goliath staring you in the face today is financial pressure that seems insurmountable. Whatever it is, Goliath is always scary, and not just because he's so huge. He's also intimidating, daring you to do anything about your problem.

Have you ever felt as if a problem was talking to you? "I dare you to try to solve me. I'm too big for you. I'll take you down." Well, if you haven't met a Goliath yet, you will. So this week I want to give you some biblical armor you can put on the next time you meet a giant. I want to talk about the power of a total commitment to God. I want you to see what the mind of Christ looks like in action as we walk in the sandals of David.

David was not on the battle line when Israel squared off against the Philistines. He was back home with the sheep. His older brothers were part of the army. You can refresh your memory on the details of the story by reading verses 1-25.

But David was there when Goliath showed up for about the eightieth time (v. 16) to defy Israel and God. Israel couldn't send anyone out to fight him and defend God's honor because this was strictly a volunteer operation. So on the day David was present, Goliath issued his challenge.

Now everyone had heard him, but David heard him in a way that ticked him off. Here is the first key to the power that comes from commitment. All that the Israelites saw was Goliath. But David said, "Wait a minute! This man is coming out threatening God's people. He is uncircumcised [meaning that he had no part with God's people and God's privileges]. Our God is not on this man's side. He is with His circumcised people Israel. That's us!"

David was saying, "God is alive, right? We are God's circumcised people, right? God has made His covenant with us, right? Then let's go." Are you a part of God's people? Then your problem is not too big, right?

——— **Think About It** ———
Goliath was nine feet, nine inches. How tall is your God?
You only have power when you are able to measure the size of
your God against the size of your problem.

"Commit your way to the LORD, trust also in Him,
and He will do it." Psalm 37:5

BIG BROTHER
Read It: 1 Samuel 17:28-30

Did you know there are some people out there who don't want to see you carry out your commitment to God and tap into His power? You can see this very clearly in today's reading, an interesting exchange between David and his older brother Eliab. David was only in the camp because Jesse had sent him there with food for Eliab and David's other brothers. And David was only upset about Goliath's challenge because Goliath was making God look bad.

But Eliab wasn't plugged into any of that. So he challenged David. "Now, boy, you know you belong with those sheep. Leave this mess to the men. What are you doing down here anyway? You and I know that you think you are something. You think you can do a lot. I remember when you were little. You would be running around the house talking about what you could do. Go home."

Now you ask, "Where does it say Eliab said all that?" It's in the Hebrew. Eliab was burning with anger against David probably because he was burning with embarrassment that he didn't have the guts to face Goliath.

See, Eliab was utterly powerless because he wasn't plugged into the power source. All he could see and hear was big, bad Goliath. So he tried to deflect the attention away from his inadequacies by attacking David and accusing him of having all kinds of wrong motives.

But when you're thinking with God's mind, you don't have to be intimidated by anyone—be he a giant *or* big brother! I love the way David answered Eliab in verse 29. You can see right here why God wanted David to be His king. I mean, this cat wasn't taking any stuff even as a kid.

David protested that he was just asking a question, and then he checked again to make sure the others hadn't heard him wrong. Now Eliab probably didn't know he was stifling the work of God in David's life and in Israel. So he wasn't the real enemy, and neither is the person who may be trying to hold you down.

——————— **Think About It** ———————
Sometimes the people who want to stifle you are in the enemy camp.
Sadly, at other times they may be in your own household.
Either way, you can't let them intimidate you.

"Those who know Thy name will put their trust in Thee."
Psalm 9:10

POSITIVELY BIBLICAL
Read It: 1 Samuel 17:31-33

Let me tell you, my man David had confidence. Now there is every-thing wrong with a confidence that totally rests in yourself. But there is everything right with a confidence that rests in the fact that your God is bigger than your problem.

If you've been reading along with us this year, you probably know by now that I'm not a big fan of the power of positive thinking as it's usually taught. But if there is ever a time when the power of positive thinking is okay, it is when your positive thinking is powerful because it is positively *biblical* thinking.

Biblical thinking says that there is no problem so great that your God is not greater. As Corrie ten Boom put it, "There is no pit so deep that God is not deeper still." If you realize that, then you have a basis for positive thinking. When you have learned to live life this way, then you see power. The reason so many Christians aren't seeing power is because when their human resources are gone, they give up. They quit. But not David.

David's confidence mystified King Saul, because the king wasn't think-ing with a God-centered mind. So he said, "Wait a minute, David. We've got a problem. You are just a kid. This Goliath has been a warrior since he was a kid, and he's a grown man. He's got all the experience." Saul was saying, "Logically, this is a dumb idea." And many times when you try to do what God tells you to do, people will say, "You've got to be crazy."

I know that because I've already had some people tell me that. Now what these people are really saying is, "Don't apply God's principles to this problem because that's not logical."

But just like a lot of positive thinking isn't biblical, a lot of what's log-ical isn't biblical either. The question is not how things add up logically. The question is, have you measured the size of your God against the size of your problem? You will have no power until you do. If you are having trouble doing that, get on your knees today and ask God to sharpen your spiritual eyesight.

——— **Think About It** ———
If all you see is what your 20/20 shows you,
you will never be a powerful, supernatural Christian.

"God is our refuge and strength, a very present help in trouble."
Psalm 46:1

GET A HISTORY
Read It: 1 Samuel 17:34-37

David saw something no one else around him saw. He saw God. David was committed to God in a way the others were not, so he got the power of God to bring down his giant. Not only did David see what no one else saw, but here is something very important. He also had experiences with God elsewhere to let him know that Goliath would be no trouble.

Let me tell you what happens when most people run into a big problem. They never learned to call on God in their little problems, so when the big one hits, they don't know how to call on Him and tap into His power.

That's when the pastor's phone rings, because people go looking for someone spiritual to help them. The thing is to let God work where you are, so that when you get out there in the middle of a big problem, you have a history with God. That's what David had. So he gave Saul a little history lesson in the power of God. David proceeded to tell Saul a bedtime story about a lion and a bear.

Now this brother was bad. I could understand if David had said, "The lion came after me." But David said he went after the lion, talking about, "You aren't taking any lamb of mine! King of the jungle nothing."

Now what was the basis of David's power? It was his commitment to a God he knew was alive. See, if you know that your God is alive, you can go chasing after lions and bears if that's what He tells you to do. But you need to ask yourself how alive your God is to you today. Let me show you what I mean.

Is your God just a cross you wear around your neck, a picture on your wall, or a Bible that's dusty on your bookshelf? Is your God the "beddie-bye" prayers you say at night? Is that how alive your God is? Or is your God the living reality of your life? Then you need to act like it. He is a powerful God.

--------- **Think About It** ---------
If you are asking God to make you look good, you may not
get the power. But if you are telling God, "I want to make
You look good," God says, "You need some power."

"Your hand will be lifted up against your adversaries,
and all your enemies will be cut off." Micah 5:9

RAISING IT TO A HIGHER POWER
Read It: 1 Samuel 17:38-49

Let me give you one more principle about the power of commitment. It's in verse 40. David chose five stones because Goliath apparently had four brothers or four sons (see 2 Samuel 21:22; 1 Chronicles 20:5). David was ready to take on the whole family if necessary, because they were messing with God.

Here is the principle: Believing God doesn't mean you do nothing. What it means is that as you step out for Him, God infiltrates and takes what you can do and does the miraculous with it.

See, people who tell you, "I'm just going to sit here and trust God," don't understand what it means to trust God. But God didn't give you the abilities you have so you could sit on them while He becomes your heavenly genie. He gave you your abilities so that He could infuse them with His power and then use them to perform miracles.

What you must do is meet your spiritual responsibility. You must think with the mind of Christ and act on your commitment. This is not the twisted theology that says, "God helps those who help themselves," or, "Name it and claim it, because then God has to do it." No, no. God is the One doing all the empowering.

Now when you decide to step out for God the way David did, there will always be a giant around to do a little "woofing" with you. Goliath did some serious woofing with David. Here comes this little kid with a slingshot, so Goliath starts needling him. "Do I look like Fido to you, brother? Am I a dog that you come to me with sticks?" And he cussed David out.

Well now, we've already learned this week that David was kind of bad too. So he said, "Okay, we'll do some woofing before we get down." He gave it right back to Goliath, but David wasn't just talking tough.

David could talk tough because Goliath was making fun of the true God. David was there as God's representative to hold up His interests in that mess. Whose interests are you looking out for today, yours or God's?

—————— **Think About It** ——————
God wants to infuse your life and raise the power
of your power to an infinitely higher power.

REFLECTION

Do you see why David did what he did in the story of Goliath? He didn't go out there and fight the giant just so he could get TV coverage, make all the talk shows, endorse a line of slingshots, and get rich. He didn't do it so he could get the credit, so people would point to him and say, "There's the guy who brought Goliath down."

David took on Goliath so that everyone in that battle would know there is a God in Israel.

I often remind the people in my church that if we are going to build God's alternative in that place, our reason must be so that everyone in Oak Cliff will know there is a God on Camp Wisdom Road. Our motive has to be to lift Jesus up. He said, "The higher I am lifted up, the more people I will draw to Me."

If you want to experience God's power in your life, you are going to have to be sure you are plugged into His program. The power of commitment is the power you receive when you commit yourself to God's agenda, not yours.

And when you do that, then you'll see the power fall! No problem will be able to stand against you if you come against it as God's representative, looking out for His interests and committed to doing His will His way.

So my question to you this weekend is, what is your Goliath? What is scaring you to death? Pick up some stones and go for it!

"What does it profit a man to gain the whole world,
and forfeit his soul?" Mark 8:36

THE WHOLE STORY
Read It: Mark 8:34-36

One of the things I love about the Lord Jesus is that you can always depend on Him to tell you the whole story.

Jesus wouldn't hand you a rose without warning you to watch out for the thorns. He wouldn't tell you the good news and skip the bad. And He wouldn't call you to follow Him without telling you the cost involved in being His disciple.

Satan isn't like that. He only tells you half of the story. He only wants you to see the up side of sin. He doesn't want you to know you're heading toward a dead end called hell.

Sometimes you don't even get the whole story in church. Everyone is all dressed up, looking good. But if you could see behind the scenes, you would see the rest of the story. One thing you get to see in the ministry is the other half of the story. You find out where people live and how they are hurting.

So Jesus always gives you the whole story. That's what I need to do too if I'm going to be faithful to Him and to you. So this week we're going to talk about the sacrifice of commitment.

Now I know that *sacrifice* isn't a fun word. Most of us don't want to hear about what we have to give up, what we have to turn loose of, to follow Jesus. We want to know what we will be given and what we can hang onto as we walk with the Lord.

Some of Jesus' disciples really get off on talking about the kingdom, the power, and the glory. And those are all real. We just spent a week looking at the power of commitment.

But if you and I are going to apply the mind of Christ to our daily lives, we have to think with His *whole* mind. And one of the things on Jesus' mind is the cost of commitment, the sacrifice required to be His disciple.

But you know what? If you're really in love with Jesus, the stuff He asks you to give up is no big deal.

——————— **Think About It** ———————

What Jesus asks you to give up are the baubles and trinkets of this world in exchange for all the riches of heaven. What a deal!

*"No one of you can be My disciple who does not
give up all his own possessions." Luke 14:33*

THE WHOLE BALL OF WAX
Read It: Mark 10:17-31; Luke 9:57

Does today's verse make you feel a little uncomfortable? Let's talk about it. There are tremendous privileges and benefits to following Christ. But they're not gained without cost. Nothing truly worthwhile is.

The rich young man who ran up to Jesus that day asked the right question: "What shall I do to inherit eternal life?" (Mark 10:17). He just wasn't ready for the answer, because Jesus told him to sell everything he had and fall in behind the twelve.

Someone will say, "That was just for that guy, because he loved his possessions too much to give them up." It's true that Jesus was dealing with this man's particular need. But standing next to Jesus were twelve men who did give up everything they had (v. 28). You can't follow Jesus without giving Him the whole ball of wax. Whether He actually calls you to sell everything or not, your attitude needs to be that it all belongs to Him.

The would-be disciples of Luke 9:57-62 also didn't understand what they were being called to do. The context of this passage is very interesting. Jesus has just been rejected (vv. 51-56). What's more, He was on His way to Calvary. Now rejection and death weren't on the minds of the crowds who followed Him.

A lot of folk who followed Jesus had become enamored with what He could do. With just a word, He could make the blind see and the lame walk. He could pray over a boy's lunch and feed the whole county. People said, "I think I'll hang out with Jesus. If I ever get sick, He can heal me. If I ever become poor, He can feed me. If I ever get depressed, He can make me happy."

But what people forgot was that while Jesus did all of those things, He was headed to a place called Calvary. He was on His way to die. It was easy to lose track of that and get excited about Jesus because of the benefits package.

Don't get me wrong. Jesus has the best benefits going. But He also wants us to understand the sacrifice involved in being committed to Him.

———— **Think About It** ————

If our Lord suffered rejection and death, why should we expect
to kick back and float into heaven on a bed of ease?

"Whoever does not carry his own cross and come after Me cannot be My disciple." Luke 14:27

DO YOU UNDERSTAND?
Read It: Luke 9:58; 14:25-35

Remember, we said on Monday that Jesus always tells you the whole truth? Today's text is a case in point.

We saw yesterday that as Jesus made His way to Jerusalem and the Cross, a potential disciple volunteered to join up. Jesus wanted to make sure this guy knew what he was getting into, so He said, "Do you understand what you just said? You said you would go with Me wherever I go. But I don't even know where I'm going to sleep tonight. Do you understand that total commitment to Me means you are not tied into the security of this world order? Do you understand that?"

We need to ask ourselves these same questions today, especially because we are being blitzed by a pseudo-theology that goes like this: "I'm the King's kid, and the King owns everything. Since I'm His kid, He wants me to own everything too. So I'm just going to tap into my inheritance and get whatever I think I need, because God wants me to have it."

There are so many problems with this thinking that I don't have space for them all. One problem is that you can't find an example of this in the Bible. According to this teaching, Job was the biggest sinner ever because he lost everything.

Now Jesus is not saying, "To be committed to Me, you have to go and sell your house, find a little cubbyhole, stuff yourself inside it, and live miserably." That's the other extreme.

But Jesus is saying, "Commitment to Me means that if need be, you are available to give up those tokens of worldly security that everybody else clings to so hard. Following Me means that sometimes you may have noplace to lay your head."

This is the sacrifice of commitment. Jesus made no apology for it, because He will never ask you to surrender anything without providing something better in its place. That doesn't mean if you give up your Chevy, He'll replace it with a Cadillac. It may mean just the opposite. The point is, Jesus calls us to make choices that only make sense in light of eternity.

——— **Think About It** ———

If Jesus requires you to give up what looks like worldly security, don't fret. Eternal security is worth a whole lot more.

*"Jesus said to them, 'Follow Me. . . .' And they immediately
left the nets and followed Him." Mark 1:17-18*

I'M GOING TO
Read It: Luke 9:59-60

There was a second man on the road Jesus walked that day. The first man volunteered, but didn't understand what he was saying. The second guy must have had potential, because Jesus called him.

"Okay, Jesus," he answered, "You've got a deal. But I've got something to do first. I need to go home and bury my father. Let me do that, and I'll be right back to join You." Now that seems like a reasonable request. All the man wanted to do was carry out his responsibilities at home. Jesus couldn't deny that request, right?

Wrong. The man's father wasn't dead yet. One way we know this is that the Jews buried their dead within twenty-four hours. So if his father had just died, he would have already been at home overseeing the burial or else just back from the burial and ready to go.

What the man was referring to was the custom of the day that the oldest son stayed home and took care of the affairs of the house until his father died. Then he would receive his inheritance and move on with his life. So this "wannabe" disciple was not saying, "My father just died, and I've got to go home." He was saying, "Jesus, I'm not ready to follow You yet."

Does that sound like anybody you know? "Jesus, I'm going to follow You . . . as soon as I finish school, buy a new house, get my children raised."

Listen to me. Whenever you tell Jesus, "I'm not ready," you are making two dangerous assumptions. First, you are assuming that you are going to be around long enough to get ready.

Second, you are assuming that if you live long enough, you will finally come to a point where you're ready. The problem is, that's not the way life works. What normally happens is that the longer you live, the more encumbrances you gather, the more stuff you accumulate that demands your attention. If you're going to follow Jesus, do it now. If you need to make a sacrifice, make it today.

--- **Think About It** ---

Jesus is saying to you, "Let spiritually dead people deal
with death. You are no longer dead because you have met Me.
Don't get caught up in death. Get caught up in life."

"Forgetting what lies behind and reaching forward to what lies ahead, I press on toward the goal." Philippians 3:13-14

WAIT 'TIL THE PARTY'S OVER
Read It: Luke 9:61-62

The third would-be disciple on the road to Jerusalem must have heard the other two men's exchanges with Jesus, because he stated his request right up front.

Again, saying goodbye to the family doesn't seem like an unreasonable request. But let's look at it in its cultural context. When this guy said he wanted to go home and say goodbye, he wasn't saying, "Jesus, give me an hour or so to go home, pack my suitcase, and say goodbye. Stay here, and I'll be right back."

No, he was saying, "I want to go home and throw a goodbye party for my family and friends. You know how long these things last, Jesus. Give me about two weeks, and I'll catch up with You when the party's over. Just leave me Your forwarding address."

I had the opportunity to see this kind of celebration firsthand when I went to Guyana, the home country of my wife Lois. We went to an East Indian wedding. Now weddings here in America are usually over the same day they start. Not in Guyana. When those folk come together to celebrate, they *celebrate*. This party went on for over a week. They just grabbed a couple of hours of sleep, got up, and kept on jamming.

Well, that's exactly what this man wanted to do. But Jesus knew the problem with that. Verse 62 is a rough one because Jesus allowed no exceptions. Anyone who grabs a plow on His property had better be ready to keep his eyes front and center and lay down a straight furrow. Any farmer can tell you that if you turn around and look back while you're plowing, you'll lose your sense of direction and start going crooked.

So Jesus is saying, "Once you make the decision to follow Me, start following immediately. Don't delay your commitment. You can't have one hand on the cross and one hand back at home. You've got to make that decision." You can't serve Jesus while looking behind you and reaching back for the stuff you left behind. How long has it been since you checked your furrows?

——— **Think About It** ———
If you're going to plow a straight furrow for Jesus,
you need to check the position of your eyes and your hands.

REFLECTION

I hope you're planning to neglect some things this weekend. You say, "Excuse me, Tony. How's that again?"

I'm talking about planned neglect. Now I don't mean neglecting the job your wife asked you to do for her or neglecting your kids. I'm talking about the commitment it takes to neglect the thousand and one things you could be doing that won't get you where you want to go.

Someone is reported to have asked a concert violinist at Carnegie Hall how she became so skilled. She answered, "It was by planned neglect." She planned to neglect everything that was not related to her goal.

See, there are a lot of things you could be doing that you give up if you're a committed disciple of Jesus—not because those things are bad necessarily, but because they're unproductive in terms of God's kingdom.

There's nothing wrong with taking care of your family or throwing a goodbye party unless those things keep you from following Jesus. Commitment to Him always involves sacrifice.

Does this mean you shouldn't strive to be successful in business? Of course not. Just make sure your success doesn't own you. Because, remember, a true disciple puts everything he has in Jesus' hands. That means if He wants it, He can have it.

As the song says, "I have decided to follow Jesus. No turning back! No turning back!" Can you sing that today?

TWELVE

◇

JESUS' ONLY PROGRAM

"I Will Build My Church"

*The church is taking a lot of heat today.
Sometimes it seems as if there are only three
people who are determined to see the church hang
around and grow. But those three are the
Father, Son, and Holy Spirit! Jesus is only building one
thing today: His church. So if you and I want to be on His
construction crew, we had better be studying His blueprint
for the church. These next four weeks I want to share
with you the power, the program, the perspective,
and the prophecy of the church.*

"[God] put all things in subjection under [Jesus'] feet, and gave Him as head over all things to the church." Ephesians 1:22

WHAT DO YOU SAY?
Read It: Matthew 16:13-15

If we're going to talk about the Church, we need to begin at the beginning. That's where we're starting this week. The passage before us, Matthew 16:13-20, contains the first mention of the Church in the New Testament, and in all of Scripture, for that matter. In fact, the word is only used two places in the Gospels, here and in Matthew 18:17.

It's appropriate that each time the Church is mentioned in the Gospels, it's on the lips of Jesus. For He is the Head of the Church. And the Church will continue to be His until He delivers all things up to the Father (1 Corinthians 15:24), because no power on earth or below can take us out of Jesus' hands.

So before we start looking at who makes up the Church and how it should operate, we need to be absolutely straight on the identity of its Head. Interestingly enough, that's exactly where Jesus began with His disciples on this occasion when He revealed to them for the first time His plan for a brand-new entity called the Church.

In the course of their travels, Jesus and the twelve came to the region of Caesarea Philippi, twenty-five miles north of the Sea of Galilee and actually the farthest north Jesus ever traveled in His earthly ministry.

They had been up and down the land some by now, so most of the people of Israel had had time to form an opinion about Jesus. The disciples had also had time to think about who Jesus was, and it was their view He was most interested in. So Jesus got this monumentally important exchange going by asking His disciples what the talk around town was about Him. Who did people think He was?

Now as I pointed out before, Jesus never asked a question to gain information. When He asked a person something, it was a test. That's what was happening here, as we know from reading the following verses.

So the disciples offered a sampling of the current views about Jesus, and they were all pretty complimentary. But none of them was the correct answer, so Jesus asked a follow-up question—one every person must still face and answer today.

————— **Think About It** —————

How you answer Jesus' question will determine your eternal destiny.

"Thou art the Christ, the Son of the living God." Matthew 16:16

SAVIOR AND SON
Read It: Matthew 16:16-17

Chalk one up in the win column for Simon Peter. Old Pete nailed this one. His confession of the identity of Jesus Christ is one of the greatest statements in all the Bible.

Remember, Jesus was about to tell the disciples about the Church for the first time, but He didn't want to reveal His plan until they were clear about His Person. Peter's confession covered all the bases. By calling Jesus "the Christ," Peter was identifying Him as the Messiah, the Anointed One, Israel's promised Redeemer. Peter was saying that Jesus was the fulfillment of all the Old Testament's promises and prophecies. He was the Lamb of God who would come to bear the sins of His people and of the world.

Peter also recognized Jesus as deity by calling Him "the Son of the living God." This statement means He shares the very essence of deity with the Father. All that makes the Father the eternal God belongs to the Son. So Peter covered Jesus' humanity and deity.

What Peter said was enough to earn him an advanced degree in theology, except that Peter had never been to seminary. The explanation, of course, is that Peter didn't figure this all out on his own (v. 17). Knowledge like this can only come through the revelation of God. And that's still true today.

Now we have an advantage because we have the completed revelation of God. The Bible tells us very clearly that Jesus is the Son of God and Savior of the world. But the only One who can make those words come alive in our hearts is the Spirit of God.

What I'm saying is that if you are a Christian, you did not get saved just because you woke up one day and decided you'd like to believe in Jesus. You did not conjure up the faith to be saved. God came looking for you. He revealed the truth about Christ to you and burned the conviction of it into your heart.

This is important to remember, not just for personal salvation, but as we talk about the Church. The Church is God's idea from beginning to end. He just lets us in on the good stuff.

--------- **Think About It** ---------
Since the Church is God's idea, we can't make it work
merely by the force of our will and our effort.

"No man can lay a foundation other than the one which is laid,
which is Jesus Christ." 1 Corinthians 3:11

ONLY ONE FOUNDATION
Read It: Matthew 16:18; Ephesians 2:19-22

When you read Matthew 16:18, you wouldn't think it's a verse that Christendom would spend about 1,500 years arguing about.

This is not the place to argue church hierarchy and structure. I want to stick to the text, because the Bible is its own best interpreter. On Friday we'll go to Peter's own writings to see what he understood about headship in the Church. For today, let me make some observations about this important verse.

First, remember that Jesus is addressing all the disciples here, not just Peter. That's evident from the context on both sides of verse 18. So whatever Jesus said to Peter, the other apostles also had a key part in it. For example, we know from John 20:23 that all the apostles were given the authority to bind and loose.

Second, you probably know that the two words *Peter* and *rock* are a play on words in the Greek language. They both mean rock, stone. In my research I found that the word *rock* could be used of a rocky ledge or a large slab—a larger composition of stones made up of smaller stones.

I believe what Jesus is saying here is not that Peter himself is the rock on which He will build His Church or even that Peter's confession is that rock. Jesus is telling Peter, "I am singling you out as the lead stone, as the spokesman. But when I build My Church, I won't build it on just one stone. I need all the stones coming together [the other apostles] to make a mighty slab of stone on which to build My Church." Ephesians 2:20 confirms that all the apostles, not just Peter, are part of the one foundation stone that the Church is built on, with Jesus Christ as the "cornerstone."

See, no matter what your particular view of the structure or syntax of Matthew 16:18, there is one absolutely indisputable fact about the Church: Jesus Christ and He alone is the Head of the Church. He purchased the Church with His blood. And He will not share His glory with anyone.

--- **Think About It** ---

Don't miss the best part of this verse. Jesus is talking
about the Church knocking over hell, not about us trying to
hang in there while Satan knocks us to the ground!

"I was dead, and behold, I am alive forevermore, and I have the keys of death and of Hades." Revelation 1:18

HOLDING THE KEYS
Read It: Matthew 16:19-20

If there's a key anywhere in the universe that goes to anything important, it's hanging on Jesus' key ring.

A key is a symbol of authority. If I give you the key to my house, I am telling you that my house is your house. It's very interesting that here where Jesus mentions the Church for the first time, in the next breath He hands out keys.

Now the fact that Jesus has a lot of keys under His authority is evident when you compare today's verse and today's reading with Revelation 3:7, where Jesus says He also holds the "key of David." This is another reference to His total authority.

I want to show you something intriguing that I think is going on here, so stay with me. Why would Jesus need to give the Church so many keys? Because hell has so many gates (v. 18). The idea is this: Every time Satan opens a gate in hell to loose some of his forces to attack the Church on earth, God wants us to unlock a door in heaven behind which lies the power to defeat that attack.

See, if someone gives you a key, you make two assumptions. First, you assume there is a locked door that needs to be opened. And second, you assume that the key you have will fit the lock on that door.

Now that's a figurative way of speaking about the spiritual warfare the Church is engaged in with the forces of Satan. But don't miss the power behind what Jesus is telling us in verse 19. We are the aggressors. The One who has all authority, who owns all the keys—even the keys to the very gates of hell—has delegated His authority to us, His Church. We are the ones who are supposed to be calling the shots over hell.

That doesn't mean we are to be arrogant or throw our weight around. The reason we can be aggressive against Satan is that if we go in the name and authority of Jesus, we will be making decisions that already have heaven's clout behind them!

——————— **Think About It** ———————

If you're a member of the body of Christ, you have all the authority of God and His Word behind you in your daily battle with Satan.

"As living stones, [you] are being built up as a spiritual house."
1 Peter 2:5

THE ROCK'S TESTIMONY
Read It: 1 Peter 2:4-5

If you want to get the straight scoop, go to the source. That's what we have been trying to do this week as we talk about the Church. I referred to the fact that Matthew 16 has been one of the most dissected and disputed passages in the entire Bible, mainly because of disagreements over the role Jesus assigned to Peter in the building of His Church.

Well, it's not hard to establish that Jesus was not giving Peter an exclusive ruling authority in the Church that no other apostle had. Peter was the leader, to be sure. Peter was the spokesman, the "Rock," without a doubt. But, remember, Jesus was speaking to all twelve of His disciples that day in Caesarea Philippi. The authority to bind and loose, for example, was not given to Peter alone.

Now Peter did use the keys of the kingdom to open the Church to the Jews on the Day of Pentecost in Acts 2 and to Gentiles in the house of Cornelius in Acts 10, but he drops out of the narrative in Acts after the Jerusalem council (Acts 15:7).

We have said that Jesus' purpose in building the Church was to use many stones coming together to form one mighty slab and that Peter was simply one stone in that slab. But why not ask Peter what he understood Jesus to be saying? After all, Peter was there in Matthew 16. Other than Jesus Himself, Peter is the best interpreter of that event.

Well, we do have Peter's interpretation in today's text. He pictures the Church as a "spiritual house" made up of many living stones—which, by the way, includes believers like you and me today. Here, I believe, is the imagery we talked about earlier this week of a mighty slab of stone made up of many individual stones, forming the foundation of the Church.

Now if Peter alone were the rock upon which the Church was built, this would have been a perfect opportunity for him to declare his supremacy once and for all. But under the inspiration of the Spirit, Peter testified to the truth. And for that we can be eternally grateful!

―――――― **Think About It** ――――――
Since you are designed by God to be a living part of
His living Church, if you're a church dropout, you're
tearing something that was meant to be a unified whole.

REFLECTION

One of the things you notice right off when you start talking about the Church is how clear the Bible is that the Church is meant to be a unified single organism.

Think about the biblical images used of the Church: a body, a spiritual house, a family. Those are singular even though a body, a house, and a family are made up of individual members. But the call is always for oneness in heart and purpose.

That's what the Head of the Church wants for us, in fact. In John 17:21, Jesus prayed for the unity of His people. He was about to die on the cross, so this prayer is His last will and testament for the Church, if you will.

But there is someone else in the universe who is intensely interested in the Church's ministry and particularly in seeing to it that the unity Jesus prayed for doesn't happen. The Church is the biggest threat Satan has on his hands right now. When the Church is functioning the way it's designed to function, we've got a force that can bulldoze the gates of hell flat.

So if you're Satan, your primary goal has to be to smash the mighty slab of the Church into a bunch of bickering pebbles, to disable the body by getting the eyes fighting with the feet and the hands mad at the ears. To collapse the house by getting the stones in the walls to say, "I'm tired of supporting this mess."

You get the point. The unity of the Church is what Jesus wants you and me to cherish and maintain. Are we going to deny Him His will for us?

"We have not ceased to pray for you . . . that you may walk in a
manner worthy of the Lord." Colossians 1:9-10

WALK WORTHY
Read It: Ephesians 4:1-2

Don't read today's Scripture and study till you read Ephesians 1–3. I thought maybe an opening line like that would get your attention on a Monday. Now whether you actually read Ephesians 1–3 today is up to you. My point is that you can't really fulfill the instructions for Christian duty in chapters 4–6 until you have the proper doctrinal understanding of the Church that Paul lays out in chapters 1–3.

In the Bible, doctrine always precedes and undergirds duty. We can't act like the Church until we know what the Church is and what God wants us to do. We've talked about the establishment of the Church and the spiritual power Jesus has delegated to it. Now we'll study the spiritual practice or duty of the Church, drawing on classic passages in Ephesians 4–5.

When Paul tells us in 4:1 to "walk in a manner worthy of [your] calling," he refers to what he's just written. Our calling is that we're saved by the sovereign work of God's grace, equipped to do good works (1:4-6; 2:8-10), and formed into a new body, the Church of Jesus Christ (2:11-16).

That's a high calling, and we need to live up to it. The idea of the word *worthy* is equivalence or equal weight. That is, make sure your conduct is equal to your call. Don't let your theology outrun your practice. Let the doctrine in your head translate into duty in your heart.

So let's see what's involved in walking worthy of our calling. Humility simply means you recognize that you aren't the only one in God's program called the Church. The opposite of humility is thinking more highly of yourself than you ought (Romans 12:3).

To walk with gentleness or meekness means that your spirit is in check. Meekness in the Bible means "strength under control," like a horse tamed to the saddle.

Patience is a perfect partner for gentleness, because it means to practice self-restraint rather than to retaliate. Forbearance is that quality you want others to show toward you when you've messed up, so Paul says just reciprocate the favor.

——— **Think About It** ———
If these qualities make you think of Jesus Christ,
you're getting the idea! That's why you are called to be Christlike.

"[Be] diligent to preserve the unity of the Spirit
in the bond of peace." Ephesians 4:3

WALK IN UNITY
Read It: Ephesians 2:11-22; 4:3-6

If you want to know why the unity of the Church is such a big deal to God, look at the price He paid to achieve it. We're not just talking about some deal on paper here. It cost Jesus His blood to bring us together into the Church (v. 13). Paul says emphatically in verse 14 that Jesus Himself is our peace.

Last weekend I shared some thoughts on the unity of the Church and how Satan is out to destroy it, and you may want to look that page again. Let me make a couple of observations about unity.

First, if we are going to preserve the Church's unity, we have to realize that we can't come in with our own agendas. The only agenda for the Church is the one already established by its Head, Jesus Christ. He didn't consult with me when He set it, and I doubt if He consulted with you either.

If you want to see the fabric of unity in a local church unravel in a hurry, let the members start pushing their personal or group agendas. That's when you start hearing stuff like, "Well, I think we ought to," "In my church back home we always," instead of, "What does God's Word say?"

Notice secondly that we are to preserve this unity, not manufacture it. We are not striving to be one body; we *are* one body in Christ. He did the unifying work by His death on the cross. He doesn't ask us to do what only He can do. It's the unity of the Holy Spirit, not the unity of Tony Evans or anyone else. Our unity is a priceless gift to us from the Church's Head, and the best thing you can do with a priceless gift is thank the Giver and cherish the gift.

Third and finally, check out the basis of our unity (vv. 4-6). It's based on the eternal, changeless truths of the faith, not on something superficial or external. We are not called to look, think, act, or talk alike. We are called to unite around the core of truth we hold in common and the Lord we worship together.

──────── **Think About It** ────────

Have you ever thought that if those other Christians would just look, think, act, and talk like you, there'd be no problem? Think again!

"This I say . . . and affirm together with the Lord, that you walk no longer just as the Gentiles also walk." Ephesians 4:17

WALK DIFFERENTLY
Read It: Ephesians 4:17-32

If you want to know how important it is that we walk like the Christians we are, look no further than today's verse. The Apostle Paul says, "When you hear from me on this one, you are hearing from God." Now every word in the Bible is inspired by God, so when an author underscores that fact, it's like saying, "Sit up and pay attention."

What Paul wants us to do is not to walk the way we used to walk, not to follow the crowd, not to move the way the masses are moving. Now I'm not talking about being different just for the sake of being different. You aren't to go out there looking for ways to clash with your secular friends or co-workers. The believer's difference is to be a *biblical* one. That is, we step out from the crowd and walk in another direction because that's what God has called His Church to do.

One reason you don't want to follow the world's crowd is because of where they're headed—toward "futility," straight into a brick wall. As a result, they are darkened, ignorant, and hardened. Paul says that you, Christian, don't want that. And I say, "Amen, brother."

See, when you got saved and became a member of the Church, which is the body of Christ, you entered a different sphere; you acquired a different way of thinking (vv. 20-21). The truth of Jesus Christ should now be the environment of your learning. To put it another way, everything you do should be subject to divine evaluation. That's why the church is charged with teaching the Scriptures as God's standard. And that standard doesn't get any more down-to-earth and practical than the remaining verses of Ephesians 4.

Let me summarize what it means to walk differently from the world. It means, among other things, to quit lying and stealing if those are a problem for you. It means get a job and be honest in it; get control of your tongue and your emotions; quit nursing bitterness and start forgiving. Are any of these unclear to you?

————— **Think About It** —————
Christians are *supposed* to be different. Non-Christians may try to make you feel like the oddball, but they're the odd ones, not you.

"Walk in love, just as Christ also loved you." Ephesians 5:2

WALK AFFECTIONATELY
Read It: Ephesians 5:1-7

You're supposed to look like your daddy. That's what Paul says in verse 1 of today's reading. We're talking about the practice of the Church, what it means to look and act like the people of God that we actually are.

Now to walk in love as we imitate God means that we do for each other what Jesus Christ did for us. The Bible says He came to serve and to give, not to be served and to receive. He took the form of a "bond-servant," a slave (Philippians 2:7).

Therefore, for Christians to walk in love means seeking to serve one another, being ready to sacrifice for the next person. The shame of people in the church who are not involved in any way in its ministry is that they are saying, "I don't want to walk in love. I don't plan to serve anyone. Just keep serving me."

But the Bible says we should love each other so much that we are willing to die for each other. Now that's what I call an intense relationship. God has called very few of us to lay down our lives for the church, especially in this country. But too few of us are even willing to do the easy things He asks us to do: serve, give, teach, pray, or whatever.

One thing is sure. If the world doesn't see this kind of love in the church, they aren't going to find it anywhere else. What the world offers is the stuff Paul lists in verses 3-7.

In light of what he says in verses 1-2 about imitating our loving and serving God, one striking thing about this list of ungodly attitudes and actions is that these things are the opposite of love. When you walk in love, you don't use people to satisfy your impure desires; you don't take from them to satisfy your greed, and you don't abuse or belittle them with your mouth.

Instead, you distance yourself from these kinds of things and the people who practice them. We talked yesterday about Christians being different. If there's anything that ought to distinguish you and me from the world, it's the love we have one for another.

———— Think About It ————
People don't care what you know until they know that you care.

"Let us therefore lay aside the deeds of darkness and
put on the armor of light." Romans 13:12

WALK REFLECTIVELY
Read It: Ephesians 5:8-13

Light shows things as they really are. That's why as the children of light, we need to make sure that our walk matches our talk, that our practice matches our doctrine. To walk in the light is to reflect the character of God in such a way that people actually see what God looks like when they look at us. We've been seeing this week that what we believe should very definitely impact the way we live.

Paul states that in an unusual way in verse 9, mixing the metaphors of light and fruit to talk about the "fruit of the light." But there's no mistaking his meaning. As members of Christ's body reflecting His light, we are to practice "goodness, righteousness, and truth."

Reflecting God's character means reflecting His will. So our assignment is to find out what pleases God (v. 10). A few verses later Paul will tell us to understand what God's will for us is, which as we saw in our study on the Holy Spirit is to be filled with the Spirit.

Now if we're reflecting godly character in the way we live, it's going to have an effect on the darkness. Light exposes what's being done in the dark, and one of the church's tasks is to expose the "unfruitful deeds of darkness" (v. 11).

This is heavy. A lot of individual Christians and churches don't want to touch this one because it involves risks. Now I don't think Paul means we are to go around calling sinners names and all that, but neither is he talking about hiding our lights under a bushel.

The most effective way to expose wrong behavior for what it is is by displaying right behavior. The very presence of Christians in a community and a neighborhood should have this effect of bringing evil to light, because people see God's alternative.

Of course, there are those times when we have to get out of neutral and take a stand for what's right no matter what the cost. But day in and day out, your witness is the most effective way you have of letting your light shine and exposing the darkness.

——— **Think About It** ———

Are you making contact with any lost people around you who need to see your light shine? Don't keep it hidden inside the church.

REFLECTION

You've probably heard about the nervous mother who rushed up to her son's kindergarten teacher on parents' night and said, "I'm Johnny's mother. Tell me, am I bragging or complaining?"

That reminds me of what can happen in the body of Christ if we're not careful about the way we walk. If you go to witness to someone about his need of Christ and tell him how Christ will change his life, your witness may not have much clout if he has just been burned by the acid tongue of another Christian or messed over in business by someone whose business ethics did not match the fish symbol or cross on his business card.

What I'm saying is, if you name the name of Christ, it matters a whole lot how you behave yourself. If Ephesians 4 and 5 mean anything, they mean that a Christian ought to be the best employer in town. Christians ought to be the most productive employees in town.

The pagans in town ought to be able to say, "Well, I don't really care for all they teach and believe down there at the church, but I'd have to admit they're the most trustworthy people around these parts."

My friend, take some time this weekend to check out your walk. Get out the mirror of God's Word and hold it up to your life. Let the searchlight of the Holy Spirit beam in on anything that needs fixing. As the days get tough, we believers are either going to have to get our walk right or get off the street!

*"In the exercise of His will He brought us forth
by the word of truth." James 1:18*

THE NEW AND THE OLD
Read It: 1 Peter 1:22–2:1

Remember when Nicodemus came to Jesus at night in John 3? Jesus told Nicodemus he had to be born again, which threw Nick off course. So he asked a logical question from a human perspective: "How can a man be born when he is old?" (v. 4).

In other words, it doesn't make any sense to try and become a baby again when you've already been through that stage and are way beyond it. Of course, Jesus had to explain to Nicodemus that the birth He was talking about is spiritual, not physical.

Well, just as it doesn't make sense in the physical realm for an old man to try and become a newborn baby again, in the same way it doesn't make sense in the spiritual realm for a "newborn babe" in Christ to try and live like the "old man" of the flesh that he was before he met the Savior. Once you've shed the filthy rags of the old life, why would you ever want to put them on again?

That's Peter's point in the verses before us today. When we come to Christ and become members of His body, the Church, it changes our perspective on everything. So as we continue our studies on the Church, I'd like to talk with you this week about the perspective of the Church—that is, how we should see ourselves as new creations in Christ.

Peter sets the context for this new perspective when he reminds us that we have in fact been born again—not physically, as Nicodemus thought, but spiritually by the living and eternal Word of God.

See, that truth alone changes everything. Whereas physical birth actually begins the decaying and dying process, spiritual birth is the beginning of a growth process designed to last into eternity. As we have seen so often in recent weeks, the new birth is such a radical change that we are to consider ourselves dead to our old way of life. Paul says it, and now Peter says it.

Since the old life is dead and buried, don't go back and try to dig it up. Since you're a new person in Christ, start living like it.

———— Think About It ————
If you need a reason to praise God today, praise Him
for your new birth, which is as secure as His Word.

*"Grow in the grace and knowledge of our Lord
and Savior Jesus Christ." 2 Peter 3:18*

MIDNIGHT FEEDING
Read It: 1 Peter 2:2-3

I love the way Peter describes the desire we should have for the nourishment by which we grow in our Christian lives. The apostle says we should desire the Word of God the way a newborn baby desires milk. Now how does a baby desire milk? With an intensity that you can't imagine until you've heard that midnight cry.

See, when a baby gets hungry, everything else is irrelevant: the time, the fact that Mom and Dad worked hard all day and are tired, the fact that we just went through this drill a few hours earlier. A baby's agenda is about as focused and uncluttered as you can get. He wants to eat —now. If the urge is not satisfied, somebody's ears are going to pay the price.

Have you ever been so hungry for the Word of God that you couldn't sleep until you had chowed down on it for a while? When was the last time your spiritual stomach growled so bad at midnight that you just had to get up for a midnight feeding on the truth of God?

Those are convicting questions for all of us, so let's move on. I'm convinced that the reason we as Christians too often display malice and envy and slander and all that other junk in verse 1 is that we are feeding ourselves on spiritual junk food. Junk food is designed to fill a deep need with a quick fix that carries you for a while but doesn't provide any real nourishment.

What a contrast to the pure, unadulterated, unmixed Word Peter talks about here. You know, not only can you not ignore a baby's hunger, but you can't fool a baby either. Start mixing stuff into that formula that isn't designed to be there, and either that baby's taste buds or his sensitive stomach will expel that mess. Once you've tasted the good stuff, the real thing, you don't want the junk food.

And you *have* tasted the good stuff, by the way. That's the idea of the "if" in verse 3, which means since. It's a statement of fact, not doubt. You've had the real thing. Can your spiritual taste buds still tell the difference?

——— **Think About It** ———
Since you have tasted God's goodness in salvation,
don't settle for spiritual junk food.

*"Behold, I am laying in Zion a stone . . . a costly
cornerstone for the foundation." Isaiah 28:16*

UNDER CONSTRUCTION
Read It: 1 Peter 2:4-8

Why does the Bible call us "living stones?" It's because as Christians we're under construction. We're being built into a spiritual house, the Church. We're the only building program Jesus has going right now, and He's intensely interested in how construction is progressing.

If verses 4-5 of today's reading sound familiar, it's because we looked at them in detail on Friday of Week One. So I'll refer you back to that study to see how these verses fit into the context here.

Peter's message here is that Jesus Christ is accomplishing today exactly what He said He would accomplish back in Matthew 16:18: He is building His Church. And there is absolutely no doubt in Peter's mind as to who is the most valuable Stone in the project. It's Jesus Himself, the "living stone" (v. 4), the "choice [and] precious corner stone" (v. 6), the "very corner stone" (v. 7), and the "stone of stumbling and a rock of offense" (v. 8). Talk about having the right perspective on the Church. Peter is saying that no matter from what angle you view the spiritual building that is the Church, Jesus is holding the whole thing together.

Now, not everybody wants Jesus to be their Cornerstone. There are plenty of folk who will tell you, "I don't need the church. I don't need what the church is offering. I'll come to God my own way."

No, you won't. See, God only has one program. He's committed to His church the word of reconciliation (2 Corinthians 5:19-21). If you aren't into that, then your unbelief means that Jesus is not your Cornerstone but your headstone! Jesus said, referring to Himself, "On whomever [this stone] falls, it will scatter him like dust" (Matthew 21:44). That's the doom Peter is talking about (v. 8).

Now let me explain why we as individual stones in God's building need to grow up spiritually. If one side of a building goes up faster than the other side, you've got a lopsided building. If you and I are weak and can't hold up our part, the building will be out of kilter. And you can't blame the Cornerstone. He's solid for all eternity.

——— **Think About It** ———
If you're not growing, you're jeopardizing the stability
of the whole Church. It won't fit together right.

"You are a chosen race, a royal priesthood, a holy nation,
a people for God's own possession." 1 Peter 2:9

GOD'S ROYAL PRIESTS
Read It: 1 Peter 2:9-10

Today we're talking about some serious new perspectives on who you are as a part of the Church. Peter packs about as much perspective into two verses as you can get. Consider the title "a royal priesthood." *Priesthood* is a term loaded with biblical meaning. To show you all that it means, I would have to start in Genesis and go through the entire Bible. Here's the bottom line. God set aside Israel as His chosen priesthood, His special representatives on earth. Their job was to show the world what God was like. That's what a representative does.

But Israel messed up in its assignment to be God's "kingdom of priests" and "holy nation" (Exodus 19:6). In fact, Jesus told the priests and religious leaders of His day that the kingdom of God would be taken away from them and given to another nation (Matthew 21:43).

That's us, brothers and sisters! Jesus wasn't talking about a political or geographical nation. He was referring to the "holy nation" of His Church, the people who are His representatives on earth in this age. These terms Peter draws on are all borrowed from the Old Testament. They originally applied to Israel, but Peter uses them to describe the Church. In doing so, he is telling us that God is doing something brand new in the Church.

In Israel, being a priest was the highest honor you could get. Today, you and I minister as God's priests—and not just priests but royal priests. That means you're a child of the King. You have been given the incredible privilege of ministering before God in His new temple, the Church.

More than that, you and I have gone from nobodies to somebodies in Christ. What do I mean? Well, as Gentiles we were outside the covenant nation of Israel. Paul says we were strangers to God's promises, like hungry folk looking in the window of a fine restaurant (Ephesians 2:11-12).

But that's all changed now. We're somebody. We've been adopted by Jesus Christ. We're family now. If you are having trouble "finding yourself," let God tell you who you are.

————— **Think About It** —————
Now as God's priest, you don't freelance. You have only
one message to deliver: the "excellencies" of the One who
brought you from darkness to the light.

"Put on the Lord Jesus Christ, and make no provision
for the flesh in regard to its lusts." Romans 13:14

JUST PASSIN' THROUGH
Read It: 1 Peter 2:11-12

Remember the old cowboy movie where a guy would ride into town, tie his horse up outside the saloon, and go in for a drink? He'd stand at the bar as the locals stared at him intently. Finally, one of them would come over and say, "Howdy, stranger. You're new in town, ain't ya?"

"Yup."

"Will ya be stayin'?"

"Nope. Just passin' through."

Well, that's the idea Peter has in mind here. We're strangers on earth now. We're aliens to this environment even though this is where we reside and operate for the time being. But our homestead is in heaven.

If you're just passing through, you don't want to get tangled up in local hassles. That cowboy didn't have too much to worry about, because he would soon ride off and leave that town and all its problems behind him.

Now the analogy breaks down here, because our job is not just to pass through town. We're to leave a witness. God did not just save us so He could take us to heaven someday. He wants us to be walking advertisements for heaven while we're here on earth. Why? Because other folk need to know about heaven and how to get there.

But if we as God's people get all tangled up in fleshly lusts and start looking, talking, and acting like everybody else, don't be surprised if the world starts taking potshots at the church. It's one thing to be falsely accused and slandered as an evildoer when you're actually doing good. It's another thing to be called an evildoer—and have the charges stick!

Let's change the imagery from cowboys to space aliens. How do you know when an alien from outer space shows up in a science-fiction movie? Well, he looks different. He acts different. He communicates in a different way. He's not interested in "earthling" stuff because he's got higher business to tend to. He's on a mission for his master.

Do you ever feel a little different as a Christian? That's good. Just make sure you're different for the right reasons.

——— **Think About It** ———

It's true that we are a "peculiar people" (v. 10, KJV).
But that means special, called, chosen—not odd!

REFLECTION

Sooner or later, if you live your life by the standards of God's Word, someone will say of you, "That isn't natural."

To which the correct answer is, "You're right. It isn't natural. It's supernatural." See, being an alien means you function in a whole different realm. You take your instructions from another planet, from an unseen Leader.

I'm convinced that if you are a Christian, there ought to be something supernatural, something other-worldly, about the way you run your business, treat your family, handle your money. There ought to be a quality about your life that makes people say, "I can't figure this guy out, but I want what he's got."

I alluded yesterday to the fact that Christians are not called to be different just for the sake of being unusual or even odd. Unlike a movie alien with a scary face and body, we're supposed to attract people to our Leader so that they will want Him to be their Leader too.

Yes, there will always be some folk who are put off by your witness and who will slander you as an evildoer. But if your behavior is excellent among them, and if you are showing off the excellencies of your Leader, the Lord Jesus Christ, then that's their problem to deal with, not yours.

So let me ask you this weekend: Are you an attractive alien? If you're not sure, get out the Word and give yourself a look-see (James 1:23-25).

"I have not written to you because you do not know the truth,
but because you do know it." 1 John 2:21

THE WORD MADE SURE
Read It: 2 Peter 1:12-15

Imagine having Paul and Peter stand before your church and say, "We're about to depart this life and go to be with Jesus. But we wanted to leave you with a final exhortation."

I suspect that you and everyone else would be leaning forward in your pews in anticipation of what these two giants, these two foundation stones of the Church, would have to say. You'd have your pen and paper out, ready to capture their last words.

Well, you can put your pen away and quit pretending, because we already have the parting exhortations of Peter and Paul, and we're going to look at them this week. We've studied the power, the program, and the perspective of the Church. I want to conclude this section by talking about the prophetic word of the Church.

See, you and I have something better than having Peter and Paul stand before us. We have something "more sure" than if Peter were here in person to verify the truthfulness of everything that happened in the Gospels. We have the completed revelation of God, His "prophetic word" (v. 19).

Now for Peter, that meant the Old Testament in particular, since the New Testament was still being written. But now that the Scriptures are complete, the Holy Spirit wants us to understand that the entire Word of God is included in Peter's assurance.

Now, remember, Peter was writing with urgency because Jesus had revealed to him that his time was short.These verses are part of a last will and testament, his final legacy to the Church. And what parting exhortation did the great apostle leave? Not, "Remember me," but, "Hold to the Word. Obey the Word." Here we see how wise the Head of the Church is.

If Jesus had left us anything but His Holy Spirit and the written Word, it wouldn't have remained. People die and pass on. The memory of them fades. What they told us gets mixed up and lost as the years go by. That's why you don't build the Church on people. But the Spirit is the eternal God, and the Word is forever settled in heaven.

——————— **Think About It** ———————
Peter was "diligent" to remind you of the truth.
You need to be diligent in applying it to your life (see vv. 5, 10).

"Preach the word; be ready in season and out of season."
2 Timothy 4:2

PREACH THE WORD
Read It: 2 Timothy 4:1-8

Here is Paul's last will and testament to the Church. Now this gets personal for me, because Paul's charge is specifically made to pastors who are called of God to preach and teach the Scriptures. But the whole church can learn a lot about the importance of the Word from this passage.

There's no question here that Paul saw his death as imminent. These verses carry the solemnity of a will being read to the family by an attorney and then being carried out according to the wishes of the deceased. But there's nothing morbid or gloomy about this. Paul wasn't afraid of death, because he was ready. He was looking forward to hearing Jesus say, "Well done, My good and faithful servant."

And by the way, the "crown of righteousness" Paul anticipated isn't just for preachers, but for "all" who love the Lord's appearing. That includes you if you're a born-again child of God.

I want you to notice what occupied Paul's mind and heart as he wrote. It was the Word of God, the Word that Christ committed to His Church, the Word that we are commissioned to defend and proclaim, the Word that can keep the Church strong and pure if we believe it and obey it.

Why was Paul so high on the Word? Because he knew its origin. You can't fully appreciate how strongly Paul felt about the faithful preaching of the Word until you back up and read verses 10-17 of chapter 3. Paul knew that days of apostasy, times of falling away from the truth, were on the way. He wanted Timothy to be aware of the danger. But more than that, Paul wanted Timothy to know that he possessed the antidote to unbelief and error: the "sacred writings" (v. 15), the Scripture that was God-breathed and therefore totally reliable and profitable for every spiritual need we have (vv. 16-17).

See the wisdom of God's plan here? It's what we talked about yesterday. We in the Church have the inspired, infallible, inerrant Word of God to guide and guard us. That's why the Word we preach today is the same Word Paul urged Timothy to preach. God's truth doesn't change.

--------- **Think About It** ---------
If you knew you were going to die soon, what legacy would
you leave behind that would benefit the body of Christ?

"What we have seen and heard we proclaim to you also."
1 John 1:3

BETTER THAN BEING THERE
Read It: 2 Peter 1:16-18

What Peter wants us to know is that the Word of God will stand even after people are gone. He wants to make sure we understand that when he talks about the Word, he's not talking about a bunch of made-up fairy tales that we just close our eyes and believe in anyway. The apostles did not pull the Gospel, the Word, the truth about Jesus Christ, out of the air. They were eyewitnesses of the things they wrote about.

Peter is saying, "You have my solemn testimony that these things are true." In fact, there is no doubt that Peter was aware he was writing Scripture here. And he knew that for later generations of Christians like us who are far removed from the earthly days of Christ, his testimony recorded and verified in Scripture would be all-important.

So Peter wanted to remove any doubt that the Word we have is true. I don't know about you, but for me that's real important, because sometimes I have moments of doubt like everybody else. Preachers are not immune to doubt.

But when the doubts come, it's great to be able to go back to the basics, open the Word, and hear Peter say again, "When the question crosses your mind, just remember that I am not just telling you a tale I was told. I was there. I saw something. The Holy Spirit is my witness that this is true."

One of the things Peter saw was the transfiguration of Christ, recorded in Matthew 17. You'll recall that on the mountain Peter heard God speak and saw Moses and Elijah appear and talk with Jesus. Moses represented the Law, and Elijah the Prophets—the Old Testament, in other words. And Jesus was there representing the new word from God. So what Peter says is that the whole Bible was there on that mountain witnessing to the deity of Jesus Christ.

Peter never forgot that day. Neither did the Apostle John, as today's verse shows. But Peter is saying that as powerful as that experience was, what we have now is even better. We have the Word.

--------- **Think About It** ---------
Doubts are bound to come. It's what you do with them that's
important. Don't let your doubts drown out the Word.
Let the Word speak to your doubts.

"See to it that you do not refuse Him who is speaking."
Hebrews 12:25

HOLD ON UNTIL . . .
Read It: 2 Peter 1:19

Peter says we have a Word that is even better than what he saw on the mountain. That's the payoff to today's study.

Now he's not saying that there was anything unreliable about the testimony he just gave of what he saw on the Mount of Transfiguration. God forbid. Peter's testimony is now part of Scripture itself, which means the Holy Spirit has verified it.

What Peter wants us to know is that we are not stuck with second-hand goods because we didn't get to see and walk with Jesus. Actually, we have the advantage because we have the completed Word.

So what should our response be? To pay attention to the Word. Not to mess with it or ignore it, but to take heed to it as to a lamp shining in the darkness. What does a lamp do? It gives light. So even if there is darkness all around you, if you have a lamp, you have light. You may be in deep darkness right now. But Peter says if you just hold to the Word in the darkness, if you stay in the realm of the light, then the darkness will turn to dawning when the "morning star" rises and bursts upon you.

I think the rising star Peter is talking about is the breaking forth of the Word of God into your life in power. That's why he urges you to hold onto the Word in the darkness, because when push comes to shove, it's the thing that will keep you.

So my message for you today is hold onto the Word. If it looks like God has forgotten you, hold onto the Word. If it looks like Satan is winning out there, hold onto the Word. If it looks like you can't hold on any longer, get somebody else to help you hold onto the Word.

How long? "Until." Now I like that. It doesn't say if or maybe or possibly, but until—until God takes you up to the mountain like He took Peter. Then when the power and the glory of God shine forth in your life, you can tell someone else what you have seen and heard.

——— **Think About It** ———
Whatever else you do, don't let go of the Word.
It will see you through any darkness.

"All Scripture is inspired by God." 2 Timothy 3:16

KNOW ALL OF IT
Read It: 2 Peter 1:20-21

One of the tragedies of our day is people who twist the Scriptures to suit their private purposes. What's to keep people from doing that and trying to sell it as the pure Word of God? Well, we may not be able to keep people from going off on a tangent with the Bible, but Peter gives us a warrant for saying you can't do it any way you want.

Verse 20 says you can't just pick out a few verses to bolster your cause. That's the way Satan used the Bible with Jesus in the temptation in the wilderness. He tried to get Jesus to jump off the temple on the biblical premise that God would keep Him from harm.

I love what Jesus said. He didn't get into an interpretational argument with the Devil. He just said, "On the other hand," and brought up another subject that exposed Satan's scheme as illegitimate (Matthew 4:7).

In other words, you need to know the whole Scripture, not just a few verses. See, if Satan had tried quoting the Bible to some of us, we would have scratched our heads and said, "Well, sounds okay to me. I can't see anything wrong with that. After all, it's Bible."

But you can't make up your own interpretation as you go, because the writers of Scripture didn't make this stuff up as they went along. They were carried along by the Holy Spirit, who protected them from error and guaranteed that what the Bible says is what God wanted it to say.

We don't have the Bible today just because some men woke up one day and said, "Let's write a book." When someone says the Bible was written by human beings, that's only half right. The human authors of Scripture wrote as they were pushed along by the breath of the Holy Spirit, the way a sailboat is carried along by the wind.

The point is, we have a sure Word from God. We have a Word you can stake your life on. That means even when you don't want to believe it, it's still true. Even when you don't want to obey it, it's still right. It's a sure and certain Word.

——— **Think About It** ———

Jesus' example reminds us how important it is to grow in
our knowledge of God's Word. John 3:16 will get you
to heaven, but you can't stop there.

REFLECTION

I've been studying, preaching, and teaching the Word of God for more years than I care to think about, and I'm more amazed by it every time I open it.

Only a Book inspired by God could hold such depths of wisdom. I went to seminary for four years and got a master's degree in theology; then I went four more years and got my doctorate. When I graduated, I felt like I was still in kindergarten, because the Bible moves from milk to meat.

You can gulp milk down, but meat takes a little more work. You have to dig a little deeper in the Scriptures to deal with the meat. But the more you chew, the more you find that the Bible contains nourishment beyond what you can even imagine.

What am I saying? I am saying that the more you grow in grace and knowledge, the more you know what people are talking about when they talk about the peace, the joy, the encouragement, and the strength they find in the Word.

I am more committed to the Word today than the day I first opened it, for several reasons. First and foremost, because it is the truth and because I have been called to proclaim it.

But I have also discovered that the Word calms me when I am ruffled, cools me when I am frustrated, guides me when I am lost, and teaches me when I lack wisdom. It is sufficient for every need. Have you found the Bible to be all of that and more to you? If not, God is waiting to meet you in power in His Word. What are you waiting for?

THIRTEEN

◇

IT'S HIS BIRTHDAY

Deciding to Worship Jesus at Christmas

Before Christmas was a holiday, it was a birthday. Unfortunately, this has gotten lost. Apart from a few religious ceremonies, Christmas is primarily a time for sinning and shopping. For many people, Christmas is big business, and the birth of Christ is secondary. If you want to make sure that doesn't happen in your heart, if you want to worship Christ this Christmas, it has to be a decision on your part. In these final weeks together, I want to help you do that by looking at the biblical story of Christmas.

*"When the fulness of the time came, God sent forth
His Son, born of a woman." Galatians 4:4*

AN IMPORTANT LIST
Read It: Matthew 1:1-17; Luke 3:23-38

You're probably wondering why we are starting our Christmas devotional series with genealogies. Simple answer: Because that's where the New Testament starts. See, the Christmas story doesn't begin with Matthew 1:18 or Luke 1:26. It begins with "the book of the genealogy of Jesus Christ" (Matthew 1:1).

Now we're not going to work our way through all these names in the two lists, so relax. What I want you to see today is that the preparation for the birth of Jesus Christ reveals the sovereignty of God in an unforgettable way. Every name on these lists tells a story of how God controlled, ruled, and overruled in the affairs of people and nations to accomplish His will in the incarnation of His Son. Paul was right on target when he said Jesus was born not a minute too early or too late. He was right on God's time.

Matthew's record shows that Jesus was related by royalty to David. Luke's genealogy reveals that Jesus was related to David by family. Matthew says Jesus was tied to David through Solomon, so He had a legitimate right to the throne. Luke says that Jesus was related to David through David's other son, Nathan, which is Mary's line. So Jesus was the heir to David's throne and a Son of David through His family.

To arrange all this, God had to do some sovereign matchmaking. He also had to deal with an incredible array of people, good and not so good, over many hundreds of years to set the stage of history for Jesus' arrival.

The genealogies of Jesus reveal another beautiful facet of God's character: His grace. There are some messed-up folk on Matthew's list. David's name is there. He was guilty of adultery and murder. Bathsheba is there too (v. 6). Solomon is also present, the king who loved many foreign women. I also read the name of Rahab the prostitute (v. 5). And what about Manasseh? He was a wicked king for fifty-five long years.

Do you see the grace of God in action? He never excuses sin, but He forgives and uses imperfect people. That means He can use us.

──────── **Think About It** ────────
No matter how you've messed up, God can bring something
good from your life if you'll give yourself to Him.

"She will bear a Son; and you shall call His name Jesus."
Matthew 1:21

TWO RIGHTEOUS PEOPLE
Read It: Matthew 1:18-21, 24-25

A word of caution as we dive into the Christmas story today. Don't let familiarity breed a spirit of complacency, an attitude that says, "Oh yeah, I've heard this so many times. I know exactly what happens."

I say this because God's Word is always fresh, and the Spirit always has something new to teach us if we are open to His ministry. So pray for a teachable spirit. Ask God to give you a childlike sense of wonder for the next four weeks.

Matthew cuts to the chase right away. Mary is pregnant, and Joseph knows the baby is not his. So as not to publicly disgrace Mary, he makes plans to divorce her quietly. But then he hears from God. The angel tells Joseph that this baby is the Savior, the fulfillment of God's program.

You have to love Joseph's response (v. 24; I'm saving vv. 22-23 for tomorrow), because it is a response of pure faith. When he hears from the angel, he embraces God's word so completely that he completely reverses his plans. Instead of divorcing Mary, he takes her as his wife and cooperates fully in carrying out the will of God.

Think about this. Do you know why God could do a miracle through Joseph and Mary? Because they were righteous people. The Holy Spirit was free to do His Holy Spirit thing because they were righteous people.

Now Joseph wasn't perfect, and neither was Mary. But the driving passion of their lives was honoring God in their attitudes and actions. If you don't have a passion for holiness, you are not a good candidate for God's miracle. They had a passion for holiness.

Because a holy God was getting ready to produce a holy Son, He wanted to work through holy people. The Bible says that Joseph protected Mary's virginity. He would not touch her sexually during the entire betrothal period and pregnancy. And we know from Luke's account the kind of godly woman Mary was. I wonder what God could do if He could find two righteous people like that today? There's no telling.

——————— **Think About It** ———————
Joseph had a moral code that would not allow him to compromise.
Mary had a godly character. And they were both obedient.
Any Josephs and Marys out there today?

*"The Lord Himself will give you a sign: Behold, a virgin will be
with child and bear a son." Isaiah 7:14*

A CANDIDATE FOR MIRACLES
Read It: Matthew 1:22-23

I want to step back a little today and talk about the greatest miracle God ever performed and about this whole area of miracles. The greatest miracle in history is Christmas—God becoming a man. A pregnant virgin is indeed a miracle. Mary's pregnancy was the result of the activity of the Holy Spirit. As I began to reflect on the miracle of Christmas, I began thinking about miracles.

The reason miracles happen is that God the Holy Spirit is at work in our world. And wherever He is at work, the miraculous is possible. But God does not dispense miracles on demand, nor does He grant them to make us feel good and fulfill all of our wishes. His miracles always serve *His* purposes, not any man's. Let me show you what I mean.

The miracle of the virgin birth occurred because it was the "fulness of time." Mary became pregnant because in God's plan it was time to send us a Savior who would pay the penalty for our sins. So the miracle of a pregnant virgin was to accomplish God's salvation program.

What I am saying is this: If you are living for God's glory and are plugged into His will and His agenda, you are a candidate for a display of His miraculous power. Now just saying that scares some people, because they think of the excesses of what I call the "miracle-chasers" who try to get God to perform on demand, usually for personal gain.

That's not what I'm talking about. But we usually run too far the other way and rule out the possibility of God using us in a truly miraculous way. Joseph and Mary weren't looking for a miracle. But when they realized their situation would glorify God and accomplish His will, they were ready to go.

God does miracles to achieve His will and bring glory to Himself. Now there will never be another virgin birth. There doesn't need to be. But faith says that the God who can form a baby in a virgin's womb when it accomplishes His plan can do miraculous things through ordinary people like you and me if we are committed to Him.

——— Think About It ———
If you believe the Bible, you know that miracles do happen.
Is there a miracle needed in your life that will glorify God?

"It is he who will go as a forerunner before Him . . . to make ready a people prepared for the Lord." Luke 1:17

ANOTHER MIRACLE
Read It: Luke 1:5-25

Today we meet the supporting cast of the Christmas drama. Mary and Joseph weren't the only righteous couple in the story. Their relatives Zacharias and Elizabeth were also righteous (v. 6). But they had a problem. They were old and cold (v. 7).

Zacharias was one of twenty thousand priests who served at the temple in those days, divided into twenty-four orders or "divisions" that rotated (v. 5). Therefore, the odds were against a priest like Zacharias being chosen for the honor of burning incense in the temple. If a priest got to do this once in a lifetime, he was fortunate.

But Zacharias's number was called, because God doesn't pay any attention to odds. So Zacharias was performing his priestly duty in the temple when an angel suddenly appeared to him. That would be enough to scare most of us. But that wasn't the only reason Zack was scared. When a priest was offering sacrifice in the Holy Place in the temple, there would be only one reason for an angel to appear. Zacharias had done something wrong—and when you do something wrong in the temple, you die.

So Zacharias was getting ready to meet God. He was scared to death. But instead he got his own miraculous birth announcement, like the one God gave to Abraham and Sarah, another "old and cold" couple.

Now Zacharias and Elizabeth must have been married for a long time. They had probably been praying for a child for many years, since barrenness in Israel was still a disgrace (v. 25). They may have even given up. But the angel said, "It's prayer-answering time."

See, they wanted a child, but it was not yet God's time. He didn't just want Zacharias and Elizabeth to have a child. He wanted them to be the parents of Jesus' forerunner, John the Baptist. In order to give them this special child at the right time, God didn't answer their prayer earlier.

Zacharias questioned Gabriel, so Gabriel said, "Excuse me? I've just come from God's presence to speak to you. Since you don't believe God's word, you don't speak for nine months." It doesn't pay to doubt God!

——— **Think About It** ———

God wants you to believe Him just because He said it.
In His case, saying it makes it so.

"Nothing will be impossible with God." Luke 1:37

SO BE IT
Read It: Luke 1:26-38

Today's text is one of the most beautiful and moving in Scripture. But it's not a pretext for worshiping Mary. She was a godly and virtuous young woman, but God never instructed anyone to worship or pray to Mary. Mary needed a Savior just like you and me (see 1:47). As we said the other day, Mary was righteous, but she wasn't sinless. She was privileged, but she wasn't perfect.

The announcement to Mary came in the sixth month of Elizabeth's pregnancy with John the Baptist. Both births would be miraculous, but there was a huge difference between them. John the Baptist would come through the normal means of human conception, as unlikely as conception was between an older couple like Zacharias and Elizabeth.

Mary, of course, was a virgin. So this would be a miracle of God from beginning to end. This helps to explain why Gabriel did not rebuke Mary for asking a question (v. 34) the way he rebuked Zacharias. Mary was asking a logical question, given her virginity. Besides, her response in verse 38 shows that she was not expressing doubt or unbelief in God's word.

Jesus could not have a human father because He had to be a perfect man to die for the sins of imperfect people. So Joseph could not be Jesus' biological father, or Jesus would have been tainted by the virus of sin. Jesus needed a Father who was as perfect as He had to be. The only Father who meets that criterion is God. So in Jesus we have perfect God and perfect man, the God-Man who was fully man and fully God simultaneously.

So Mary believed the word of God over against her physical circumstances. She did not know how, but she did know *who*.

See, too many of us try to figure God out. But His methodology isn't always clear, and He's under no obligation to explain every detail to us. All we need to know is that He is accomplishing His glory and His program through His people.

Mary's question was: "How is this possible?" When God answered her, all she needed to say was, "So be it."

--------- **Think About It** ---------
When you know God, you don't have to know how
He's going to do what He said He would do. You just have
to know that it's God who is going to do it.

REFLECTION

Sometime during this Christmas season, you'll probably hear a sermon decrying the continued secularization of Christmas. So let me get my sermon in early!

In the introduction to this section, I mentioned the fact that for most people Christmas is big business, a time for sinning and shopping. I also said that if you want to make your Christmas a time of worship, it will take a definite decision on your part.

See, it bothers me when kids have more affection for Santa Claus than they do for Jesus Christ. I'm concerned when people are more interested in what's under the tree than who was in the manger.

Now don't get me wrong. Claus is my boy. There's nothing wrong with Santa Claus as long as we understand that he has nothing to do with Christmas. Let's just call it what it is, toy time, and try not to confuse it with the worship of Jesus Christ.

Same thing goes for a tree or lights or whatever else you want to put up as decorations. That's fine, but just don't let those things serve as a substitute for your worship this Christmas.

In fact, you can use all the symbols of the Christmas season as an object lesson to help your family understand the difference between a winter holiday of gift-giving and bright lights and God's act in history of sending the Savior to redeem us. May God bless you and help you to make worship a priority this Christmas.

*"My soul exalts the Lord, and my spirit has rejoiced
in God my Savior." Luke 1:46-47*

THE POWER OF GOD
Read It: Luke 1:39-56

I love this part of the Christmas story, because now it starts getting real good. Now we are talking about the power of God.

First, we have an elderly woman who was barren now in the sixth month of her pregnancy. And the child she is carrying is John the Baptist, the forerunner of Jesus Christ.

Now we've got a miracle working here because we already know the Holy Spirit is at work. The Spirit's power is evident in today's text when Elizabeth heard Mary's voice. All Mary had to do was say, "Hi, Liz," and the baby in Elizabeth's womb started leaping for joy. Then people go around talking about, "Human life doesn't begin in the womb." But that's another lesson.

Anyway, when Elizabeth heard Mary's greeting and felt the baby jump, she knew immediately that Mary was pregnant and that her baby was the Messiah. How did Elizabeth know all of that? Because it was the Holy Spirit talking. Luke says she "was filled with the Holy Spirit" (v. 41).

So the Holy Spirit was confirming to Mary through Elizabeth what the angel had told Mary earlier, that she would become pregnant and carry the Savior. Mary knew she was expecting, not because she felt something, but because God was telling her and confirming it through Elizabeth. Here we see the power of God in action as the Holy Spirit brought these two women in contact with one another, validating His work in the miraculous conception of Jesus.

When Mary heard all of this, she quickly drew on her Bible memory program and began a beautiful song of praise that is known as the "Magnificat," from the Latin word for magnify (KJV). Mary did not say, "I don't believe it. Give me a doctor to substantiate it." She did not ask for any of that. She simply said, "Holy Spirit? That's all I need to know."

See, when the Holy Spirit is involved, He is not necessarily going to use a method you are familiar with, a normal means. Mary gave glory to God without knowing all the details. She simply believed Him.

──────── **Think About It** ────────

If you believe that God can and God does, then the only question left is: "Will He do it at this time for me?" And that's His call.

*"She gave birth to her first-born son; and she wrapped Him in
cloths, and laid him in a manger." Luke 2:7*

IRS TIME
Read It: Luke 2:1-7

Now I'm not an artist, but I want to paint a word picture for you today, because I think it will help you appreciate even more the miracle we call Christmas.

The first-century world into which Jesus was born was a chaotic place. It was a world of political turmoil, an environment of endless intrigues and plots and revolutions. The Jews had their own super-patriots, called Zealots, who were dedicated to overthrowing Rome. One of Jesus' disciples was "Simon who was called the Zealot" (Luke 6:15).

The bully of the world into which Jesus was born was, of course, mighty Rome. Rome crushed nation after nation to expand its rule across the known world. It taxed its subjects until they were bled dry. Israel was under Roman rule and basically helpless to do anything about it.

The king on the throne in Judea was a crazy man named Herod the Great, whom we'll meet again later this week. He was legendary for his cruelty, putting members of his own family to death when he suspected they might be plotting against him. He held Judea in his iron grip. As an occupied people, the Jews had little choice but to submit to Rome's rule. But the tensions were always high.

Religiously, Israel hadn't heard from God for nearly four hundred years. There were no prophets, no miracles, little true worship of and reverence for the God of Abraham, Isaac, and Jacob. Nobody seemed to be really looking for or expecting Messiah to come. All in all, things were in a mess.

What's my point? Just this. You can take all of that mess and all of that intrigue and all of that fighting for power and position and set it aside when God gets ready to move! When He says it's time for His Son to come, He moves men and nations to accomplish His plan.

Case in point: Mary and Joseph had to get to Bethlehem so Jesus would be born there and fulfill Scripture. No problem. God just says, "It's IRS time," and the job is done. When God gets ready to move, don't worry about the mess around you!

--------- **Think About It** ---------
If God hasn't answered yet, don't stop praying.
When He gets ready to act, obstacles are irrelevant.

*"Today in the city of David there has been born for you
a Savior, who is Christ the Lord." Luke 2:11*

THE RIGHT IDEA
Read It: Luke 2:8-20

The great artist Rembrandt was one of the many artists who attempted to portray the scene in Bethlehem's manger. But nobody did it better than the Dutchman. His nativity scene focuses your attention exclusively on the baby in the manger. Rembrandt captured the biblical idea by painting a shaft of light so that it fell on the baby Jesus and illuminated Him alone. Rembrandt put the other figures in the painting, but he wrapped them in the shadows so that all the adoration goes to Jesus.

Centering all the attention on Jesus is just what God the Father had in mind that first Christmas night. We'll see tomorrow that the magi were only interested in worshiping Jesus. And we know from this famous story in Luke 2 that the shepherds had the right idea too.

When I try to picture a scene like the one described in verses 8-14, I can see why people want to become artists and try to capture moments like this on canvas. This is Christmas card stuff: a great choir of angels filling the sky while a band of shepherds look up in terrified wonder.

See, you have to like these shepherds, because they caught on right away and got in the spirit of this thing. They wanted to worship this new King too, so they went running off to Bethlehem with real joy and anticipation in their hearts. What I like about these men is that ordinarily they had little to get excited about. Shepherds in that day were a pretty despised group. They were poor. Their occupation was on the bottom rung of the career ladder.

Now they didn't get excited that first Christmas because they thought they were going to get some presents. They didn't get pumped to go see baby Jesus because they heard the manger was all lit up with pretty lights. And they weren't looking for an overweight man in a red suit. They just wanted to worship their Messiah.

There's nothing wrong with pretty lights. Ornaments are fine. But if all we had this Christmas was Jesus, would it be enough to send us jumping for joy? I hope so. I pray it would.

———— Think About It ————
If you can't get excited about Jesus this Christmas,
better check your spiritual pulse.

"Where is He who has been born King of the Jews? We . . . have
come to worship Him." Matthew 2:2

THE INCONVENIENCE OF WORSHIP
Read It: Matthew 2:1-6

Let's talk about the amazing magi for a few days. They were professional astronomers. But they were more than just stargazers, because when the star appeared they knew the true God was up to something.

Maybe they knew the prophecy of Numbers 24:17: "A star will come out of Jacob; a scepter will rise out of Israel." A scepter means a king is coming. The magi must have been familiar with Israel's Scriptures because they knew the One they were looking for was "King of the Jews."

So they set off on a journey that took well over a year, maybe as long as two years. No price was too high to find this King and worship Him.

Now you can imagine the stir the magi made when they arrived in Jerusalem. These men were from the east. They were Gentiles, so they were not even the ones who were supposed to be expecting Jesus.

King Herod got shook up. I guess so. If you are the king and some folk show up to worship another king born in your neighborhood and you don't even know who he is, you are going to be a little upset.

So Herod called in the preachers. Now they knew the answer. "Oh yeah, we know who they're talking about. He's just down the road in Bethlehem. Says right here in Micah 5:2."

This shows that knowing the Bible and worshiping God aren't the same thing. These preachers knew the Bible, but they weren't even looking for Messiah. But some Gentiles living a thousand miles away spent a year or two searching for Him.

See, knowing the Word of God does you little good until you give the God of the Word the worship He's due. These men had the right answers, but not the right worship. They didn't want to be inconvenienced.

Jesus had been born down the street. By now He was almost two years old, still living in Bethlehem, but they hadn't even bothered to check it out. The only reason they brought it up was because Herod grilled them.

If you haven't inconvenienced yourself to worship Jesus, you haven't worshiped yet.

──────── **Think About It** ────────
You'll know your worship is getting serious when neither the inconvenience nor the price of worship can stop you from worshiping God.

"When they saw the star, they rejoiced exceedingly with great joy."
Matthew 2:10

GO WEST, BOYS
Read It: Matthew 2:7-10

I find it interesting that Herod secretly called the magi and sent them to Bethlehem to check out this new King. Why didn't he send his own men? They were more dependable than those Eastern "tourists," weren't they? Herod didn't think so. He didn't send the preachers, because he figured if they had kept this thing quiet this long, he wasn't going to let them mess up now. Besides, as Jews they might not like what he had in mind for this new King. So he sent the magi to Bethlehem.

Now we know these men were driven by a passion to worship the true God. As a result, they also enjoyed His guidance. God led them to Jerusalem by means of His star, the Shechinah glory that we read about in the Old Testament, the brightness of God's glory.

Now when they got to Jerusalem, they didn't know where to go from there. So they did the logical thing and started asking around. As we saw yesterday, Herod didn't have a clue, but his court preachers knew where Jesus was from their study of the Scriptures. So God used an ungodly king and ungodly preachers to lead the magi to the next step.

There's a great truth here I want you to see. God's guidance is such that if you follow what you do know, He will show you what you don't know until you get where you are supposed to go.

People ask, "How come God won't lead me?" Because you haven't followed Him in His general leading, so He won't give you specifics. The magi started out knowing only that God was telling them, "Go west."

So they made their way west. Then all they knew was that they were in the general vicinity of their destination, so they asked questions and got some nifty specifics from Herod's crowd. Then the star led them right to the house.

That's specific guidance. It took a lot of faith for the magi to head west. But God sharpened the direction signs each step of the way, and the result was that they experienced the "exceedingly great joy" they anticipated when they left.

--- **Think About It** ---

God will never show you the specifics of His will if He
can't trust you to obey Him in His general will.

REFLECTION

When you talk about Christmas being a time of worship, you can see why the magi, the wise men, are my boys.

They're on the scene for only one purpose: to worship the newborn King. Now Herod claims he wants to worship the Babe of Bethlehem too, but he's on another track altogether.

See, even if Herod's motive had not been to murder Jesus, his claim to worship Him was still no good. Herod would probably have legalized the holiday, giving it government recognition and mixing the sacred and the secular all up. Herod was not a worshiper. In fact, he would have wanted to take a big slice of the glory for himself.

So God sends the magi back home another way. By doing so, God is saying, "If you are going to worship Me, worship Me only." See, you can't worship God and anyone or anything else: Santa, Bloomingdales, Saks, whatever. This is no corporate deal. If you are going to worship God this Christmas, worship Him alone.

God was born in the form of man so that we might be related to Him. That's the message of Christmas. This means that the only time over this holiday season that you will have Christmas is when you and your family are worshiping and focusing on Christ.

Now as I said last weekend, if you want to have a happy holiday time with family, friends, fireplace, laughter, lights, and all that, that's great. Just make sure you don't miss the uniqueness of Christmas: God with us!

*"All nations whom Thou hast made shall come
and worship before Thee, O Lord." Psalm 86:9*

NO LEFTOVER ATTITUDE
Read It: Matthew 2:11-12

By the time the magi arrived in Bethlehem, Jesus was no longer a new-born. He was probably a toddler, living not in a stable but in a house.

The main thing is that when the wise men saw Jesus, they fell down and worshiped Him. This child had created them. He had created His parents. He had created the ground on which the house stood.

The magi understood who Jesus was. They understood that this moment was worth the trip, that Jesus Christ deserved to be worshiped. And they gave Him gifts worthy of a King: gold, frankincense, and myrrh.

Now I want to show you something. Joseph and Mary were dirt poor. We know that from the poor people's sacrifice they offered later for Jesus (Luke 2:24). They also had a problem. Herod was going to come looking for Jesus to kill Him. They needed to flee to Egypt.

Jesus' folks didn't have the money to go to Egypt and live there till Herod died—until the magi presented their gifts. God became their sufficiency because they worshiped Him. Remember, they were there worshiping Jesus along with the magi.

My focus for this Christmas is worship. When you're willing to pay the price to worship God, He becomes your sufficiency. He meets your needs.

Because Joseph and Mary and the magi were His worshipers, God was able to supply the needs of His Son's parents to protect Him from Herod. Worship puts you in a context where God can meet your needs. Worship also brings God's protection. He wasn't going to let the magi come all that way to worship Him and then be ambushed by Herod (v. 12).

What is worship worth to you? Those men came a long way for one worship service. They spent more than a year on the road just to bow before a child and present Him with gifts.

Worshiping Jesus Christ wasn't a leftover attitude for them. It was a priority. If you want to understand Christmas, worship Him. Many of us don't appreciate the high cost of worship. You don't come before a King without paying a price.

--- **Think About It** ---

Worship is costly, but so is anything in life
that has value and meaning to it.

"See to it that you do not refuse Him who is speaking . . .
from heaven." Hebrews 12:25

THE JUDGMENT OF CHRISTMAS
Read It: Matthew 2:13-18

One other thing happened that first Christmas, but you won't find it in any Christmas pageant or on Christmas cards—God's judgment.

Verse 18 is a quote from Jeremiah 31:15. Rachel was considered the mother of Israel because she was the favorite wife of Jacob, the father of the twelve tribes, and she was the mother of Joseph and Benjamin. Rachel was barren for a long time. One day she cried out, "Give me children, or I'll die!" (Genesis 3:1). God answered her prayer, and Rachel came to be viewed as the mother of Israel. In fact, she was buried near Bethlehem.

The image of Rachel weeping for her children was picked up by Jeremiah to picture the nation weeping over the children dying or going into exile into Babylon as God's judgment fell on a nation that had rejected Him. Jeremiah was the prophet of the Babylonian captivity of Israel, a time of great weeping. So he pictured Rachel crying for her children.

Matthew says this prophetic image was fulfilled in Herod's slaughter of the babies in Bethlehem. Even though this was a cruel act for which Herod was responsible, he was the instrument of God's judgment on Israel for rejecting His Son.

You say, "Tony, that's hard. That doesn't sound like Christmas." You're right. It is hard. But it is a part of the Christmas message. We must understand that whenever you reject Jesus Christ, you pay a price. Not because God is mean, but because He is holy and must judge sin. Unfortunately, the sins of the fathers often fall on the innocents.

When you reject Christ, you remove His protection from yourself, your family, and even your nation (Hebrews 10:26-27). But when you accept Him, He protects you as He carries out His will so that nothing can happen to you outside of His plan.

Christmas is more than a baby in a manger. It is "God with us." That's a wonderful message worth celebrating and singing about. But when God shows up, you've got a decision to make. You either worship Him, or you turn away. Both decisions are costly, but only worship is worth the cost.

——— **Think About It** ———

Many people will wind up in debt because they want a nice Christmas. How much are you willing to pay to worship the King?

*"God [has] bestowed on [Jesus] the name
which is above every name." Philippians 2:9*

THE HIGHEST NAME
Read It: Isaiah 9:6

The essence of Christmas is captured in this phrase: "God with us." That's what it's about. The theological term is the Incarnation, the "becoming flesh," of God. The reason we have a holiday is that God became man. To only admire Christ as a great person, a great prophet, or a great teacher is to devalue and insult Jesus. He is God in the flesh.

You can see this truth in Isaiah's prophecy. The two amazing verses we will study today and tomorrow actually take in both comings of Christ, first as the baby in Bethlehem and then as the mighty King ruling on David's throne.

Notice how Isaiah 9:6 distinguishes between the birth of Jesus and His eternal existence. As a child He is born, but as the Son He is given. Jesus was never born as the Son of God. He is eternal God, the second Person of the Trinity.

When we talk about Christmas, we are talking about God coming to dwell among us. Now, one of these days someone may come knocking on your door, trying to tell you that Jesus is less than God. But the term "Son of God" does not mean Jesus is less than God. "Son of God" describes His essence as God.

See, if I call myself a son of man, what I am saying is that I bear the essence of *Homo sapiens.* All that makes *Homo sapiens* distinctly human makes me who I am. Therefore, I am a child of man or a son of man. I bear all the characteristics of humanity.

The same is true of Jesus. All that makes God who He is, Jesus possesses. No one less could be the "Wonderful Counselor," picturing a Person of supernatural wisdom. Certainly no one less than God could claim the title "Mighty God."

Even though Jesus is the Son of God, He is to His people the "Everlasting Father." Who else but Jesus bears claim to being the "Prince of Peace"?

Hundreds of years before Bethlehem, Isaiah let us know that this child, this Son, is unique. And it's His birthday.

——————— **Think About It** ———————

Evidently, a lot of folk don't understand who Jesus is, because if they did, Christmas would be a far different holiday than what we see today.

"At the name of Jesus every knee [shall] bow." Philippians 2:10

THE RIGHT SHOULDERS
Read It: Isaiah 9:7

The wise men and the shepherds were ahead of the game when they bowed before the baby Jesus on that first Christmas. As we've been saying, worshiping Jesus, "God with us," is what Christmas is all about. That's a biblical Christmas. Falling on your knees before Jesus Christ is the heart of Christmas. All the other stuff is nice, but it's not really necessary.

It's good that we have Christmas to practice bowing, because someday the whole world is going to drop to its knees before Jesus, the Apostle Paul tells us. That will be when He rules in His millennial kingdom, a time that the Prophet Isaiah looks forward to in today's verse.

We always have a problem with governments today. The problem is that the government is usually resting on the wrong shoulders. In other words, we don't know whom to trust. We don't know whom we can depend on. We don't know who is going to come through when the need is there. Even when the right people are in places of authority, they are often so overburdened they can't get very much done.

But the Son will have no such problem when He takes David's throne. His shoulders are broad enough to handle the righteous rulership of the whole world. In fact, His kingdom will continue to grow and expand without end. Now that's a hard concept to grasp, but that's what Isaiah said.

This prophecy is still future, but we in the Church today are the recipients of many of the blessings God will give the world someday. Even though Jesus is the Prince of Peace, He is not yet providing world peace, because the world has rejected His rule.

But you and I as members of His body are enjoying peace with God and the peace of God because we have bowed our knees in submission to Jesus Christ. The world may get off on the cute scene of a helpless baby in a manger. But unless you understand that that baby is the eternal God who is going to rule the nations with total justice and righteousness and with a rod of iron, you've missed the point of Christmas.

———— **Think About It** ————

People can either bow voluntarily to Jesus today in worship,
submission, and acceptance, or they will be forced
to bow before Him later. Which is it for you?

"All this took place that what was spoken . . .
might be fulfilled." Matthew 1:22

FULFILLED
Read It: Matthew 1:22-23; 2:15, 17, 22-23

The truthfulness of God is clearly seen in Christmas. He cannot lie. The key word in the verses cited above is *fulfilled*. Time and again the events of Christmas fulfilled biblical prophecy. How do I know Christianity is true and every other religion is wrong? How can I answer a person who says, "Evans, how do you know Christianity is the only true faith?"

The answer is fulfilled prophecy. The Christmas story alone has many prophecies written hundreds of years before the events occurred.

Now the critics will explain to you that you cannot have this kind of specificity recorded hundreds of years ahead of time, because that would mean the Bible is true, and God forbid that this should be the case. That's impossible, they say, so what really happened is that after the events occurred, people went back and wrote about these things as if they were future. Well, that view is so discredited that it just doesn't do anymore.

There's no way around it—the Bible is a book of prophecy that has come true, and one of the most amazing prophecies is in Matthew 2: the prediction of Jesus' birthplace (vv. 5-6).

Now if you were going to pick a place for Messiah to be born, Bethlehem wouldn't be the spot. It's a small town even today. In Jesus' day, it was really a two-by-four place, a one-stoplight town. To narrow down the location of Jesus' birth was an incredible piece of predictive prophecy. And although the word *fulfilled* is not used in these verses, the prophecy was fulfilled to the letter. Even Jesus' enemies admitted the accuracy of Micah 5:2.

We saw earlier in our Christmas series that the virgin birth of Jesus was in fulfillment of prophecy. Even the flight to Egypt and the return to Galilee were said by Matthew to be a fulfillment of Old Testament prophecy. Herod's slaughter of the babies and Joseph's and Mary's decision to settle in Nazareth were also fulfillments of prophecy.

Just the fulfilled prophecies I've named today would be evidence enough of the truth of what we believe. But, of course, they are just five out of hundreds throughout the Bible.

--- **Think About It** ---

The problem is never a lack of evidence, but a lack of faith.

REFLECTION

Since we've been talking a lot about the difference between a biblical Christmas and the world's version, and about the importance of worship at Christmas, let me show you something.

By obeying the emperor's order to go to Bethlehem to be taxed and then by obeying God's order to take Jesus and flee to Egypt to hide from Herod, Mary and Joseph were obeying a command and living by a principle that had not even been enunciated yet.

In Matthew 22:21, the adult Jesus, in response to a trick question from His enemies, asked for a Roman coin and said, "Render to Caesar the things that are Caesar's; and to God the things that are God's." In other words, give Caesar your taxes but not your worship.

That's exactly what Jesus' parents were doing here, more than thirty years before Jesus said that. Rome would have their taxes but not their final loyalty.

More than any other day of the year, Christmas gives us a clear opportunity to draw a line between what is Caesar's and what is God's. That's the difference I've been trying to show you between the secular holiday and the biblical event of Christ's birth. The state can have our silver but not our souls. Jesus is to reign supreme in our hearts.

This Christmas, is your loyalty divided between God and Caesar? Bow before Jesus and make Him supreme ruler of your life. He deserves and will settle for no less.

"Freely you received, freely give." Matthew 10:8

JESUS' BIRTHDAY WISH
Read It: Matthew 25:31-36

Do you have any idea what Jesus wants for His birthday? Christmas is first and foremost Jesus' birthday, right? Where I come from, the birthday boy is the one who gets the gifts, not the guests.

Unfortunately, Jesus doesn't get a lot for His birthday. Christmas has become largely a day when everyone seems to get something except Jesus, a day when He winds up watching us make each other feel good. And a lot of the gifts you will get this Christmas are things you either don't need or don't want, or maybe both.

Sometimes we get an inappropriate gift for someone because we fail to ask that person what he or she really wants. Well, when the receiver of your gift is Jesus Christ, you don't want to miss the mark and give Him something He doesn't want.

Now maybe you're asking yourself about now, "How can I know what Jesus wants for His birthday?" My friend, I'm glad you asked, because I believe it's possible to answer that question. I believe we can know a great deal about what Jesus wants, because He has left us His "gift wish list" in the Bible.

This list is what I want to talk with you about on our last week together. See, my premise this week is really very simple. If we as Christians are going to celebrate Christmas as it was meant to be celebrated—as the birthday of our Savior and Lord—then we ought to treat it like a birthday party and try to find out what the guest of honor wants for His birthday.

The easiest way to do that is to ask. So let's imagine we have just asked Jesus what would really make Him happy this Christmas. Our main Scripture text, the latter portion of Matthew 25, is the Lord's answer.

Now Jesus is talking about a judgment yet future, at the beginning of His millennial kingdom. But don't miss the point that the judgment is based on how people were treated here on earth. What Jesus wants for His birthday is for you and me to serve people who can't do anything for us, because that's the way He operates Himself.

──────── **Think About It** ────────
Another way to know what someone wants is to know him
or her so well you don't even have to ask. That's
how well Jesus wants you to know Him.

"Let the man who has two tunics share with him who has none;
and let him who has food do likewise." Luke 3:11

SEEING JESUS IN OTHERS
Read It: Matthew 25:37-40

It's interesting that in Jesus' description of this judgment, the righteous are not even aware that they were ministering to Jesus when they reached out to the needy.

Verse 40 is the key. Here it is, what Jesus wants for Christmas. I said yesterday that He wants us to help the poor and needy, people who can't pay us back for our service. But it's even more direct here in today's text. According to these verses, what Jesus wants—what Jesus needs—for His birthday is something to eat because He's hungry. He's thirsty and would love something to drink. He's naked and needs some clothes. He's lonely and needs a friend. And He's in prison and needs a visitor. That's what Jesus wants and needs for Christmas.

But the righteous say, "Jesus, I don't remember ever seeing You hungry, thirsty, lonely, naked, or in prison." Jesus tells them, "If you helped anyone in need, you were looking at Me." See, what Jesus wants is for you and me to do something for another one of His children who cannot do something for us in return. He wants us to touch a life, to meet a need in another part of His family. He wants us to invest in the lives of other brothers and sisters. When we do that, we're acting like kingdom people, and we get a kingdom reward.

Jesus is telling us to do exactly what He did when He walked among us. So what I am saying is that we Christians are the continuation and extension of the Incarnation. God became flesh that He might minister to men. Now He works through you and me (people of flesh) to keep on ministering to men.

If you want to exchange gifts with people who are going to give you a gift in return, that's fine. That's how the world defines Christmas. But it's not necessarily Christmas.

Christmas happens when you and I do what Jesus did for us. He gave us a gift we could not repay Him for, the gift of salvation. The only kind of people Jesus helps are those who can't repay Him—and that's all of us!

——— **Think About It** ———

We've got to stop letting the world define our holidays.

"Even so faith, if it has no works, is dead, being by itself."
James 2:17

CALL IT WHAT IT IS
Read It: Matthew 25:41-46

You know, things would be a lot less spiritually confusing at Christmas, and the lines between the sacred and the secular wouldn't get so blurred if people who only wanted to have a party at the holiday season would have their party and call it what it is: party time.

But no, they have to call it Christmas. Well, I hope that by the time this week is over, you'll see that not everything that goes by the name Christmas fits God's definition of Christmas. Christmas is Jesus' birthday, and you haven't had Christmas until you've answered Jesus' question, "What did you get Me this year?" For the people in today's text, the answer unfortunately is nothing.

You say, "Tony, I don't want to be like that. This year I want to get Jesus something for His birthday that He really wants. I want to put a smile on His face. How can I do that?"

Well, I think you start by recognizing that what Jesus wants is not what most people want to do for Christmas, so it will take a conscious decision on your part to be counterculture here. What you do is gather the family together and say, "We are going to celebrate Jesus' birthday this year by using it as a time to minister to others who are in need."

Do I mean no gifts for your kids? No, that's not what I'm saying. I'm saying make sure your family understands: "This is what we are going to do for Jesus. This is our birthday present to Jesus." Each Christmas the Evans family identifies another family in need and goes over on Christmas Eve with gifts and bags of groceries. We sit down with the family, spend some time with them, and share Christmas together.

My friend, that's Christmas. Sure, we get up on Christmas morning and open up our presents from each other. But that's not Christmas. That's family. That's a good time, but Christmas was when we went to that family who could give us nothing in return.

———— Think About It ————
You should be celebrating Christmas regularly, because a regular part of your life should be touching people who can do nothing for you in return—the kind of people Jesus Himself touched.

"I was a stranger, and you did not invite Me in." Matthew 25:43

LEAVING JESUS IN THE COLD
Read It: Matthew 25:1-13

It occurred to me in looking at Matthew 25 that the story of the ten virgins was a good parable of what happens to us at Christmas if we're not alert. I'm not saying this parable has anything to do with Christmas per se. It's a parable of the coming kingdom. But I want you to see that it's possible to let Christmas come and yet miss the heart of it. After all, almost everyone in Israel slept through the birth of Jesus and missed it. I'm saying this because I came across a very interesting and sobering piece, a "retelling" of Luke's Christmas story, which I want to share with you:

> *And there were in that same country, children keeping watch over their stockings by the fireplace. And lo! Santa Claus came upon them, and they were sore afraid. And Santa said unto them, "Fear not, for behold I bring you good tidings of great joy which shall be to all the people who can afford them.*
>
> *"For unto you will be given great feasts of good turkey, dressing, cake, and many presents. And this shall be a sign unto you. You shall find presents wrapped in bright paper, lying beneath a Christmas tree adorned with tinsel, colored balls, and lights.*
>
> *"And suddenly there will be with you a multitude of relatives and friends, praising you and saying, 'Thank you so much! It was just what I wanted!'*
>
> *"And it shall come to pass as the friends and the relatives have gone away into their own homes, the parents shall say to one another, 'Darn it! What a mess we have to clean up. And I'm tired. Let's go to bed and pick it up tomorrow. Thank goodness Christmas only comes once a year.' And they shall go with haste to their cold beds and find their desired rest."*

That's how most people will experience December 25 this year, and they'll call it Christmas. But make no mistake about it. You can do all of that while leaving Jesus standing out in the cold like an unwelcome stranger, the guest of honor not even invited to His own birthday party.

--------- **Think About It** ---------

What is there about your celebration of Christmas that marks it as a distinctively Christian event of worship and thanksgiving to Jesus?

"Do good, and lend, expecting nothing in return;
and your reward will be great." Luke 6:35

BLESSED TO SHARE
Read It: Matthew 7:7-12

Jesus says Christmas is when you keep doing unto Him what He did unto you. Let me explain what I mean. If you have tomorrow's bread, you aren't poor by the standards of the Bible. In Bible days, poor was when you weren't sure of today's bread. That's why the Lord's Prayer says, "Give us this day our daily bread." Any people who had a day's worth of bread could say their needs were met.

Most of us not only have bread for today and tomorrow but enough for a month. We are well stocked. But the Bible only promises you today's bread, so if you've been blessed beyond that, that's wonderful!

But you are never blessed so you can forget someone else who isn't so blessed. One of the great tragedies today is that Christians are ungrateful. See, only people who really understand where their blessings come from can be truly grateful for them and unafraid to share them.

I'm afraid Christmas surfaces the ingratitude in some people's hearts. Have you ever known kids who would open their presents on Christmas morning, check what they got against their wish list, and want to know why everything on the list isn't under the tree?

You say, "Oh, well, that's just kids for you." Well, guess what? God's adult children can be the same way. We can cuss and fuss and say, "God, how come I don't have this? How come I didn't get that?"

And God says, "If you only knew what I've already given you! If you only understood what it cost Me to give you My Son. If you only knew the price I had to pay to give you eternal life, then you'd stop complaining and start giving thanks! If you understand what I have given you, you will be happy to give of what you have to meet someone else's need, because you will understand that what you have, you have because I've been good to you."

This Christmas season it's time to be grateful for the grace of God. And there's no better expression of gratitude than to help someone else who has less than you have.

———— **Think About It** ————
If you want to gauge how much God is working in you,
check the level of your love to people who can't pay you back.

REFLECTION

A re we done already?
It doesn't seem possible that we've come to the end of a full year of studies in God's Word together.

If you're reading this at Christmas, you're probably thinking about the New Year and maybe even making some resolutions for next year.

So let me ask you a final question. Where will the new year find you? I don't mean what state you will be living in. I mean where will the new year find you spiritually?

For example, will you be able to wake up on January 1, look back over this year, and see some real steps of progress you've made in your walk with God? Will you be able to say you know and love God's Word more than you did this year? If you can, and if this book has helped, I am very grateful.

But if the new year finds you fighting the same old addictions, losing the same old battles, and making the same old promises to yourself, to your family, and to God, let me offer you a parting word of hope.

The resurrected Jesus said, "I am the Alpha and the Omega, the first and the last, the beginning and the end" (Revelation 22:13). That means He rules from A to Z and everything in between. Whatever your need or problem may be, if it fits between those two extremes, Jesus Christ can do something about it! God bless you as you begin a new year with Him.